D1191211

AMERICAN REVOLUTIONARY WAR SITES,
MEMORIALS, MUSEUMS AND LIBRARY COLLECTIONS

American Revolutionary War Sites, Memorials, Museums and Library Collections

A State-by-State Guidebook to Places Open to the Public

by DOUG GELBERT

McFarland & Company, Inc., Publishers
Jefferson, North Carolina, and London

British Library Cataloguing-in-Publication data are available

Library of Congress Cataloguing-in-Publication Data

Gelbert, Doug.
 American Revolutionary War sites, memorials, museums and
library collections : a state-by-state guidebook to places open to
the public / by Doug Gelbert.
  p.   cm.
 Includes index.
 ISBN 0-7864-0494-9 (library binding: 50# alkaline paper) ∞
  1. United States — History — Revolution, 1775–1783 —
Battlefields — Guidebooks.   2. United States — History —
Revolution, 1775–1783 — Monuments — Guidebooks.
3. United States — History — Revolution, 1775–1783 —
Museums — Guidebooks.   4. United States — History —
Revolution, 1775–1783 — Libraries — Guidebooks.   5. Historic
sites — United States — Guidebooks.   6. United States —
Guidebooks.   I. Title.
 E230.G45   1998
 973.3 — dc21   98-7159
                                                              CIP

Manufactured in the United States of America

McFarland & Company, Inc., Publishers
 Box 611, Jefferson, North Carolina 28640

CONTENTS

INTRODUCTION

The War for American Independence possessed many of the features that would come to fascinate students of future wars. Like the American Civil War, neighbor was often pitted against neighbor, and in the Revolution's bloodiest clashes there was often not a British soldier on the field. Like the Confederacy the Patriots were outmanned and its leaders forced to rely on guile and daring to sustain the war effort.

The American cause also attracted the talents of freedom fighters around the globe. This truly "world war" involved contributions from the French, Germans, Spanish, Polish, Scottish, black slaves, free blacks and American Indians. Buried in the descriptive site profiles and visitor information of this book is the rich historical background of American Revolution.

The scope of the book spans the period from the punitive taxations of the American colonies by the British crown in the 1760s until the adoption of the U.S. Constitution in 1787. Birthplaces and homesteads that pertain to important Revolutionary figures which fall outside the time frame of 1767–1787 are also included.

The war stretched across the Canadian border to the north and to the Atlantic coast of Spanish Florida in the south; it was fought in the wilderness of the Northwest and at outposts on the Mississippi River.

Sites include preserved battlefields, undeveloped sites of action, gravesites and buildings connected to the Revolution. Most of the sites are open to the public; those which are private can be viewed from the outside and are included for their significance to the Revolution. Whenever possible, notice of regular reenactments and celebrations is provided for site entries.

Memorials to the heroes of the Revolution began appearing sporadically in the 1820s. After the Civil War many communities erected monuments to that conflict as plans for remembering the War for American Independence were eclipsed. In time, many of these memorials came to be rededicated to "veterans of all American wars."

Collections include museums with permanent American Revolution displays and libraries with important collections relating to the war.

The book is arranged alphabetically by state, with the country of Canada, for the sake of coherence, treated likewise. Prior to each state section is a brief profile of that state's status at the time of the Revolution and a corresponding timeline, if appropriate. Under each state the relevant cities are alphabetically listed, and within each entry are addresses, phone numbers, operating hours and admission policies. Following the main body of the text is a general index to people and places.

THE SITES, MEMORIALS AND COLLECTIONS

Arkansas

Revolutionary Status: Spanish territory

Gillett

Arkansas Post County Museum (col)

Route 169 off Route 165, south of town, 501-548-2634; Wed–Sat, 9:30–4, Sun, 1–4. Free.

Although the exact location is not known, somewhere near this site in 1686 Henri de Tonty, a friend and lieutenant of Rene Robert Cavalier, Sieur de LaSalle, established the first permanent French settlement on the lower Mississippi River. The French landlords, however, took sporadic interest in Arkansas Post and in 1765 the region was ceded to Spain.

The Spanish recognized the importance of controlling the Indian trade and developed Arkansas Post to limit British influence in the area. During the American Revolution, the Spaniards reluctantly joined forces, nominally, with the American Patriots; not, certainly, out of any sympathy with the rebel cause, but as a matter of advancing their fortunes in the West.

With Spain's formal entrance into the war in 1779, Spanish governor Bernardo de Galvez seized Mobile and the British posts along the lower Mississippi River. Although suffering more urgent crises in America, the British were not willing to let their interior trade disappear so easily.

In 1782, a band of British partisans attacked a Spanish convoy and captured Señora Cruzat, wife of the Spanish commandant, at St. Louis. She secured her release from her captors and hurried to New Orleans to warn of an impending attack on Spanish river ports, including Arkansas Post (Fort Carlos III to the Spaniards).

On the morning of April 17, 1783, British commander James Colbert and a force of 81 Indian, black and Loyalist troops moved on Arkansas Post, defended by Captain Jacobo Dubreil. The attackers were unable to penetrate the forewarned fort but overran the nearby village and took several prisoners. A Spanish expeditionary force extricated the captives a few days later.

Occurring 18 months after Yorktown and after a preliminary peace treaty had been signed, the "Battle of Arkansas Post" is considered the westernmost action in the Revolution. The community itself was destroyed during the Civil War. The museum at the site of the National Memorial contains artifacts revealing the history of the post.

Canada

Revolutionary Status: British colony

Chambly

Fort Chambly National Historic Park (site)
2 rue Richelieu, off Highway 112, Quebec, 514-658-1585; Jun–Labor Day: daily, 9:30–6; May: Tue–Sun, 9–5; Sept: Tue–Sun, 10–5, Mon, 1–5; Mar–Apr and Oct–Dec: Wed–Sun, 10–5. Admission charged.

The French built the first wooden fort here in 1665; a stone fort replaced the original in 1711. The British took command in 1760 and shortly thereafter all French possessions in Canada were in the hands of England. When the American colonies rebelled the British did not have the manpower to control its widespread system of forts along the frontier.

Fort Chambly was one fortification left lightly guarded as the British regulars massed at Fort St. Jean, ten miles south. The American invasion "force" of 1775 took St. Jean at great cost and quickly seized Chambly. It was a particularly valuable prize as the British neglected to destroy vital stocks of food and weapons before surrendering. The Americans used the fort as a base for deeper incursions into Canada before deserting and burning the post in 1776.

The fort has undergone extensive restoration since the Canadian government began making repairs in 1882. Several buildings have been restored and orientation films describe not just the fort's history but the restoration as well. The cemetery, southwest of the post, is the final resting place of many Revolutionary War soldiers, including a promising American general, John Thomas, who perished of smallpox on June 2, 1776.

Montreal

Montreal History Centre (col)
335 Place d'Youville, Quebec, 514-872-3207; May–Sept: daily, 9–5; Oct–Apr: Tue–Sun, 10–5. Admission charged.

Montreal was never a military stronghold but seven months of its history were spent under American control. Invading American troops met no resistance when they took the city in November 1775. In addition to exhibits and interactive displays, the museum features a film depicting the events that shaped the development of Montreal.

General Richard Montgomery, heading the occupation forces, stayed at the Chateau Ramesay, built in 1701 for Montreal's governors. Converted into a museum in 1895, it is still open for tours.

Quebec

The Fort Museum (col)

10 rue Ste-Anne, Quebec, 418-692-2175; Jul–Aug: daily, 10–6; Apr–May and Sept–Oct: Mon–Fri, 10–12:30 and 2–5; Sat–Sun, 10–5. Admission charged.

The elaborate sight-and-sound diorama depicts the six sieges of Quebec between 1629 and 1775. The final assault was a marginally coordinated New Year's Eve attack by Benedict Arnold and Richard Montgomery. Montgomery swept up the St. Lawrence River after capturing Fort St. Jean and Montreal. Arnold was fighting his way along the Chaudière River, making one of the most arduous military expeditions ever undertaken on the North American continent, to approach from the north.

Montgomery was killed near the base of today's Citadel and his column dissolved. Arnold was seriously wounded in the leg and was replaced in the field by Daniel Morgan, who was captured with 400 men when Montgomery's assault withered. With Royal governor Guy Carleton planning the Canadian defenses it would never become the "fourteenth colony."

Sackville

Fort Beausejour National Historic Site (site)

Highway 2, five miles east of town, New Brunswick, 506-536-0720; Jun–Oct: daily, 9–5. Admission charged.

The French did not construct this fort until 1751 and four years later it was under British control. Now known as Fort Cumberland, it never left British hands until abandoned in 1833, withstanding an American assault in 1776. Restored ruins are in the park and a military museum is maintained at the visitor center.

Saint-Jean-sur-Richelieu

Fort Lennox National Historic Park (site)

Saint-Paul-de-Île-aux-Noix in the Richelieu River, 12 miles south of town, Quebec, 514-291-5700; Victoria Day–Labor Day, Wed–Sun, 10–6. Admission charged.

In 1753 this swampy island was uninhabited, save for a retired French soldier who purchased its entire 210 acres for a bag of walnuts; hence its name. By 1775, when American invaders made it their base as they advanced on Montreal, there was but a single farm on the desolate island. The intervening 22 years were not without intrigue, however.

The French covered half the island with a star-shaped fortification, home to 3,000 men. Log barriers stretched to each shore. It took 7,000 British soldiers and 40 cannon to batter the defenses of one of the largest forts ever built in

Canada into retreat in 1760. The British destroyed the fort when they abandoned the Île aux Noix.

In June 1776 a ragged retreat from Montreal crowded 8,000 men onto the island. Scores succumbed to smallpox and malaria before they could be fully evacuated. A month later the Hessians occupied the island, which became a British base for raids into the United States. Stone fortifications were begun in 1782 but soon abandoned.

The massive stone ruins date to the naval base built by Great Britain for the War of 1812. A museum recounts the history of the wars prior to that time when the men of four nations protected the Richelieu River.

Saint John

Fort Howe Lookout (site)

Magazine Street, New Brunswick; Open daily, 24 hours.

The British built this blockhouse (now reconstructed) in 1777–78 to protect the area from American privateers and Indian raids. The lookout provides a sweeping view of Saint John.

Loyalist Burial Ground (site)

Sydney Street and King Street East; New Brunswick; Open daily, 24 hours.

It is estimated that more than 100,000 Loyalists left the new United States during the Revolution, many of them persecuted for their ties to the monarchy. Saint John was a popular destination and the burial site was established in 1784, once used by United Empire Loyalists.

Windsor

Fort Edward Blockhouse (site)

Fort Edward Street, off King Street, Nova Scotia, 902-542-3631; Jun–Labor Day: daily, 9–6. Free.

Fort Edward is reputed to be the oldest original blockhouse in Canada. It and the earthworks are all that remain of Fort Edward, built by British major Charles Lawrence in 1750. It was an important base, never challenged, in the American Revolution.

Connecticut

Revolutionary Status: Original colony
Estimated Colonial Population: 198,000
Colonial Capital: rotated between Hartford and New Haven
Last Colonial Governor: Jonathan Trumbull
Troops Provided: 8 Continental regiments

Revolutionary Timeline

September 6, 1776: David Bushnell launches America's first submarine, the *Turtle*, against the British

April 27, 1777: Battle of Ridgefield occurs after British plunder Danbury

September 6, 1781: Benedict Arnold begins conquest of New London

---

Ansonia

General David Humphreys House (site)

37 Elm Street, 203-735-1908; Mon–Fri, 1–4:30. Free.

The house, built around 1698, was the home of General David Humphreys, a local manufacturer who served as an aide to General Washington during the Revolution. After the war he became an early U.S. ambassador and a renowned poet.

Coventry

Nathan Hale Homestead (site)

2299 South Street, 860-742-6917; May 15–Oct 15: daily, 1–5. Admission charged.

Connecticut state hero Captain Nathan Hale was born on this site in 1755. Nathan and five of his brothers served in the Revolution. His family pulled down the house of his birth in 1776, perhaps incorporating it into a newer home on the property. Hale never saw the new house; he was hanged as a spy a month earlier.

Danbury

Danbury Scott-Fanton Museum (col)

43 Main Street, 203-743-5200; Wed–Sun, 2–5. Free.

The heritage of Danbury has been preserved in house museums and exhibits. Artifacts and displays from the Revolution are contained in the collection. A library is also available.

Enoch Crosby (mem)

Hartell Avenue, off Crosby Street.

A memorial statue has been erected to the famous Patriot spy, Enoch Crosby, who was living in Danbury at the start of the Revolution. Crosby was the model for James Fenimore Cooper's Harvey Birch in *The Spy: A Tale of the Neutral Ground*.

Sybil Ludington (mem)

Danbury Public Library courtyard, 170 Main Street.

Sybil Huntington was a 16-year-old girl who, on April 26, 1777, rode bravely through "the enemy-infested countryside for thirty miles in Putnam County, New York, to warn the local militia that British troops were attacking and plundering Danbury."

Ludington began her ride in Fredericksburg (now Ludingtonville), New York, about 17 miles from Danbury. She went south to Carmel Village, then to Mahopac, north through forests and steep hills of Kent Cliffs and Mead Corners, then east to the villages of Stormville and Pecksville.

The monument shows Sybil raising the stick she used to bang on doors as she rode, shouting, "The British are burning Danbury. Muster at Ludingtons." Ludington is shown nearly life-size, riding side-saddle on the proper left side of a large horse. The metal statue was dedicated on September 11, 1971.

Wooster Cemetery (site)
Ellsworth Avenue; Open daily, dawn to dusk.

In Wooster Cemetery stands a monument to General David Wooster, fatally wounded chasing the British in the Battle of Ridgefield in April 1777. He died five days later. Congress voted to erect a memorial to Wooster but it never happened. The present monument was erected by the Masons in 1854. Carved into the side of the imposing sandstone tower is a description of the battle. Wooster is buried beneath the tower; his remains were moved after 77 years from an unmarked grave in the town's oldest cemetery.

East Granby

Old New-Gate Prison & Copper Mine (site)
Newgate Road off Route 20, 860-566-3005; May–Oct: Wed–Sun, 10–4:30. Admission charged.

America's first chartered copper mine began extracting ore in 1707. Mined out by 1773, the shafts and underground tunnels and rooms were converted into the first working state prison in the United States. The decidedly inhospitable conditions in the 70-foot mine spawned the name "New-Gate" after the notorious cellblock in London. The Continental Congress sent captured Loyalists into the underground cells beginning in 1776. As many as 60 Tories were held here during the Revolution and escape attempts — several successful — were commonplace. The primitive prison was abandoned in 1827. Tours include the dank underground cells.

East Haddam

Nathan Hale School (site)
Main Street, 860-873-9547; Memorial Day–Labor Day: Sat–Sun, 2–4. Free.

Hale taught in this one-room school from November 1, 1773, to May of 1774, following his graduation from Yale College. Hale signed on with the Continental Army and was commissioned as a lieutenant on July 1, 1775. After Washington retreated from the rubble of the Battle of Long Island to Manhattan on August 29, 1776, he desired intelligence on the British activities back on Long Island. The 21-year-old Hale, now a captain, volunteered.

He returned to Connecticut, gathered his Yale diploma as a prop for his disguise as a Dutch schoolmaster, and sailed across the Long Island Sound to Huntington. He diligently sketched and mapped the British positions and began his return to Manhattan, unfortunately stopping at a tavern known as the Cedars, where a Tory relation betrayed him. He was barely a mile from his quarters.

Taken to British commander Sir William Howe, Hale's gathered intelligence was discovered and he was hanged the next morning.

Enfield

Martha A. Parsons House (col)

1387 Enfield Street, 860-745-6064; May–Oct: Sun, 2:00–4:30. Free.

The house was built in 1782 by John Meacham but its Revolutionary interest is derived from its wall coverings. This is the only house remaining in the nation with "George Washington Memorial" wallpaper.

Thomas Abbey (mem)

Enfield Congregational Church, 1295 Enfield Street.

The sculpture was erected by the descendants of the Abbey family at the cost of $20,000 in 1916 to commemorate Thomas Abbey's part in the American Revolution. Legend maintains that Abbey beat a drum to alert the townspeople that the Revolution had begun. A longtime veteran of the French and Indian War, Abbey, born in 1731, took up arms against the British as well. The standing Thomas Abbey created by Sherry Edmundson Fry is dressed in eighteenth century clothing. There is a drum behind him draped with a cloak.

Essex

Connecticut River Museum (col)

67 Main Street, at the Steamboat Dock on the Connecticut River, 860-767-8269; Tue–Sun, 10–5. Admission charged.

Included in the displays on shipbuilding and maritime history is a replica of America's first submarine, *Turtle*. The single-man underwater contraption, designed for battle by David Bushnell, was used briefly during the Revolution to minimal effect. The *Turtle* was launched against Lord Howe's flagship, anchored off New York City, but failed to sink its target.

Fairfield

Old Town Hall (col)

611 Old Post Road, 203-256-3000; Jun–Labor Day: Mon–Fri, 8:30–4:30. Free.

A prosperous place before the Revolution, Fairfield was wiped out by a British raid in July 1779. More than 100 houses and buildings were looted and burned. A Fairfield resident away at the time was Captain Samuel Smedley, a mere youth who had captured so many prized ships by the end of the Revolution that a captured British officer was moved to remark, "There is little hope of conquering an enemy whose very schoolboys are capable of valor equaling that of trained veterans of naval warfare." The Old Town Hall on the green was rebuilt in 1791 and contains records and documents dating to 1648.

Greenwich

Israel Putnam Cottage (site)

243 East Putnam Avenue (Route 1), 203-869-9697; Wed, Fri, Sun, 1–4. Admission charged.

Maj. Gen. Israel Putnam, commander of the wintering Continental troops in Redding, was surprised by a British foraging party in this outpost on March 26, 1779. Local tradition, probably apocryphal, has the 61-year-old Putnam driving his horse down a rocky embankment to escape the British dragoons — feared infantry who rode their horses into battle before dismounting to fight. A large stone and plaque nearby tell the tale of "the famous ride down 'Put's Hill.'" The small building was known as Knapp's Tavern in the Revolution and has been restored to its appearance at that time.

Groton

Fort Griswold (site)

Monument Street and Park Avenue, 860-445-1729; Memorial Day–Labor Day: daily, 9–5; Labor Day–Columbus Day: Sat–Sun, 10–5. Free.

Late in August 1781, with General Washington marching to Virginia and the war's conclusion, Benedict Arnold, now in the employ of the crown, proposed a diversionary strike on New London, a major storage depot in his native state of Connecticut. Lt. Gen. Henry Clinton placed 1,700 men under his command and Arnold set sail on September 6, 1781.

Two forts protected New London at the mouth of the Thames River: the sparsely garrisoned Fort Trumbull on the west bank and Fort Griswold, with 140 militia under Lt. Col. William Ledyard, occupying the stronger position east of the river. The British split their force, Arnold leading the western invasion and Lt. Col. Edmund Eyre commanding the assault on Fort Griswold. Around 9:00 A.M. Arnold landed and easily displaced the two dozen men at Fort Trumbull, who fired one volley, spiked their cannon and fled.

Eyre did not have such easy going. He struck the fortress from three sides but met such heavy fire from the defenders that the British had to retreat, losing Eyre to a mortal wound. A second assaulting force was thrown back and finally the British stormed the walls in desperate fighting. After 40 minutes of bloody work, Ledyard ended the gallant defense by offering his sword to Lt. Col.

Abram Van Buskirk of the 3rd Battalion of New Jersey Tories. Van Buskirk, according to American accounts of the battle, accepted the sword and thrust it through Ledyard's body. The Americans reported more than 70 men being murdered after the offer to surrender.

Arnold completed his raid by setting New London afire and destroying over 100 buildings. He had achieved no military objective in this, the last important battle in the North, and further discredited his once outstanding record.

Portions of the earth and stone fortifications remain in the 17-acre park. Buildings on the property include the Ebenezer Avery House, where wounded were treated, and the Monument House, which contains relics of the Fort Griswold massacre. It was moved from its original location on Thames Street in 1971.

The Groton Monument in Fort Griswold, soaring 134 feet high from a hilltop, was dedicated in 1830 to the victims "when the British, under the command of the traitor, Benedict Arnold, burnt the towns of New London and Groton, and spread desolation and woe throughout this region." A tablet on the monument bears their names.

Hartford

Hartford Ancient Burying Ground (site)

Gold and Main streets, 860-525-6610; Tours Jul–Aug, 10–1:45. Free.

Hartford escaped any crippling military action during the war but many Revolutionary War soldiers, as well as its earliest settlers, are buried here.

Old State House (site)

800 Main Street, 860-522-6766; Mon–Sat, 10–5, Sun, 12–5. Free.

Charles Bullfinch designed this building, the oldest state house in the nation. The senate chamber has been restored and on display is a Gilbert Stuart portrait of George Washington.

State Capitol (col)

Capitol Avenue and Trinity Street, 860-240-0222; Apr–Oct: Mon–Fri, 9:15–1:15, Sat, 10:15–2:15; Nov–Mar: Mon–Fri, 9:15–1:15. Free.

Crafted from white Connecticut marble, the building dates to 1880. Among the statues and relics inside are Israel Putnam's tombstone and a camp bed used by Lafayette. At the North Entrance is a work by Paul Bartlett, "Israel Putnam Leaving His Plow."

Lakeville

Salisbury Cannon Museum (col)

Routes 44 and 41, 860-435-0566; Memorial Day–Labor Day: Sat–Sun, 1–5. Free.

The museum is devoted to the American Revolution, focusing on seven individuals and the events that occurred in 1775. Interactive programs and special events are offered. Nearby is a 1762 iron blast furnace erected by Ethan Allen and three partners, which produced cannon for the American armies and navies.

Lebanon

Governor Jonathan Trumbull House (site)
West Town Street, on the Green, 860-642-7558; May–Oct: Tue–Sat, 1–5. Admission charged.

Known in England as "the Rebel Governor of Connecticut," Jonathan Trumbull was the only governor in 1775 who supported the war and held his job before *and* after the Revolution. Trumbull arranged numerous cattle drives from Hartford to Continental Army camps; so many, in fact, that Connecticut came to be known as the "Provisions State." Trumbull himself came to be known to George Washington as "Brother Jonathan." Trumbull retained his office throughout the conflict, retiring in 1784 after 15 years.

From this two-story frame house sprung the leading family of the Revolution from Connecticut. His eldest son Joseph was appointed commissary general for the Continental Army in 1775, a position of such stress it put him in a premature grave in 1778 at the age of 41. Jonathan Trumbull, the patriarch's namesake, was paymaster of the American Northern Department. He later served in the U.S. Senate and as governor of Connecticut.

The youngest Revolutionary Trumbull was John, a Harvard graduate like his brothers. He served as a 19-year-old aide-de-camp to Washington in 1775 and later under Horatio Gates. Then he devoted his life to art, sailing to England in 1780 to study under Benjamin West. In 1824 John Trumbull completed seven years of work on four Revolutionary scenes in the rotunda of the nation's capitol.

Revolutionary War Office (site)
West Town Street, 860-642-7558; Jun–Aug: Sat, 1:30–5:00, Sun, 1:30–4:30; Sep: Sat, 1:30–5:00. Free.

Jonathan Trumbull made his fortune in the mercantile trade and this store, built in 1727, used to adjoin the family home. Trumbull's experience as a merchant proved valuable in the Revolution, when shopping for supplies with practically worthless Continental notes required delicate diplomacy. During the Revolution it was where the Connecticut Council of Safety planned the crucial supply lifeline of the war. It is estimated that more than 1,200 meetings took place here.

Meridien

Count Casimir Pulaski (mem)
Broad Street.

Julius Gutzwa sculpted this memorial in honor of Count Pulaski, the "Father of the American Cavalry." A bas-relief depicts Pulaski standing in full dress. It was dedicated in 1934.

New Haven

Black Rock Fort (site)

Woodward Avenue, 203-946-8790; Open daily, dusk to dawn.

New Haven evolved into the major port of the West Indies trade — much of it illicit — in the 1750s. It was an ideal breeding ground for anti–British sentiment and on the New Haven Green on April 22, 1775 — two days after the fighting at Lexington and Concord — Benedict Arnold, a local shopowner, organized his 2nd Company, Connecticut Governor's Foot Guard. Arnold forced the New Haven guards to surrender the keys to the municipal powder house.

In 1779 New Haven was the prime objective of General Sir Henry Clinton's punitive expedition against the Connecticut coast. When British raiders arrived to sack the town, however, the local militia — including Yale College students — was stronger than anticipated and the invaders withdrew without being able to give New Haven "the conflagration it so richly deserved." At Black Rock on the east side of the harbor is a reconstructed fort where most of the skirmishing occurred.

Memorial to the Defendants of New Haven (mem)

Columbus and Congress avenues.

James Edward Kelly created three life-sized male figures — a soldier, farmer and student — and an artillery piece on a caisson. The monument was dedicated in memory of the heroism against the British on July 5, 1779.

Nathan Hale (mem)

Connecticut Hall, Yale University.

The monument to Hale, Class of 1773, was created by Bela Lyon Pratt and dedicated in 1913. Around the edge of the bronze base in incised print are the famous words attributed to the doomed spy: "I only regret that I have but one life to lose for my country."

Pardee-Morris House (site)

325 Lighthouse Road, 203-772-7060; Jun–Aug: Sat–Sun, 11–4. Admission charged.

The Pardee House, built in 1685, was one house the British managed to burn. Partially destroyed, it was rebuilt in 1780. The restored eighteenth century Colonial home carries the tale of the British plundering of New Haven.

New London

Nathaniel Shaw Mansion (site)

305 Bank Street, 860-443-1209; May–Oct: Wed–Fri, 1–4, Sat, 10–4. Admission charged.

Captain Nathaniel Shaw, Jr., built the two-story granite building in 1756. During the Revolution it housed the Naval Office for Connecticut. Guided tours include its history in the Revolution, in colonial New London and in the West Indies trade.

Old Town Cemetery (site)
Hempstead Street, north of Bulkeley Square; Open daily, dawn to dusk.
To New London's misfortune, Benedict Arnold spent much of his childhood in the town and knew the terrain. He chose it as a target for his raiding party on September 6, 1781, destroying 150 buildings. Arnold claimed that most of the destruction was the fault of accidental fires but townspeople contended he stood at this cemetery viewing the flames "with the apparent satisfaction of a Nero." The cemetery is the final resting place of some 100 Revolutionary War veterans.

Statue of Nathan Hale (mem)
Williams Park.
The statue of the 21-year-old Connecticut spy is a duplicate of the rendering in City Hall Park, New York City. Hale taught school in New London for over a year, leaving in July 1775 to become a lieutenant in the 7th Connecticut Militia.

Newtown

Hillbrow House (site)
1715 Main Street (Route 25), Private residence.
The blue-dormered structure was built in 1715 and was the home to an alleged Loyalist who refused to share his freshly baked bread with Rochambeau's hungry French troops. Down the street, in the center of town, are bullet holes in the golden cock weathervane on top of the 1719 Meeting House, supposedly made by the French soldiers. Rochambeau's force was camped on the site of the Cyrenius Booth Library, at 25 Main Street, on the way to the siege at Yorktown.

Norwich

Christopher Leffingwell House (site)
348 Washington Street, 860-889-9440; May–Oct: Tue–Sun, 2–4. Admission charged.
The tavern room dates to 1675, having been built by Norwich's leading founder, Thomas Leffingwell. Christopher Leffingwell, his son, turned to manufacturing and operated the state's first paper mill. A fervent patriot, he funded a light infantry company and operated the public house as a Revolutionary War meeting place.

Redding

Putnam Memorial State Park (site)
Routes 107 and 58, 203-938-2285; Open daily, dawn to dusk. Free.
Maj. Gen. Israel Putnam grew larger than life during a career fighting in the

frontier and in the French and Indian War. He is said to have survived a burning at the stake, an imprisonment in Montreal and a shipwreck off the coast of Cuba. During the Revolution, however, after distinguished service at Bunker Hill, he lost forts Clinton and Montgomery in the Hudson Highlands and by the winter of 1778, in his sixtieth year, he was given the less rigorous task of commanding the camp at Redding. Here "Old Put's" most notable achievement was squelching a looming mutiny as soldiers threatened to march on Hartford for more food and supplies.

The palisade and blockhouses of "Connecticut's Valley Forge" have been restored but crumbling chimneys and other traces of buildings are the most discernible relics of any remaining Revolutionary camp. A stone obelisk was erected by the state in 1888 to honor the men who suffered through an exceptionally severe winter here. The dramatic statue of Putnam at the park's entrance is the work of Anna Hyatt Huntington.

Reenactment: Each fall, the Second Continental Light Dragoons stage Revolutionary War reenactments during a two-day encampment of American and British forces. This is the only continuous program in the northeast to honor veterans and male and female patriots from 1775 to the present.

Ridgefield

Keeler Tavern Museum (site)

132 Main Street, 203-438-5485; Feb–Dec: Wed, Sat, Sun, 1–4. Admission charged.

Danbury, 15 miles to the north and a vital manufacturing center in Colonial days, was a storage supply depot for the Patriots — and an obvious target for the British. The inevitable invasion came in April 1777, when 2,000 Loyalist and British troops under New York governor William Tryon overwhelmed the region and burned Danbury. They were headed back to their ships in Long Island Sound on April 27 when a force of Continentals and militia headed by General Benedict Arnold blocked their escape in Ridgefield. Behind the British was General David Wooster with 200 militia.

The superior British numbers forced Arnold to withdraw, and the next morning a Tory guide led Tryon around the American lines to their fleet. Arnold, who had been in nearby New Haven on personal business and stewing about a lack of recognition for his military exploits from Congress, was finally promoted to major general for his daring on this battlefield. At Ridgefield he had one horse killed beneath him and another wounded and narrowly avoided capture. Wooster was not so fortunate. He died five days later from wounds and is buried in Wooster Cemetery in Danbury. The British placed a gun at Keeler Tavern, which still boasts a cannonball wedged in a wooden beam behind a panel on the exterior of the building.

Southington

Rochambeau Monument (mem)

Marion Avenue.

The monument, sculpted by James Edward Kelly, was erected by the Irish Historical Society of Providence in recognition of the fact that an Irish brigade accompanied Rochambeau's army when he stopped in Southington in June 1781 on his way to Yorktown and again in November 1782 on his return. It was installed in 1912.

Tolland

Benton Homestead (site)

Metcalf Road, May–Oct: Sun, 1–4. Admission charged.

This center-chimney Colonial building, constructed around 1720, housed Hessian prisoners during the Revolutionary War. The paneling is original, the furnishings reproductions.

Westbrook

Military Historians Headquarters-Museum (col)

North Main Street, 860-399-9460; Tue–Fri, 8–3:30. Free.

The museum is said to house the largest collection of American military uniforms in the country, including an interesting array from the Revolution. A research and video library is also available.

Westport

Compo Beach Minuteman (mem)

North Compo Beach Road and Compo Beach Road.

Daniel Webster created the bronze soldier on a base of small boulders. Dedicated in 1910, it depicts a local militiaman kneeling in wait for advancing British troops. British raiders landed near Compo Beach to begin their plundering of Danbury.

Wethersfield

Webb-Deane-Stevens Museum (site)

211 Main Street, 860-529-0612; May–Oct: Wed–Mon, 10–4; Nov–Apr: Sat–Sun, 10–4. Admission charged.

By the spring of 1781 Washington had seemed to have wrung every last bit of effort out of his struggle for independence. Replacement quotas were not being met by the states and his army was starving. He had been promised fresh French troops but had no idea when they would arrive to bolster his army. There seemed no way to strike the final blow against the British. Comte de Rochambeau, commander of the French Army in America, suggested a meeting to prepare strategy. On May 21, 1781, the two leaders met in the Joseph Webb House.

Rochambeau, knowing he had 3,200 troops coming from the West Indies but under instructions not to disclose the information, proposed an attack on Lt. Gen. Cornwallis in Virginia. Washington could not envision any scenario where his ragged army could march successfully to Virginia and thought a move on New York more prudent. A successful attack here, he reasoned, would draw enemy troops from the South.

After heated discussion, Rochambeau accepted Washington's plan but he dispatched the arriving French fleet to the Chesapeake anyway. The combined Franco-American forces moved on New York but an assault soon proved untenable. By this time Washington learned of the French arrival in Chesapeake and immediately moved south, knowing he could trap Cornwallis on the Virginia coast. The final step in the war had been taken.

Silas Deane, who built the second of three houses in the museum complex, laid a successful groundwork for his life with a Yale College education in 1758. Two favorable marriages followed in the next decade as his law practice and social position flourished. He was elected to the First Continental Congress in 1774 and in March 1776 Congress authorized him to travel to France as America's first foreign envoy. He was later joined in Paris by Benjamin Franklin and Arthur Lee and the trio succeeded in signing commercial alliances with France in February 1778.

Later that year Deane was recalled by Congress to defend himself against charges from Lee that he was engaging in dubious commercial activities. Neglecting to bring his records, he was unable to clear his name, if indeed he could have. He returned to Europe and while there wrote to American friends that he believed America and England should be reconciled. When the letters appeared in a Tory newspaper his allegiance to America was in serious question and he disappeared to the Netherlands. Regarded as a traitor, Deane lived out his life in England and died on board ship while headed for Canada in 1789. He was 52 years old.

In the Webb House is a 1916 mural of the Battle of Yorktown, although the strategy for that final conflict was not actually formulated in its chambers, as local tradition holds. The Webb House is furnished as it supposedly looked when Washington and Rochambeau conducted their tumultuous summit.

Windsor

Oliver Ellsworth Homestead (site)

778 Palisado Avenue, 860-688-8717; May–Oct, Tue, Wed, Fri, 10–5. Admission charged.

Oliver Ellsworth attained fame in Windsor, Connecticut's oldest town, as an ardent Revolutionary patriot, jurist and statesman. He built this house in 1781 and returned to Philadelphia to help frame the Constitution. The house remained in the Ellsworth family until 1903.

Delaware

Revolutionary Status: Original colony
Estimated Colonial Population: 37,000
Colonial Capital: New Castle
Last Colonial Capital: Under Pennsylvania jurisdiction
Troops Provided: 1 Continental regiment

Revolutionary Timeline

August 29, 1777: British defeat local militia at Cooch's Bridge
December 7, 1787: Delaware becomes the first state to ratify the Federal Constitution

---

Claymont

Robinson House (site)

Naamans Road (Route 92) and Philadelphia Pike (Route 13), Sun, 1–4. Admission charged.

The main section of the 1723 building was better known as Naaman's Tavern, a place where many revolutionaries stayed — the inn resided on the main road to Philadelphia, some 25 miles away. Washington rented a room in late August 1777 before the Battle of Brandywine. British officers also imbibed at the inn and three were taken prisoner in 1778 as they ate breakfast. Later, Revolutionary War hero General Thomas Robinson lived here. A blockhouse on the property dates to 1649.

Dover

The Green (site)

Off State Street.

Named after Dover, England, and first settled in 1670, the town was planned by William Penn, but not formally platted until 1717. The Green was a prominent feature of Penn's plans and was laid out in accordance with his design. The Declaration of Independence was read to the citizens here and soldiers were mustered on the grass for the Revolution. Dover became the capital of Delaware in 1777 and on December 7, 1787, the U.S. Constitution was ratified in the Old State House on the Green, the first state assembly to do so.

John Dickinson Plantation (site)

Kitts Hummock Road (County Road 68), six miles south of town, east of Route 113, 302-739-3277; Tue–Sat, 10–3:30, Sun, 1:30–4:30. Free.

The two-story brick house along the banks of the St. Jones River was built by Samuel Dickinson in 1740, and John Dickinson, the "Penman of the American Revolution," spent his boyhood here. Schooled extensively in law, John

Dickinson began his practice in Philadelphia in 1757 at the age of 25. He won a seat in the Delaware assembly in 1760 and one in the Pennsylvania legislature in 1762.

Dickinson's was a moderate voice amidst the cacophony of radicalism which arose around him. He worked vigorously against British rule but believed any differences could be settled peacefully. He stated his views in a series of letters which came to be published as the influential *Letters from a Farmer in Pennsylvania to the Inhabitants of the British Colonies*.

As a member of the Continental Congress he spoke against independence as the leader of the conservative faction of Congress. He voted against the resolution and did not sign the Declaration of Independence. Nevertheless, he was one of only two Congressmen who immediately took the field for military duty in the Continental Army. He served briefly and held various political offices in Pennsylvania and Delaware during the Revolution, although his national influence was now greatly reduced. After the war he returned to prominence and assisted in writing the U.S. Constitution.

Throughout his legal and political career carried on elsewhere, John Dickinson remained a farmer. He inherited his father's Kent County property upon his death in 1760 and extended the holdings for miles. A fire gutted the plantation house in 1804 and Dickinson rebuilt it, using the original walls, before his death in 1808. Guides in historic clothing interpret the daily life on an eighteenth century plantation, including those of the tenants and slaves.

Old Christ Church (site)

Water and State streets; Open daily, dusk to dawn.

In the cemetery is buried Caesar Rodney, signer of the Declaration of Independence. The church was built in 1734 and later enlarged; the Rectory at 502 South State Street was finished in 1770.

New Castle

Immanuel Church (site)

The Green. Open daily, dawn to dusk.

Founded in 1689, it was the first Church of England parish in Delaware. The nave dates to 1703; additions were made in 1820 and 1848. George Read, a signer of the Declaration of Independence, and other prominent Delaware statesmen are buried here.

Old Court House (site)

211 Delaware Street, between Market and Third streets, 302-323-4453; Tue–Sat, 10–3:30, Sun, 1:30–4:30. Free.

Delaware was granted home government and its own Assembly in 1704 and New Castle was its capital until 1777. The centerpiece of the town, which still looks much as it did in Colonial and Federal times, is the Old Court House. Built in 1732, the cupola on the Old Court House is notable as the center of the 12-mile radius, surveyed by Mason and Dixon, which forms Delaware's unique circular boundary with Pennsylvania. The Declaration of Independence was read here in 1776 and Delaware's first Constitution was adopted on September 20, 1776. Walking tours of the historic town depart from the Old Court House.

The Strand (site)

Along the Delaware River.

New Castle's finest Colonial homes are located along this stretch which evolved from a seedy riverfront into inns and townhouses. Included on the street is the law office of Thomas McKean, a delegate to the Continental Congress of 1774, at Number 22. A fire swept the street in 1824 and one home that did not survive was George Read's. His son's house next door, which he built as Delaware's largest private home in 1804, did.

Newark

Cooch's Bridge Battlefield (site)

Old Baltimore Pike, off Route 896; Open daily, 24 hours.

In the summer of 1777 it became apparent that the British would launch an attack on Philadelphia from New York. But from which direction would the assault come? Would the British move overland through New Jersey or storm the colonial capital from the sea, taking advantage of their vast naval superiority?

In July part of the suspense lifted when the British set sail down the Atlantic Coast. But scouts lost track of the armada for three weeks. General Howe sailed around the Delmarva Peninsula and landed unopposed at Head of Elk, now Elkton, Maryland, on August 28, 1777. Once detected, skirmishing continued along the road to Philadelphia with the heaviest fighting at Cooch's Bridge in Delaware.

The little state of Delaware provided only a single regiment to the Continental Army but the unit distinguished themselves in nearly every battle of the Revolution, earning the nickname the "Blue Hen Chickens" after a particularly fierce breed of fighting gamecock. The state nickname survives today but the engagement at Cooch's Bridge was the only fighting on Delaware soil. Only three British soldiers were killed.

Legend has it that Betsy Ross' Stars and Stripes flew for the first time at Cooch's Bridge. There is no formal display preserving the battle, except for a small memorial of cannons and a descriptive plaque. The terrain can be viewed from a 90-foot observation tower in nearby Iron Hill Park.

Wilmington

Caesar Rodney Equestrian Statue (mem)

Rodney Square at Market Street between 10th & 11th streets.

A delegate to the Continental Congress, Caesar Rodney was at his home in

Dover on July 1, 1776, when he received word that Congress was voting on a Declaration of Independence the following day. Rodney, ill and near death, set out immediately for Philadelphia, 80 miles distant. Traveling along dark, unmarked roads he arrived at the Pennsylvania State House (now Independence Hall) the next morning in time to cast a deciding vote for independence for Delaware.

Rodney remains one of Delaware's great heroes and his ride is immortalized in the equestrian statue by James Edward Kelly, a specialist in military personages. Dedicated on July 4, 1923, it is a unique rendering in that Rodney's horse is in full gallop with two front legs in the air. The entire assembly rests on only a few square inches of the two rear hoofs. Kelly achieved the precarious balance by weighting the tail and positioning Rodney slightly back of center. Caesar Rodney's historic ride is depicted in scenes around the granite base.

District of Columbia

Revolutionary Status: Nonexistent; created under new Constitution

American Army Crossing the Delaware (mem)

Hirschorn Museum and Sculpture Garden; Independence Avenue at 8th Street, S.W.

Thomas Eakins cast the men of the Continental Army crossing the Delaware River, on their surprise attack of the Hessian troops at Trenton, in bronze in 1893. The figures, standing and sitting, were presented by the Commonwealth of Pennsylvania. Also in the garden is Eakins' work of "The Battle of Trenton."

Anderson House (col)

2118 Massachusetts Avenue N.W., 202-785-2040; Tue–Sat, 1–4. Free.

George Washington and the officers of the Continental Army and Navy founded the Society of the Cincinnati in 1783. The large stone house, once the residence of Lars Anderson, minister to Belgium and ambassador to Japan, is the national headquarters, library and museum of the Society. Exhibits and Revolutionary War artifacts are available.

Benjamin Franklin (mem)

10th Street at D Street N.W.

The execution of patriot and diplomat Benjamin Franklin was executed by Ernest Plassman. It stands in the center of a small open park.

Captain Nathan Hale (mem)

Department of Justice, Pennsylvania and Constitution Avenue at 9th and 10th streets N.W.

On the south side of the extensive building complex is a memorial to the Connecticut captain who "in the performance of his duty resigned his life, a sacrifice to his country's liberty at New York, September 22, 1776." The bronze sculpture by Bela Lyon Pratt carries Hale's words at his execution: "I only regret that I have but one life to lose for my country."

Commodore John Paul Jones (mem)

Potomac Park, Northwest corner of Tidal Basin.

Charles Henry Niehaus sculpted the Revolutionary naval hero from bronze in 1912. Jones is depicted in full naval dress, his left hand on the pommel of his sword. Inscribed are his words: "Surrender? I have not yet begun to fight!" To the west of the Jones statue, Mrs. William Howard Taft planted the first of Washington's famed Japanese cherry trees.

Congressional Cemetery (site)

1801 E Street S.E., 202-543-0539; Open daily, dawn to dusk. Free.

The Washington Parish Burial Ground was established on 4½ acres of ground in 1807. In 1816 room was set aside for 100 burial sites for interring the members of Congress. Thereafter America's first national cemetery was known as Congressional Cemetery. First New York governor George Clinton was originally buried here before being removed to his home state. Elbridge Gerry, a signer of the Declaration of Independence, is still buried here, under a truncated pyramidal shaft.

Count Pulaski (site)

13th Street and E Street.

The bronze equestrian statue honors Pulaski, credited with forming the American cavalry in the Revolution. The depiction by Polish sculptor Casimir Chodzinski was dedicated in 1910.

Daughters of the American Revolution Museum and Constitution Hall (col)

1776 D Street N.W., 202-879-3241; Mon–Fri, 8:30–4, Sun, 1–5. Free.

The Daughters of the American Revolution was founded in 1890 with women descended from patriots in the cause of liberty. The national society, which included nearly 3,000 local chapters at one time, is headquartered in three main buildings.

Memorial Continental Hall houses the museum, consisting of 33 period rooms. The 13 Ionic columns of the south portico were donated by state chapters and legislatures of the original 13 colonies. Over 2,000 Revolutionary-era relics are preserved, mostly nonmilitary items. Busts of great Revolutionary War leaders are displayed in special niches. A library is also available for researchers.

Lectures and concerts are presented in Constitution Hall, built of Alabama limestone with seating for 3,476. The expansive stage is decorated with four

Revolutionary War scenes painted by James Monroe Hewlett — the Boston Tea Party, the inaugural of George Washington as first president, Jefferson reading the Declaration of Independence, and Colonel Moultrie accepting plaudits for his victory at Sullivan's Island.

George Washington (mem)

Washington Circle, Pennsylvania and New Hampshire avenues and K and 23rd streets.

The bronze equestrian statue of George Washington was designed by Clark Mills. He is shown with a uniform copied from one the general was known to wear. It was unveiled in 1860.

George Washington (mem)

Lisner Hall, George Washington University, between 19th and 24th streets and F Street and Pennsylvania Avenue.

George Washington left 50 shares of Potomac Canal Company stock to endow a national university, which was opened in 1822. The Marquis de Lafayette was among those attending the first commencement two years later. The university's bronze of General Washington is a replica of the life-size statue in the rotunda of the Virginia state capitol at Richmond. It was done from life by French sculptor Jean Antoine Houdon.

George Washington (site)

Washington National Cathedral, Massachusetts and Wisconsin avenues N.W., 202-537-6200; Apr–Sep: Mon–Fri, 10–9, Sat, 10–4:30, Sun, 12:30–4:30; Oct–Mar: Mon–Sat, 10–4:30, Sun, 12:30–4:30. Free.

Only completed in 1990, the medieval National Cathedral is the world's sixth largest church and features a statue of George Washington.

John Witherspoon (mem)

Connecticut Avenue at N Street.

The bronze statue honors John Witherspoon, signer of the Declaration of Independence and president of the school which would eventually become Princeton. William Couper conceived the work, which was dedicated in 1909.

Lafayette Square (site)

Pennsylvania Avenue between Madison Place and Jackson Place.

At each corner of the square across from the White House are statues of men of foreign lands who contributed to American independence — the French Lafayette and Rochambeau, the Polish Kosciuszko and the German von Steuben.

The statue of Marquis de Lafayette, in the southwest corner, is a heroic bronze by Alexandre Falguiere and Antonin Mercie. On the east side of the base Comte d'Estaing and Comte de Grasse are represented as offering French naval support, and on the opposite side Comte de Rochambeau and Chevalier Duportail provide military aid.

Rochambeau stands on the southwest corner, holding a chart in one hand and pointing with the other. The statue, a copy by Ferdinand Hamar of the memorial at Vendome, France, was accepted in 1902 as a gift from France.

Anton Popiel presented freedom fighter Thaddeus Kosciuszko with globes representing North America and Europe. The tribute is in bronze and the pedestal bears a line from Thomas Campbell's *Epic of Pleasure*—"And Freedom shrieked as Kosciuszko fell."

The statue of Baron von Steuben immortalizes the drillmaster in the teaching of young recruits with weaponry. Albert Jaeger has included portrait heads of Colonel William North and Major Benjamin Walker of von Steuben's staff.

Library of Congress (col)

Independence Avenue S.E., 202-707-5458; Mon–Fri, 8:30–5. Free.

Started by legislative enactment in 1800, the original collection of the Library of Congress was burned by the British in 1814. Thomas Jefferson offered his private collection of 6,487 volumes — considered the finest in the New World — to rebuild the library. The offer was accepted in 1815 and Jefferson was paid $23,950 amidst heated debate due to the atheistic bent of many of the former president's readings. Another fire destroyed much of the collection, including the Jefferson legacy, in 1851.

The present building of Italian Renaissance design dates to 1897. The collection has now expanded to more than 100 million items. Once the home of both the original Declaration of Independence and the Constitution of the United States, the Library of Congress now protects Jefferson's "rough draft" of the Declaration.

Memorial to the Signers of the Declaration of Independence (mem)

Constitution Gardens, between Constitution Avenue and the Lincoln Memorial Reflecting Pool.

Across a footbridge, on an artificial island, are large granite blocks carved with replicas of the 56 signatures affixed to the bottom of the Declaration of Independence. The waterside memorial centers a landscaped garden in a 42-acre park.

National Archives (col)

Constitution Avenue between 7th and 9th streets N.W., 202-501-5205; Apr–Labor Day: daily, 10–9; Sept–Mar: daily, 10–5:30. Free.

In the Exhibition Hall are the two fundamental documents of the United States: the Declaration of Independence and the Constitution. Two murals by Barry Faulkner portray the signing of the former and the adoption of the latter. The Bill of Rights is also on permanent display.

National Museum of American History (col)

Constitution Avenue between 12th and 14th streets N.W., 202-357-2700; Daily, 10–5:30. Free.

The Smithsonian Institution is home to one of the Revolutionary War's most sensational relics — the 54-foot gunboat *Philadelphia* that was part of Benedict Arnold's hastily assembled fleet used in the Battle of Valcour Island. In the summer of 1776 Arnold directed 150 soldiers and craftsmen in the construction of five two-masted galleys and eight gunboats.

In the battle, a 24-pound shot with the Crown's "broad arrow" blasted the planks in the *Philadelphia*'s bow and flooded Captain Benjamin Rue's boat. It sank to the bottom, with the top of the white pine mast barely ten feet below the surface of Valcour Bay. The craft, remarkably preserved by the icy waters of Lake Champlain, was dredged up in 1935 and restored. The holes from musket and cannon fire remain in the original timber.

Many actual items of iron and wood and pewter from the *Philadelphia* are displayed along with reproductions of eighteenth century shipboard items. The *Philadelphia* was outfitted with several 9- and 12-pound cannon and swivel guns for firing 1-pound shot and bar shot at enemy rigging.

Relief & Spandrel (mem)

Interstate Commerce Commission, 13th Street and Constitution Avenue S.W.

The limestone panels show General Washington planning the Battle of Trenton with generals Nathanael Greene, holding a map, and John Sullivan. Washington is further honored in the work by Edmond Amateis for his years of public service to America.

Thomas Jefferson Memorial (mem)

Southeast side of Tidal Basin, 202-619-7222; Daily, 8–midnight. Free.

The circular domed structure of white marble was dedicated on the 200th anniversary of Jefferson's birth on April 19, 1943. Congress authorized $3 million for its construction five years earlier, ending a long period of obscurity for the Declaration of Independence author. The circular appearance evokes the spherical influences of Jefferson's architecture. The central memorial room contains a heroic bronze statue of Jefferson by Rudolph Evans. Panels inscribed with the Virginian's most significant writings encircle the monument.

Thomas Jefferson would no doubt be uncomfortable at the splendor with which he is remembered. "I desire as my monument," Jefferson wrote on how he should be honored, "a plain die or cube of three feet, without any mouldings, surmounted by an obelisk of six feet height, each of a single stone." His instructions were followed for his modest grave in the family graveyard at Monticello.

United States Capitol (col)

Capitol Hill, 202-224-3121; Memorial Day–Labor Day: daily, 8–8; Sept–May: daily, 9–4:30. Free.

The 550-room national landmark is adorned with memorials to America's Revolution. In the Rotunda are four murals by John Trumbull: "Signing of the

Declaration of Independence," "The Surrender of Burgoyne," "The Surrender of Cornwallis," and "Washington Resigning His Commission." The "Revolutionary War Door" at the Senate Wing consists of six panels and two medallions depicting the life of George Washington and the early history of the United States.

Revolutionary figures in Statuary Hall, to which each state was invited to send statues of two distinguished deceased citizens, include George Washington, Thomas Jefferson, Marquis de Lafayette, Alexander Hamilton, Samuel Adams, Charles Carroll, Robert Livingston, Roger Sherman, Ethan Allen, Caesar Rodney and Richard Stockton.

Washington Monument (mem)

On the Mall, 202-619-7222; Apr–Labor Day: daily, 8–midnight; Labor Day–Mar: daily, 9–5. Free.

The history of the Washington Monument dates to 1783, when the Continental Congress passed a resolution providing for "an equestrian statue of George Washington." Washington scoffed at the pursuit as a needless waste of scarce government money and the matter was dropped. His death in 1799 revived interest in a lasting memorial to the great man. Bureaucratic dickering and a lack of consensus delayed positive action for another half century until ground was broken on a monument on July 4, 1848.

Money problems delayed construction and by the Civil War all that stood was a 150-foot stub. It was not until February 21, 1885, that the monument was dedicated. It was opened to the public on October 9, 1888, with a steam hoist lifting visitors to the top of the 555-foot, 5⅛-inch monument. Five minutes later they reached the observation level of the world's tallest building. Today the Washington Monument, an unadorned marble obelisk, is still the world's tallest all-masonry structure.

Florida

Revolutionary Status: Spanish Territory

St. Augustine

Castillo de San Marcos (The Fort) (site)

One Castillo Drive, 904-829-6506; Daily, 8:45–4:45. Admission charged.

Settled by the Spanish, America's oldest settlement has been fortified since 1565. Spain and Britain tussled over East Florida often and one motivation behind the British settling of Georgia in the mid–eighteenth century was to dislodge the Spanish. Under the British during the Revolution, St. Augustine was a Tory refuge and jumping off point for military operations in the American South. Prominent political prisoners seized during the war were exiled here.

Three times the Patriots attempted to invade East Florida, moving against the British defensive headquarters at Cowford, along the St. Johns River in Jacksonville. In January 1777 a small force of Patriots advanced to the St. Johns before being repulsed by Britain's Indian allies.

A more serious, if completely mismanaged, threat appeared in May in the form of a combined force of Georgia militia under Colonel John Baker and Continental troops under Lt. Col. Samuel Elbert. The British were led in Florida during the Revolution by the extremely able Patrick Tonyn. Promoted to major general before war's end, Tonyn easily coordinated a defense that routed the amateurish American assault at Thomas Creek on May 17.

The last invasion of Florida was mounted in the summer of 1778 and once again it was highlighted by uncoordinated movements between the Continental Army and Georgia militia at Alligator Bridge. Elijah Clark and 300 Georgia militia had routed an enemy detachment before coming upon a British stronghold held by more than 700 British regulars under Major Marc Prevost. Although 400 Continentals camped less than 15 miles away, Clark threw his 300 troops against the field fortifications without support. He was turned away, fortunate to only suffer the loss of nine dead.

East Florida remained a bastion for the British, Loyalists and sympathetic Indians throughout the war. After the Revolution, St. Augustine was regarrisoned by the Spanish. The field sites of these actions in northeast Florida have been swallowed by development or remain in their wilderness state. The stone fort at Castillo de San Marcos interprets the region's colorful history where Spanish, French, British and American armies battled for more than two centuries.

Georgia

Revolutionary Status: Original Colony
Estimated Colonial Population: 28,000
Colonial Capital: Savannah
Last Colonial Governor: Sir James Wright
Troops Provided: 1 Continental regiment

Revolutionary Timeline

November 25, 1778: John McIntosh repels initial British assault on Fort Morris

December 29, 1778: British troops seize Savannah

February 14, 1779: American victory at Kettle Creek cripples Tory hold on upper Georgia

March 3, 1779: British troops surprise and defeat 1,700 Carolinians and Georgians at Briar Creek

October 9, 1779: American and French invasion forces fail to retake Savannah

September 9, 1780: Elijah Clark unsuccessfully invades British-held Augusta

June 5, 1781: Americans liberate Augusta behind Andrew Pickens and "Light Horse" Harry Lee

---

Augusta

Cotton Exchange Building (site)

32 Eighth Street.

On this site American invasion forces erected a Maham Tower, first used at Fort Watson in South Carolina, to break the siege at Fort Cornwallis. The earthen-filled log tower enabled Patriot sharpshooters to fire into the fort and helped effect its surrender. The Cotton Exchange was the nerve center of the Augusta cotton market, at one time the second largest inland cotton market in the world.

Ezekiel Harris House (site)

1822 Broad Street, 706-724-0436; Tue–Fri, 1–4, Sat, 10–1. Admission charged.

Thomas Brown was a wealthy Yorkshire, England, merchant who emigrated to Georgia in 1773 to manage a 5,000-acre family investment. Openly scornful of the revolutionaries, he was grabbed by Patriots in New Richmond on August 2, 1775, and tarred and feathered. Brown's indignation was completed when he was placed in a cart and paraded in front of the citizenry while forced to renounce King George III. The Americans had galvanized a formidable enemy.

Joining the Loyalists, Brown quickly showed a useful knack for recruiting Indians to the British cause. After the British captured Augusta, Brown returned to northern Georgia as commander of the occupation forces. Despite the harsh treatment inflicted upon him previously at the hands of the Whigs, Brown proved to be a relatively lenient governor.

On September 9, 1780, an ill-advised patrol of rebel forces led by Colonel Elijah Clark invaded Augusta. Brown and a force of some 50 Tories and Chero-kees took refuge at the plantation located on this site, hastily erecting earthworks and fortifying the manor house. Clark lacked the firepower to assault the fortress but he had cut off Brown's access to food and water and demanded surrender. The Tories refused, hoping to be reinforced from the British stronghold of Ninety-Six, South Carolina.

Four days later conditions inside the makeshift fort had become desperate when the reinforcements — 500 strong — arrived. Clark made a quick retreat, leaving 29 of his wounded in Tory hands. American reports filtering out of Augusta claimed that 13 of the prisoners were hanged and the rest subjected to torture. Accurate or not, Tory reprisals against Patriots in backcountry Georgia escalated dramatically.

The temporary fort used by Brown has been replaced by a 1797 Federal-style mansion used to house tobacco merchants bringing their crop to market. Revolutionary artifacts are on display.

Fort Cornwallis (site)
6th and Reynolds streets.

As protection for traders at the head of navigation on the Savannah River, James Oglethorpe founded his second city in Georgia in 1735 by building a small fort on this site. He named it Fort Augusta, after the Princess of Wales. In 1749, St. Paul's Episcopal Church was built "under the curtain of the fort."

In the Patriot attack on Augusta in September 1780, Fort Augusta — renamed Fort Cornwallis — was captured as it was being refortified by the British. After the Americans fled, Fort Cornwallis became garrisoned by more than 250 Loyalists. A satellite fort with 80 men under Colonel James Grierson was built a mile to the east to complete the Augusta defenses.

In 1781 Nathanael Greene ordered Augusta besieged again. With Andrew Pickens and "Light Horse" Harry Lee leading the detachment, more than 500 Patriot troops arrived in Augusta on May 23. Fort Grierson was quickly taken and on June 5 the garrison in Fort Cornwallis surrendered in exchange for parole. All of northern Georgia would remain in American hands to the end of the war.

In 1786, the original Fort Augusta was torn down; the current church building is the fourth on the site. Behind the church is a Celtic cross marking the site of Fort Augusta. One of James Oglethorpe's cannons stands at the foot of the cross.

Fort Grierson Site (site)
Reynolds and 11th streets.

This is the approximate location of the temporary British stronghold commanded by Colonel James Grierson during the occupation of Augusta under Colonel Thomas Brown. Harry Lee and Andrew Pickens invested the fort on May 23, 1781, and, after vigorous attack, Grierson and his men attempted to escape under protection of the river bank to Fort Cornwallis. Few escaped, and while a prisoner Grierson was murdered by an unidentified Georgia rifleman.

Meadow Garden (site)
1320 Independence Drive, 706-724-4174; Mon–Fri, 10–4. Admission charged.

Born in Virginia in 1749, George Walton migrated to Savannah in 1769 to practice law. An ardent supporter of the growing Revolutionary sentiment, Walton was elected by the Georgia Provincial Congress to the Second Continental Congress where, at 26, he became the youngest signer of the Declaration of Independence.

Walton returned to Georgia during the war and participated in the defense of Savannah on January 9, 1778, where a British musket ball shattered his thigh. Captured as the British took the city, he was exchanged in September 1779. Walton then headed for Augusta, which was then serving as state capital, and was elected governor of Georgia in 1779.

George Walton continued his political career after the Revolution and settled into this Sand Hills cottage in the early 1790s. A primary architect in the building of Augusta, Walton lived at Meadow Garden, the oldest documented house in Augusta, until his death in 1804.

Signer's Monument (mem)
Intersection of Greene and Monument streets.

Beneath this unadorned 50-foot obelisk lie the remains of two of Georgia's three signers of the Declaration of Independence. George Walton, six-time Georgia congressman, and Dr. Lyman Hall, a Connecticut-born rice planter and state governor, are buried here. The last of the trio, Button Gwinnett, was an extreme Revolutionary who served briefly as Georgia governor in 1777. His military ambitions led him to clash with Lachlan McIntosh over leadership of a Georgia invasion of Florida, and the two men fought a duel outside of Savannah. Both were injured but Gwinnett died three days later of gangrene in his leg wound. Insolvent at the time of his death, Gwinnett was buried in an unknown location and is not interred in Augusta.

Midway

Fort Morris State Historic Site (site)
2559 Fort Morris Road, off Route 38, seven miles northeast of town, 912-884-5999; Tue–Sat, 9–5, Sun, 9:30–5:30. Admission charged.

The Continental Congress commissioned Fort Morris in 1776 to protect the thriving port of Sunbury, a town of more than 1,000 people during the Revolution that completely disappeared by the Civil War. The large earthworks were built by slave labor on a bluff overlooking the Midway River.

The British first sailed against the garrison on November 25, 1778. Colonel L.V. Fuser demanded the surrender of the fort's 200 defenders and was abruptly rebuffed by Colonel John McIntosh, who replied, "Come and take it." Fuser declined to do so.

After Savannah fell in late December the British returned to Fort Morris with a more formidable invasion force. A brief bombardment brought 159 Continentals and 45 militia into British hands. The ruins of the site are interpreted with a walking tour and a museum.

Midway Museum (col)
Route 17, 912-884-5837; Tue–Sat, 10–4, Sun, 2–4. Admission charged.

The museum in the eighteenth century cottage features exhibits on the area's Colonial influence, including a diorama of Colonel John McIntosh rejecting British surrender demands at Fort Morris. Next door to the museum is the historic Midway Church, founded in 1729. Two of Georgia's Declaration of Independence signers — Button Gwinnett and Dr. Lyman Hall — and two future Revolutionary War generals were members of the congregation.

Rincon

Georgia Salzburger Society Museum (site)

Jerusalem Lutheran Church, End of Route 275, off Route 21; Wed, Sat, Sun, 3–5. Free.

Like Savannah, the town of Ebeneezer thrived in the early history of Georgia. In 1736, 200 Salzburg Lutherans settled here to begin a bustling silk industry. The first church in Georgia was built here in 1741, replaced in 1769 by the handsome brick structure that stands today.

Ebeneezer was fortified by the Continentals in 1776 but was easily captured by Colonel Archibald Campbell on January 2, 1779, just days after the fall of Savannah. The British used Ebeneezer as a staging ground for assaults on Augusta and Charleston. The Jerusalem Church was used as a hospital for the sick and a stable for the horses.

Anthony Wayne took Ebeneezer back in 1782 and for a short time it was the capital of Georgia as the Georgia Legislature assembled in the town. But Ebeneezer never recovered from British occupation and gradually receded into oblivion. The Salzburger farmhouses have all disappeared and only the church, which includes the small museum building, remains.

Monument to John Adam Treutlen (mem)

End of Route 275, off Route 21.

John Treutlen was a plantation owner who rose to prominence when he helped thwart British and Indian invasions in the region; later he opposed South Carolina efforts to annex Georgia. He mortgaged his personal property to defray expenses of the government in the Revolution and went to serve on the Continental line. Under the state constitution in 1777 Treutlen was elected the first governor of Georgia.

After this term as governor, Treutlen retired to his plantation, north of the location of this stone monument. By 1779, however, after constant harassment by bitter Tories, he left for South Carolina, his farm in ruins. In 1782 John Treutlen was murdered by a band of a Tories.

Savannah

Casimir Pulaski (mem)

Monterey Square.

The American Revolution rescued Casimir Pulaski from a difficult exile after being given a death sentence in his native Lithuania for attempted regicide in 1771. After the intrigue against the Russian-imposed king, Pulaski continued to battle against Russia, this time on the side of the Turks. The Turks' defeat forced him to retire restlessly to France.

In May 1777 the 30-year-old Polish nobleman received a letter of recommendation from Benjamin Franklin with which he sailed to America and reported to George Washington. Pulaski saw action almost immediately, leading a counterattack at the Battle of Brandywine that helped cover the American retreat. On September 15, 1777, on Washington's recommendation, the Continental Congress appointed Casimir Pulaski general of the cavalry.

Pulaski sought to mold his cavalry into a highly mobile fighting force separate from the main army and gained the consent of Congress on March 28, 1778. But the American command could not find a suitable role for "the father of the American cavalry." Finally, on February 2, 1779, he was sent to South Carolina to reinforce the southern American forces under British attack.

On October 9, 1779, Pulaski's legion joined the combined French and American assault on Savannah and he was fatally wounded leading a final cavalry charge. Carried to a ship to be taken back to Charleston, Pulaski never regained consciousness. On October 11, 1779, the Polish horse soldier died aboard ship.

One of the enduring mysteries of the Revolution is what became of Pulaski's body. It was always thought that he was buried at sea but a local tradition persisted that he was buried at Greenwich Plantation near Savannah. As this monument was being planned in 1853 a grave was opened at Greenwich and bones were found that a doctor claimed conformed to a man of Pulaski's build and age at death. With no more evidence than that the bones were reinterred in Monterrey Square.

The elaborate monument to Casimir Pulaski was created by Robert Eberhard Launitz, a Russian sculptor. It is surmounted by a statue of liberty, embracing with her left arm the banner of the Stars and Stripes.

Colonial Park Cemetery (site)

Oglethorpe Avenue between Abercorn and Habersham streets; Open daily, dawn to dusk.

The town's second burial ground was used from 1750 until 1853. Button Gwinnett, the controversial signer of the Declaration of Independence, is most likely buried in the cemetery; a monument marks where his remains are thought to lie. Nathanael Greene was buried here for more than a century.

Nathanael Greene (mem)

Johnson Square.

Johnson Square was the first of the city's 24 "jewels" to be laid out by James Oglethorpe and William Bull in 1733. On August 10, 1776, the Declaration of Independence was read here to an "enthusiastic audience."

After the Revolution the State of Georgia gave General Nathanael Greene, second only to Washington in Patriot esteem, the confiscated plantation of Royal Lt. Gov. John Graham, Mulberry Grove. In 1785 Greene sold his holdings in his native Rhode Island and moved to Savannah, where he died a year later from sunstroke. He was only 44 years old.

The cornerstone for the 50-foot marble obelisk was laid on March 21, 1825, by Lafayette. The finished work by William Strickland was dedicated in 1830. In 1902, a controversy over Greene's final resting place was solved when his and his son's remains were located in Colonial Park Cemetery and reinterred beneath this monument.

Savannah History Museum (col)

303 Martin Luther King, Jr., 912-238-1779; Daily, 9–5. Admission charged.

The British began turning their full attention to the American South by sending an expeditionary force from New York in December 1778. Lt. Col. Archibald Campbell landed at Girardeau's Plantation, a mile from Savannah, and on December 29 he took the city. Within six weeks, Georgia, the youngest and weakest of the colonies, was completely under British control.

In the fall of 1779 the French offered the Americans the service of Adm. Gen. Count Charles-Hector Theodat d'Estaing and his 40 warships and 4,000 troops to break the hold on Savannah. D'Estaing sailed into the Savannah River on September 16 and demanded the surrender of the city, which the British had fortified under Maj. Gen. Augustine Prevost. The British ignored the demand of submission.

D'Estaing undertook an ineffective siege of Savannah, and on October 9 a combined force of 4,000 French and 1,500 Patriots under General Benjamin Lincoln stormed the city. The fiercest fighting occurred at the Spring Hill Redoubt, on the western edge of the city, where the Allies were repulsed with some of the heaviest losses of the Revolution. A bloody British counterattack left more than 1,000 men killed or wounded.

Despite the disastrous assault, Lincoln wanted to continue the siege, but the French force withdrew. The British would not leave Savannah until July 11, 1782. The museum, in a restored Central of Georgia Railroad train shed, is on the site of the Spring Hill Redoubt. It interprets Savannah's Revolutionary period with exhibits and multimedia displays.

Sergeant William Jasper (mem)

Madison Square

William Jasper became one of the first heroes of the Revolution in the South when he bravely kept his regiment's colors flying during the bombardment of Fort Sullivan in Charleston on June 28, 1776. He furthered his legend when he and a companion ambushed a British escort outside of Savannah and liberated Patriot prisoners being taken to trial and, most probably, execution.

During the American assault to reclaim Savannah on October 9, 1779, Sergeant Jasper was mortally wounded as he once again rescued the colors of his regiment. The 15½-foot heroic bronze depicts Jasper with his right hand clutching a saber pressed against a wound in his side while his left hand triumphantly holds a flag aloft. In bas-relief around the pedestal are the three major episodes of the South Carolinian's Revolutionary career: Fort Sullivan, the Jasper Springs raid, and the assault on Savannah. The monument was executed by Alexander Doyle of New York and dedicated in 1888.

The southern defense lines of the British ran through Madison Square during the occupation of Savannah.

Telfair Mansion and Art Museum (site)

Telfair Square at 121 Barnard Street, 912-232-1177; Tue–Sat, 10–5, Sun, 2–5. Admission charged.

This 1818 Regency-style mansion by William Jay occupies the site of the Government House, the residence of Georgia's royal governors from 1760 until the end of the Revolutionary War.

Sylvania

Brier Creek Battleground (site)

Brier Creek Bridge, East Ogeechee Street, eleven miles east of town.

After the British evacuated Augusta in February 1780, American Brig. Gen. John Ashe mounted a pursuit force of 1,400 men to chase the Tories down to Savannah. At Brier Creek the redcoats destroyed a bridge and the Patriots camped while they rebuilt the crossing.

Meanwhile, British commander Maj. Gen. Augustine Prevost sent a diversionary force out from Savannah while his younger brother, Lieutenant Mark Prevost, circled around the Americans with a detachment of 900 professional soldiers. The bungled American leadership was caught completely by surprise and quickly routed by the efficient British assault. Nearly 200 Americans were killed, many drowning in a desperate swim across the Savannah River. The Patriots would not retake Georgia until after the British left in two more years.

The battlefield is undeveloped but marked with an interpretive sign.

Washington

96 Kettle Creek Battlefield (site)

Warhill Road, off Route 44, west of town; Open daily, dawn to dusk.

Early in 1779 Colonel John Boyd led a force of 700 North Carolina Tories on a plundering march through South Carolina, heading for Augusta to join British units at the backcountry Georgia headquarters. Such a linkup could prove disastrous for rebel resistance in the region. Boyd's army brushed off occasional sniping from Patriot patrols as he pressed on, crossing the Savannah River into Georgia and gaining Loyalist support as he went.

Near the Little River, north of Augusta, Boyd camped to give his hard-marching troops a rest. Feeling confident, he even put the horses out to graze and ordered hot breakfast cooked for his men. On the morning of February 14, Patriot forces numbering about 300, under the joint command of Andrew Pickens, John Dooly and Elijah Clark, struck the camp.

The first surprise assault by Pickens carried the hilltop and drove in the pickets. Colonel Boyd organized 100 men into a counterattack which gave his army an opportunity to organize a defense, but he himself was mortally wounded. Coordinated flanking attacks from Clark and Dooly were able to cross the creek and soon overwhelm the Tory troops.

More than 100 Tories were killed or wounded and many more deserted the cause. Fewer than 300 of the North Carolinians continued on to join the British in Augusta, and the Patriot victory at Kettle Creek did much to strengthen the desire for independence in the Georgia upcountry. Colonel Boyd was buried on the site.

The battlefield is undeveloped and features a stone obelisk commemorating the decisive battle of the war in Georgia.

Illinois

Revolutionary Status: Part of the Virginia colony

Bloomington

McLean County Soldiers' and Sailors' Monument (mem)

Miller Park, Summit and Wood streets.

The bronze sculpture on a base of light grey granite was created by Frederick Cleveland Hibbard. The structure is an ornamental arch with a walk-through tunnel. It is dedicated to soldiers of all wars that have touched Illinois citizens.

Chicago

George Washington (mem)

51st Street and King Drive.

This equestrian rendering of George Washington is a copy of one by Daniel Chester French in Paris. Edward Potter sculpted the horse on which the commander-in-chief sits.

Lincoln Park (mem)

Lake Shore Drive from North Avenue to Hollywood Avenue.

Chicago's largest park features many monuments, including a tribute to Alexander Hamilton by John Angel. A sculpture of Benjamin Franklin was donated to the printers of the community by Joseph Medill, founder of the *Chicago Tribune*. Also in the park, near the intersection of Clark and Wisconsin streets, is a boulder marking the grave of David Kenison, believed to be the last survivor of the Boston Tea Party.

Nathan Hale (mem)

Tribune Tower Court.

This tribute to executed spy Nathan Hale by Bela Lyon Pratt shows the young prisoner passively awaiting execution. The picture of the upper portion of this statue appeared on one billion half-cent stamps issued in 1931.

Thaddeus Kosciuszko Memorial (mem)

Burnham Park, Solidarity Drive.

In 1886 the Kosciuszko Society, Chicagoans of Polish descent, initiated the idea of honoring the Polish freedom fighter with an equestrian statue. The original was dedicated in Humboldt Park in 1904 before the greatest assembly of Poles ever in America. The memorial bronze by Casimir Chodzinski was moved to Burnham Park and rededicated on October 22, 1978.

Robert Morris–George Washington–Haym Salomon (mem)

Herald Square.

Washington is flanked by two leading financiers to recognize the role the moneymen played in the creation of this nation. Morris, to Washington's right, controlled the financial operations of Congress from 1776 to 1778 and is much better known.

Haym Salomon was born into a Jewish family in Lissa, Poland. In his early thirties he sailed to New York City and established a mercantile business in 1772. Salomon embraced the movement for independence and was arrested as a spy during the early days of the British occupation of the New York. He was paroled to serve as an interpreter for Hessian officers but was arrested for a second time in 1777. A bribe to his jailer secured his freedom.

Moving to Philadelphia, he became a leading broker in government securities, a paymaster for the French army in America, and primary broker for the issue of U.S. Treasury notes. By the end of the Revolution, Haym Salomon became known as the lender of last resort for the perennially empty U.S. Treasury. He had used his personal credit to furnish the Continental Congress with over $600,000 in gold or silver in loans.

After the Revolution, Salomon suffered heavy losses as his assets remained frozen by the new government. He died insolvent on January 6, 1785, still only 45 years of age. Despite sacrificing his entire fortune for the cause of freedom, Salomon's heirs were never compensated from Congress for his losses.

Danville

Minuteman (mem)

Federal Building and United States Courthouse, 201 North Vermilion Street.

This monument, featuring Daniel Chester French's "Minuteman," was dedicated in 1915 to the memory of soldiers of the War for Independence who are buried in Vermilion County. The names of 14 men are inscribed on a concrete walk.

Ellis Grove

Fort Kaskaskia State Historic Site (site)

Off Route 3, ten miles north of town, 618-859-3741; Open daily, dawn to dusk. Free.

The French started the fortifications along the Kaskaskia River in 1736 and the settlement grew into the largest French colonial settlement in the Illinois region with about 80 stone homes. It was partially destroyed before the British takeover in 1763. They fortified a Jesuit mission in the village and called it Fort Gage.

During the Revolution many of the former French outposts had been left lightly defended by the British, who were massing their western forces at Detroit. George Rogers Clark, only 23 years old at the time but a seasoned explorer of the Ohio Valley, saw the possibility of capturing the entire Northwest and opening the Mississippi and Ohio rivers to Spanish supplies from New Orleans. He proposed his ambitious plan to Virginia governor Patrick Henry, who authorized funds for the mission.

Clark's forces numbered fewer than 200 as he sailed down the Ohio River. He landed at the site of Fort Massac, planning to execute a surprise overland attack from this point. His well-drilled expedition covered the 120 miles in five days and, after a night crossing of the Kaskaskia River, surrounded the town. The fort was surrendered without a shot being fired.

Clark's benevolent leadership soon won the affection of the French locals, who rapidly switched their allegiance to the state of Virginia. These new allies would be of considerable value in his conquering of the region.

Shifts in the Mississippi River have swallowed the original site of Fort Kaskaskia but a 275-acre park preserves the history of the area. Garrison Hill Cemetery is also on the grounds.

Evanston

Flagpole Memorial (mem)
Patriots Park.

The French settlement here dates to 1674, when Father Jacques Marquette landed in the natural harbor. In 1929 the Fort Dearborn chapter of the Daughters of the American Revolution erected a circular structure with relief carvings and sculpture in the round. Stephen Beames executed the copper and limestone sculpture on a limestone base.

Metropolis

Fort Massac State Park (site)
1757 Fort Massac, off Route 45, two miles east of town, 618-524-9321; Open daily, dawn to dusk. Free.

The French fortified the area in 1757, but their Fort Massac was long abandoned in 1778 when General George Rogers Clark and his Kentucky Long Knives rested at the fort before beginning the arduous overland march to capture Kaskaskia. A reconstructed American fort of 1796 and a statue of Clark mark the site. A plaque near the tattered monument reads: "In memory of George Rogers Clark — and his faithful companions in arms who by their enterprise and courage won the Illinois country for the Commonwealth of Virginia and so for the American Union."

Reenactment: The park now includes nearly 1,500 acres. On the third weekend in October the fort celebrates its eighteenth century heritage with an encampment, musket demonstrations and exhibitions of period arts and crafts.

Indiana
Revolutionary Status: Part of the Virginia colony

Hymera

Nathan Hinkle Monument (mem)
Bethel Cemetery, Route 48.

This limestone monument of a Revolutionary War soldier honors veteran Nathan Hinkle, who was born on June 7, 1749, and fought in the War for Independence. He died on Christmas, 1848, just short of his 100th birthday.

Vincennes

George Rogers Clark National Historical Park (site)
401 South Second Street, 812-882-1776; Daily, 9–5. Admission charged.

In 1731 François Morgnae de Vincennes built and commanded a French military post in this area and watched as a small community grew up around the fort. By 1763, when the French ceded most of its land east of the Mississippi River to England, Vincennes was home to about 85 French families. The British ignored the French village until 1777, when a garrison arrived and renamed the area Fort Sackville.

By 1778 word had spread in the region that the French were aligning with America, and Captain Leonard Helm organized the French militia to take over the fort. British Lt. Col. Henry Hamilton rounded up a force of British troops and loyal Indians and marched on Fort Sackville from Detroit. Hamilton set off in early October as one of the most severe winters on record closed in on the Midwest. It took his small army, numbering 500 by the end of the march, 71 days to reach Vincennes. Helm's small patrols scattered at the news of this expedition and only one soldier stood by him as the British captured the fort.

When he heard of Hamilton's audacious taking of Fort Sackville, George Rogers Clark knew his ambitious scheme to seize all the land northwest of the Ohio River for Virginia was in serious jeopardy. He began to march to Vincennes with a force of 200. The spring thaw left the country flooded with icy water and ground was gained at barely a mile a day in some spots. Worse, when he arrived at Fort Sackville, Clark knew he did not have the manpower to overpower the fort.

Clark cleverly arranged his forces to make his 170 remaining men seem like a thousand. He learned that 40 of Hamilton's 120-man garrison were on an expeditionary forage and during the night of February 23-24 American snipers began to fire into the fort. By the next night he had forced Hamilton to turn over the fort. Helm was sent out to capture the foraging detachment. Clark's victory at Fort Sackville was the largest land conquest of the Revolutionary War — the lands he claimed were as vast as the original 13 colonies combined.

Clark renamed the fort for Virginia governor Patrick Henry, but the lawlessness on the frontier continued. In 1784 the land was given to the United States as a public domain — the birth of the country north of the Ohio River.

The park features a granite and marble memorial building with a heroic statue of George Rogers Clark, conqueror of the Northwest and the man whom Lafayette ranked next to George Washington as a military leader. Frederick Hirons won a national architectural competition to design the memorial with his classic Greek design featuring 16 huge columns. Seven large murals in the interior depict Clark's vital role in the region west of the Appalachians. The memorial is on the approximate site of Fort Sackville. A visitor center displays exhibits and screens a comprehensive 23-minute film about Clark's exploits during the Revolution.

Other important frontier forts in Indiana include the first French encampment, Fort Miami, which was constructed about 1712. The town of Fort Wayne, named for General Anthony Wayne, grew up around the site and the historic fort is currently closed. Fort Ouiatenon was the second outpost constructed, on the Wabash River four miles south of present day Lafayette, named for the French general of the Revolution. Fort Ouiatenon is on South River Road, although no action took place here during the Revolutionary War.

Reenactment: The Spirit of Vincennes Rendezvous takes place Memorial Day Weekend and includes a battle reenactment at this historic park.

Kentucky

Revolutionary Status: County of the Virginia colony

Carlisle

Blue Licks Battlefield (site)

Route 68, seven miles north of town, 606-289-5507; Apr–Oct: open daily, 24 hours. Free for park; admission to museum.

British captain William Caldwell led a band of Indian raiders against American outposts on the frontier in the waning days of the Revolution. On August 18, 1782, Caldwell moved on Bryan Station, an unprotected settlement northeast of present-day Lexington. Caldwell failed to achieve surprise and the woodsmen repulsed the attackers after two days of fighting.

Caldwell began a retreat to the Ohio border but the frontiersmen, numbering about 180, foolishly took off in pursuit. The British ambushed the Kentucky volunteers at the Licking River and killed about 70 patriots, including a son of Daniel Boone, in just 15 minutes of fighting.

A granite obelisk honors the men killed at Blue Licks and victims of the ambush are buried in the park. Landmarks of the battle are interpreted in the park and the museum offers artifacts, a diorama and an audiovisual program of the last battle of the Revolution in Kentucky.

Danville

Isaac Shelby Cemetery State Historic Site (site)
Route 127, five miles south of town; Open daily, dawn to dusk.

Shelby led several contingents of "mountain men" to the patriot cause in the Southern Department during the Revolution. Shelby was the chairman of the first Kentucky Constitutional Convention and was both the first and fifth governor of Kentucky. The old warrior took up arms again in the War of 1812.

Frankfort

Daniel Boone Gravesite (site)
Frankfort Cemetery, 215 East Main Street, 502-227-2403; Summer: daily, 7:00–8:30; Winter: daily, 8:00–5:30. Free.

Daniel Boone was born on November 2, 1734, and at the age of 20 was driving wagons in the British Army. He sat in the Virginia House of Burgesses but joined the fight for liberty and was commissioned a colonel in the Kentucky militia. During Boone's two decades on the frontier he survived many skirmishes and ambushes from Indians but he claimed to be positive of killing only one warrior, whom he shot at Blue Licks in 1782.

After the Revolution, Boone's claims for 12,000 acres he settled in Kentucky were all lost due to faulty titles and improper surveys. He migrated to the Osage Femme Valley in Missouri in 1799, where he died on September 26, 1820. His body was returned to Frankfort in 1845 and buried, along with his wife, on a hilltop overlooking the capital city.

Kentucky's Revolutionary War Veteran Senators (mem)
Old State Capitol, Broadway and Lewis streets.

A marker at the corner of the historic former capitol building honors the six Revolutionary War veterans who emigrated to Kentucky and became United States senators: John Brown, a private in the Virginia militia; John Edwards, a drummer in the Pennsylvania line; Humphrey Marshall, a captain in the Virginia cavalry; John Breckinridge, a subaltern in the Virginia militia; George Walker, a private in Morgan's Rifle Corps; and John Adair, a brigadier general in the South Carolina line.

Liberty Hall Historic Site (site)

218 Wilkinson Street, 502-227-2560, Mar–Dec: Tue–Sat, 10:30, 1:30, 3:00, Sun, 1:30 and 3:00. Admission charged.

Virginian John Brown was a delegate to the Continental Congress and served as an aide to Lafayette in the Revolution. Moving to Kentucky he became the first senator from the fifteenth state. Liberty Hall, named for Brown's boyhood school, was the lavish Federalist-style mansion that he built in 1796.

Georgetown

Royal Spring Park (site)

Water Street and West Main Street.

John McClelland built and defended a fort here, on the site of Kentucky's largest natural spring, during the Revolution. A monument to Scott County's fallen soldiers of the Revolution marks the location. In 1789 Georgetown founder the Reverend Elijah Craig reputedly invented bourbon whiskey at the Royal Spring.

Harrodsburg

Old Fort Harrod State Park (site)

Routes 127 and 68, 606-734-3346; Jun–Aug: daily, 8:30–8; Mar–May and Sept–Oct: daily, 8:30–5; Nov–Feb, daily 8–4:30. Admission charged.

James Harrod, a Pennsylvania woodsmen, led 30 men to this site in 1774 and commenced the building of cabins. His efforts were interrupted by a call back to fight in the Battle of Point Pleasant but he soon returned to Fort Harrod and established the first permanent settlement west of the Alleghenies.

During the Revolution, Harrod escorted military supplies along the Ohio River and fought against Indian raiders. His settlement was one of the few to survive the plundering by Indians, but after the Revolution the fort disappeared. So, too, did Harrod, having never been heard from after 1793. The most popular story is that he was lured from home by the search for a mystical silver mine and murdered by a rival.

Kentucky's first settlement has been recreated, including the first schoolhouse and pioneer cabins. Also on the grounds is a memorial to George Rogers Clark.

Henderson

Nancy Morgan Hart Gravesite (site)

Book Cemetery, Frog Island Road.

Revolutionary War heroine Nancy Hart is buried in the old Hart Graveyard, now known as Book Cemetery. Nancy's son John Hart, a Henderson County resident, is also buried in the Book Cemetery. He served in the Revolutionary War with his father Benjamin and brothers Morgan and Thomas.

Louisville

Cave Hill Cemetery (site)
East end of Broadway, 502-584-8363; Daily, 8–4:45. Free.

Buried in this cemetery and botanical garden is Revolutionary War general George Rogers Clark, whose exploits in the "Old Northwest" won the United States legal right to the frontier between Virginia and the Mississippi River. Originally buried at Locust Grove, Clark's body was moved to this burial ground in 1869.

Fort Nelson (site)
7th and Main streets, historical marker only.

At this spot in the Ohio River the water drops 26 feet in less than two miles. Above this point the Ohio is wide and calm. Thus the site of present-day Louisville was a natural terminus to navigation on the Ohio River.

In the summer of 1778 George Rogers Clark led some 20 families and 120 soldiers to a small peninsula above the falls and fortified the camp with a blockhouse. Leaving the settlers in charge of the supplies in the blockhouse, Clark and his small army shot the rapids — during a total eclipse of the sun — and continued further west. The next winter the settlers built Fort Nelson at the spot of the memorial plaque.

"The Falls of the Ohio" was changed to "Louisbourg" in 1780 in honor of King Louis XVI, who was already helping America to independence.

Locust Grove Historic Home (site)
Blankenbaker Lane, off Route 42, 502-897-9845; Mon–Sat, 10–4:30, Sun, 1:30–4:30. Admission charged.

George Rogers Clark, who accomplished so much for the new United States in the Revolutionary War, found little glory with the cessation of hostilities. He struggled to find his place in the new world and for many years operated a grist mill across the river from Louisville, living in a spartan cabin. In 1809, after a paralyzing stroke and having a leg amputated, Clark moved into his brother-in-law's elegant Georgian brick mansion. He spent the final nine years of his life in the home.

Pisgah

Pisgah Cemetery (site)
Pisgah Presbyterian Church, Pisgah Pike.

The first Pisgah Church on the site was built of logs and opened for services in 1785. Seven men who served in the Revolutionary War came to be buried in the churchyard. The last, William Martin, was only 13 when the Revolutionary War began. He was interred in 1836.

Richmond

Fort Boonesborough (site)

Route 627, north of town, 606-527-3131; Apr–Labor Day: daily, 9–5:30; Labor Day–Oct: Wed–Sun, 9–5:30. Admission charged.

Daniel Boone and his men began work on Kentucky's second permanent settlement on April 1, 1775. Boone built four blockhouses and a palisade by July 1776; he would need them all during the wave of Indian attacks that engulfed the area in September 1778. Only Boonesborough, Harrodsburg and one other settlement remained after the onslaught. No trace of Daniel Boone's fort remains but a re-creation features demonstrators and artisans. An orientation film chronicles the struggles of a frontier fort in the Western Department during the Revolutionary War.

Maine

Revolutionary Status: Part of the Massachusetts colony

Augusta

Fort Western (site)

16 Cony Street, 207-626-2385; Independence Day–Labor Day: Mon–Fri, 10–4, Sat–Sun, 1–4; Memorial Day–Independence Day and Labor Day–Columbus Day: Sat–Sun, 1–4. Admission charged.

In the summer of 1775, General Washington conceived a plan to march troops north from Massachusetts to seize Quebec in a surprise attack before the British could organize defenses in the early stages of the war. He chose to lead the mission an impressive young colonel, Benedict Arnold, who was already attracting notice in the Continental Army for his daring and resourcefulness. Washington called for volunteers, men "active as woodsmen and well acquainted with bateaux [flat-bottomed boats used on rivers to haul bulky loads]." More than 1,000 adventuresome troops, bored with siege life in Boston, signed on.

Preparations were hastily arranged and by late September Arnold had 200 light bateaux in his fleet. He estimated the route, reconnoitered in 1761 by British Army engineer Captain John Montresor, would cover 180 miles to Quebec. He brought along food for 45 days, figuring the journey would last 20. The Americans departed Cambridge, Massachusetts, on September 19, 1775, in high spirits, embarking on one of the epic adventures of the Revolution.

Unfortunately, the plan had been conceived too late in the season for Arnold's men to enjoy good traveling weather. Worse, an early winter turned into one of the worst in Maine history. The 180 miles was in reality 300. Still, Arnold would not be deterred from his objective. Through dint of sheer determination and will he brought a force of about 700 men, subsisting on starvation rations, against Quebec after 46 days. Once there, however, the British were able to defeat the invaders. On November 9 many Americans were taken prisoner.

After entering Keenebec River on September 22, Arnold's expedition stopped at Fort Western and gathered full force for the first time on the 23rd. The men stayed two days, enjoying a great feast of bear meat, venison, wild fowl and other treats before setting off in earnest.

The entire Arnold Trail has been included on the National Register. The post at Fort Western was established in 1626, but the restored cedar-shaked fort building dates to 1754. The fort complex, including the original main house and reproduction blockhouses, watchboxes and palisade, is furnished to interpret early settlement and military themes.

Castine

Fort George State Historical Site (site)

Battle Avenue and Wadsworth Street; Open daily, dawn to dusk.

Over the decades the attractive deep-water port at Castine in the Penobscot Bay attracted the attention of many suitors. The French, Dutch and British flags all flew here before the Revolution. When Patriot privateers began harassing British shipping between Nova Scotia and New York, General Francis McLein and 900 men arrived from Halifax to fortify Castine on June 17, 1779. A rectangular fort about 200 feet square was constructed on a high ridge on the west side of the village.

The state of Massachusetts acted swiftly to dislodge the British. Without bothering to consult with the Continental Congress or the Continental Army the state organized an expedition of 40 vessels and the largest amphibious force of the entire war — 800 marines and 1,200 militia. Captain Dudley Saltonstall, a Continental Naval officer, commanded the force; among his officers was Lt. Col. Paul Revere in charge of the artillery.

What the expedition made up for in numbers, it lacked in ability. The amateurish attack failed to achieve surprise and it engaged the British on July 25, 1779, with no coordination. An initial opportunity to destroy the British garrison, which was unfinished and sported only 3 ships and 400 men, went wanting and the Americans set about constructing siegeworks. Just as they were about to launch their assault a British force arrived from New York with 10 vessels, including a 64-gun warship. The American landing forces scrambled back onto their ships and they were forced up the river, where their transports were beached. The Americans returned to Massachusetts on foot, carrying with them the burden of the most humiliating and devastating naval defeat of the Revolutionary War.

The ramifications from the fiasco at Fort George lasted years. Saltonstall was dismissed from the Continental Navy and returned to privateering. Revere was charged with disobedience, unsoldierly conduct and cowardice and was not cleared until a court-martial dismissed all accusations.

The British finished fortifications at Fort George and held it until the war ended, using the base to attack New England coastal towns. During the War of 1812 the British again manned the post but destroyed most of it when the town was abandoned on April 25, 1815. Fort George, partially restored, is maintained as a memorial.

Kittery

Fort McClary State Historic Site (site)

Route 103, two miles east of town, 207-439-2845; Memorial Day–Oct: daily, dawn to dusk. Free.

In the park are fortifications that appeared on this site as early as 1722. An early name for the breastwork was Fort William but after the Battle of Bunker Hill it was renamed for Major Andrew McClary, the senior officer killed in Boston. The current incarnation of the fort dates to 1846.

Kittery Historical and Naval Museum (col)

Rogers Road, off Route 236S, 207-439-3080; Memorial Day–Oct, Mon–Fri, 10–4. Admission charged.

Across the water from the Portsmouth Naval Yard, Kittery was itself an important shipbuilding center. The *Ranger*, under the command of John Paul Jones and the first ship to fly the Stars and Stripes, was launched at Kittery on May 10, 1777. The flag was created by a Congressional resolution on the day Jones was given command of the *Ranger*. Museum exhibits display 350 years of Kittery's maritime heritage.

Machias

Burnham Tavern Museum (site)

Main and Free streets, 207-255-4432; Mid-Jun–Oct: Mon–Fri, 10–5. Admission charged.

The Colonial inn, one of the oldest buildings in eastern Maine, was the meeting place for patriots scheming to capture the captain of the British four-gun schooner *Margaretta* while its officers were in church. The plot was botched and the resulting naval action in Machias Bay has been termed, parochially, the "first naval battle of the American Revolution" and the "Lexington of the Sea." The tavern is now a museum with articles from the Revolutionary period.

Machiasport

Fort O'Brien State Historical Memorial (site)

Route 92; Open daily, dawn to dusk.

After the disturbance at Lexington and Concord in April 1775, the British sent two sloops, *Polly* and *Unity*, to Machias to collect lumber for its Boston troops. The two ships were escorted by the *Margaretta*, wielding four guns on its deck. Local patriots attempted to capture the ships by surprising the captain of the *Margaretta* on land but the kidnap plot was aborted and the Machias men took up chase of the British boats in the harbor. About 40 ill-equipped colonists, behind Jeremiah O'Brien and Joseph Wheaton, caught up with the *Unity* on June 11 and captured the *Margaretta* the next day. Total losses were seven men killed and wounded on each side, including the *Margaretta*'s commander, who died in Machias the next day.

O'Brien was given the command of *Unity* and he rechristened the ship the *Machias Liberty*. A few weeks later O'Brien was able to take the British schooner *Diligent* without firing a shot. These two warships became the nucleus of the Massachusetts Navy, separate from the Continental Navy, and O'Brien captured several more prizes before his small fleet was put out of commission in late 1776.

Fort Machias was built on bluffs overlooking the Machias River shortly after the Revolutionary War began. Strengthened in 1777, the fort stood until 1814 when the British destroyed it. The breastworks that remain are earthen works from a fort built here in 1863.

Popham Beach

Fort Popham State Historic Site (site)
Ocean terminus of Route 209, 207-389-1335; Jun–Oct: daily, dawn to dusk. Free.

The granite and brick fortification here is an incomplete Civil War fort but defenses have been on this site since the first colonists in 1607. The Arnold Expedition stopped here in 1775 to take on a river pilot to guide them up the Kennebec.

Portland

Maine History Gallery (col)
489 Congress Street, 207-879-0427; Jun–Oct: Tue–Sun, 10–4, Nov–May: Wed–Sat, 12–4. Admission charged.

In addition to the artifacts pertaining to Maine's role in the Revolution, the Maine Historical Society owns the twenty-fifth copy of the Declaration of Independence.

Stockton Springs

Fort Pownall (site)
Fort Point State Park, on the Penobscot River, east of town; Open daily, dusk to dawn.

During the French and Indian Wars the British fortified the Penobscot River with a small bastion approximately 30 yards square. Fort Pownall was again occupied by a British force early in the Revolution. The garrison drove away an American invasion force in March 1775 and shortly thereafter carried away their heavy guns and ammunition. The Americans retreating from Fort George set fire to the timber fort in 1779. The earthworks of the fort have been preserved in the park.

Thomaston

Montpelier (site)
Routes 1 and 131, seven miles east of town; May–Oct: Tue–Sat, 10–4, Sun, 1–4. Admission charged.

Montpelier is a full-scale replica of the 30-room mansion built by Maj. Gen. Henry Knox, Revolutionary War hero and Washington's first secretary of war. Knox built the first house in 1793; it was razed in 1871. Montpelier contains some of Knox's original belongings, but most were lost in a 1970 burglary.

Winslow

Fort Halifax (site)
Route 201, south of town; Open daily, dawn to dusk.

One of the oldest surviving blockhouses in the United States, Fort Halifax was built in 1754 on the orders of Massachusetts governor William Shirley to "awe the Indians and cover the frontiers of New England." Fort Halifax, built of massive timbers, was covered by two small blockhouses on a nearby hill, both of which were destroyed after the Revolutionary War. Arnold and his Canadian invasion force stopped here on September 30, 1775.

Maryland

Revolutionary Status: Original colony
Estimated Colonial Population: 245,000
Colonial Capital: Annapolis
Last Colonial Governor: Governed by committee chairmen
Troops Provided: 8 Continental regiments

Revolutionary Timeline

May 23, 1774: Chestertown Tea Party staged in support of Boston

March 21, 1783: The Revolution's last naval action occurs when a Maryland ship under Captain John Lynn captures several British supply barges at Devil's Island in the Chesapeake Bay

September 3, 1783: The Treaty of Paris, which will be ratified in Annapolis, is negotiated to end the American Revolution

December 23, 1783: George Washington resigns as commander-in-chief of the Continental Army in the Maryland State House

Annapolis

The Barracks (site)

43 Pinkney Street, 410-267-7619; Open by appointment. Free.

The small, wooden structure in the middle of the narrow downtown street is typical of the buildings leased by the Maryland colonial government to house soldiers awaiting sea passage to battle areas in the Revolution.

Charles Carroll House (site)

Off Duke of Gloucester Street, private building, being restored.

The oldest section of the house dates to the 1720s, shortly after the planned town of Annapolis was chartered in 1708. Charles Carroll of Carrollton, the only Roman Catholic signer of the Declaration of Independence, is thought to have been born in this house and lived here until 1821. Carroll also was the only signer to include his address — "of Carrollton" — to the document because his father, grandfather, and many cousins were all named Charles.

Chase-Lloyd House (site)

22 Maryland Avenue, 410-263-2723; Mar–Dec: Tue–Sat, 2–4; Jan–Feb: Tue, Fri–Sat, 2–4. Admission charged.

This large brick Georgian town house by noted architect William Buckland was begun in 1769 by Samuel Chase, a signer of the Declaration of Independence.

The Crypt of John Paul Jones (site)

United States Naval Academy, Gate 1, 52 King George Street, 410-263-6933; Mar–Nov: daily, 9–5; Dec–Feb: 9–4. Free.

Scottish sea captain John Paul arrived in America in 1773 after killing the leader of a mutiny upon his ship *Betsey* as it lay in dock at Tobago in the West Indies. Paul, who had set to sea at the age of 12 and had become a merchant captain in 1769 at the age of 22, sought refuge with his brother in Fredericksburg, Virginia. He sought to further his anonymity by adding the ubiquitous surname "Jones."

When the Revolution began he received a lieutenant's commission in the Colonial Navy and quickly distinguished himself as an officer. The Continental Congress gave him a command in June 1777. He oversaw the construction of the *Ranger*, desiring a fast ship because he intended "to be in harm's way." He successfully raided the English seacoast in 1778, going ashore at Whitehaven burning ships and spiking cannons.

The French recognized his exploits and gave him command of a wearied 40-gun warship that he renamed *Bonhomme Richard* as a tribute to Benjamin Franklin. In August 1779 Jones once again peppered the British coast until he was engaged by the *Serapis* on September 23. Jones was clearly outgunned by his modern enemy and decided to attach ships to join the fight. As he struggled to join the vessels he shouted down British hecklers with his immortal taunt, "I have not yet begun to fight." Although sinking and on fire, Jones carried the fight to the *Serapis* until the British vessel succumbed late into the night.

Jones continued to serve the American cause until the Revolution was over and in 1788 he joined the Russian Navy before returning to Paris, where he died in 1792. He was buried in the St. Louis Cemetery, upon which houses would eventually be constructed. In 1905 a former ambassador to France, General Horace Porter, found what he identified as the remains of John Paul Jones. Amidst great ceremony, the remains — identified because the French had pickled his body in rum to preserve it — were returned to the United States and entombed at the Naval Academy in 1913.

The Crypt of John Paul Jones is in the back of the chapel on Blake Road. Circled around the ornate black marble crypt are remembrances of Jones' career, including swords and paintings of his famous ships. The tomb is styled after that of Napoleon.

The Academy Museum in Preble Hall features intricate ship models dating to the seventeenth century and displays on the American Navy in the Revolution.

Liberty Tree (site)

St. John's College, College Avenue; Open daily, 24 hours.

Beneath this yellow tulip poplar tree the Sons of Liberty gathered many times in the days before the Revolutionary War. Late in the nineteenth century the giant tree failed to bloom and the students decided to fell the tree with a charge of gunpowder packed in its hollow trunk. The tree didn't fall and the next spring bloomed again.

Although enthusiastically listed on a plaque at the base as being 600 years old at the time of dedication in 1907, it is more likely 400 years old. Washington, during a visit in 1791, and Lafayette, in 1824, stayed in Ogle Hall — now the Naval Academy Alumni House — across the street.

Maryland State House (site)

State Circle, 410-974-3400; Daily, 9–5; tours at 11 and 3. Free.

The Maryland State House is the oldest state capitol in continuous legislative use. It was begun in 1772 and completed in 1779 and, because of its convenient location, was the nation's capital from November 26, 1783, until August 13, 1784. As such, the large brick structure on the hill was witness to the military and political conclusions of the Revolution.

Shortly before noon on December 23, 1783, George Washington walked into the Old Senate Chamber and, speaking emotionally in a short speech, resigned his commission as commander-in-chief of the Continental Army. He concluded, "Having now finished the work assigned me, I retire from the great theatre of action; and, bidding an affectionate farewell to this august body, under whose orders I have so long acted, I here offer my commission, and take leave of all the employments of public life."

Several months later, after years of negotiation, Congress ratified the Treaty of Paris in Annapolis, which formally ended the Revolutionary War.

Several of the historic rooms off the main vestibule are open for a self-guided tour. There are exhibits on the struggle for independence, including Maryland's original copy of the Constitution. The Old Senate Chamber recreates the occasion of Washington's resignation, including a powerful rendering of the commander-in-chief in wax. The portrait of Lafayette was executed by Charles Wilson Peale, who accepted a bribe from the French general, only 22 at the time, to make him appear older.

The capitol dome was built entirely of wood, including pegs rather than nails. On the grounds, on the west lawn, is a statue by Ephraim Keyser of Baron Johann de Kalb, who was "pierced with many wounds" leading Maryland and Delaware troops against superior numbers in Camden, South Carolina, on August 16, 1780. He died three days later.

Peggy Stewart House (site)

207 Hanover Street; private residence.

On October 15, 1774, Anthony Stewart's brig the *Peggy Stewart*, named for his daughter, docked at the Severn River. On board were hidden 17 boxes — more than 2,300 pounds — of tea. The citizenry of Annapolis was seized with patriotic fervor and to save his cargo Stewart paid the tax on the tea, even though it was consigned to another merchant. He avowed that the tea was not his and offered to land the cargo and burn it, but the crowd was not appeased. Finally, at a radical public meeting, Stewart was forced to sign an apology for even bringing the tea to Annapolis and to pacify their indignation he set fire to his own ship. He shortly fled to England.

The private 1763 Georgian home sits directly across from the Naval Academy. On the campus, on the side of Luce Hall, on Holloway Street, is a plaque marking the site of the burning of the *Peggy Stewart*. Thomas Stone, a signer of the Declaration of Independence, owned the house from 1783 to 1787.

William Paca House (site)

186 Prince George House, 410-263-5553; Mar–Dec: Mon–Sat, 10–4, Sun 12–4. Admission charged.

A colonial lawyer, William Paca entered the Maryland assembly in 1768 at the age of 28. An enthusiastic backer of freedom, he was elected to the First Continental Congress in 1774 and the Second Continental Congress in 1775, although Maryland forbade her delegates to support independence. The mood in Maryland did not shift until June of 1776 and Paca was able to cast his vote for separation from England on July 2. He signed the Declaration of Independence on July 4. William Paca helped write Maryland's first constitution and was elected governor in 1782, 1783 and 1784. He served out his public life as a federal district judge appointed by George Washington.

Tours interpret the five-part Georgian home during the period Paca lived here, from its construction in 1763 to his departure for his country home in Wye in 1780. The two-acre pleasure garden features five terraces, a fish-shaped pond and a wilderness garden.

Baltimore

Carroll Mansion (site)

800 East Lombard Street, 410-396-3523; Apr–Oct: Tue–Sat, 10–4, Sun, 12–5; Nov–Mar: Tue–Sat, 10–4, Sun, 12–4. Admission charged.

Now part of the Baltimore City Life Museums, the final home of Charles Carroll was considered one of Baltimore's finest houses when it was built just prior to the War of 1812. Carroll moved into the Federal-period mansion in 1820 and managed his investments from an austere first floor office, highlighted by a wall safe protected by an iron door. On the second and third floors were the opulent living quarters where Carroll lived until 1832, "envied by many as the wealthiest citizen of the United States and revered by everyone as the last surviving signer of the Declaration of Independence."

Fort McHenry National Monument (site)

East end of Fort Avenue, 410-962-4290; daily, 8–5. Admission charged.

The fort that spawned "The Star Spangled Banner" during the War of 1812 began life in the Revolutionary War as an earthen, star-shaped bastion called Fort Whetstone. Located far enough from Baltimore to provide protection without endangering the city, it was surrounded on three sides by water. The British never attacked Baltimore so its defenses were never tested.

Maryland Historical Society Museum & Library (col)

201 West Monument Street, 410-685-3750; Mon–Fri, 10–4, Sun, tours at noon. Admission charged.

The exhibits in the collection date back to 1720 and include rare Revolutionary War uniforms. The Society owns the original "Star Spangled Banner" manuscript.

Maryland Line Monument (mem)

Mt. Royal and Cathedral Street.

The female figure atop a 60-foot monument was sculpted by A.L. Van der Bergen in honor of "all the Patriots of Maryland who during the Revolutionary War aided on land or at sea in gaining the independence of this and of these United States and to the Maryland line."

Washington Monument (mem)

Mount Vernon Square, West Pratt and North Charles streets; Wed–Sun, 12–4. Admission charged.

The 178-foot white marble column was America's first architectural monument honoring George Washington. Money for the monument was raised in 1815 by public lottery and completed in 1842 on a design by Robert Mills, who also orchestrated the Washington D.C. monument to the Revolutionary leader. The statue of Washington at the top weighs 30 tons. A 228-step spiral staircase winds to the top of the structure and to four observation windows.

Big Pool

Fort Frederick (site)

11100 Ft. Frederick Road, off Route 56, 301-842-2155; Apr–Oct: park and museum open daily, 8:30–dusk; Nov–Mar: daily, 10–4. Free.

Fort Frederick was constructed on the Cumberland Valley frontier in 1756 to protect settlers during the French and Indian War. It was named for Frederick Calvert, Sixth Lord of Baltimore. The garrison was abandoned in 1763 but was brought back to life as a prison camp during the Revolutionary War. It was garrisoned again in the Civil War.

The fort's stone walls and two barracks have been restored to their 1758 appearance and Fort Frederick is considered the best preserved pre–Revolution stone fort in the United States. The visitor center provides an orientation film and displays military uniforms. Costumed guides demonstrate musket fire and recreate the Colonial lifestyle.

Cambridge

Christ Episcopal Church (site)

Corner of Church and High streets; Open daily, dawn to dusk.

The first church on this site was built in 1673. The stone and slate structure has been reconstructed in 1794 and 1883. In the adjoining cemetery are grouped graves of local Revolutionary soldiers. Beside the church rests Maryland colonial statesman Robert Goldsborough.

Chestertown

Chestertown Tea Party (mem)

Cross and High streets; Open daily, 24 hours.

A plaque and Revolutionary War cannon mark the spot where, on May 23, 1774, "a group of Chestertown citizens undisguised and in broad daylight boarded the brigantine *Geddes* and threw its cargo of tea into the Chester River." The town then became a faithful supplier of provisions to the town of Boston, then suffering under the Boston Port Act.

Reenactment: Chestertown remembers its Revolutionary heritage during the Chestertown Tea Party Festival held during the Memorial Day weekend.

Washington College (site)

Route 213.

Chestertown, a port of entry for Maryland's Eastern Shore in the 1700s, sat squarely on the most heavily traveled North–South road in Colonial America. George Washington is known to have made at least eight visits to the town, including Worrell's Tavern at Queen and Cannon streets, where he ate on May 23, 1791. He was returning from Philadelphia on presidential business that time. Many of the town's colonial buildings remain, although nearly all are private.

Washington donated money and lent his name to the college, which opened as Maryland's first, in 1782. He served on the board of directors and was given an honorary degree of doctor of laws in 1789. The bronze standing figure of Washington was executed by Lee Oskar Lawrie.

Church Creek

Old Trinity Church (site)

Route 16, just south of Route 335; cemetery open daily, 24 hours. Free.

The simple brick church on the banks of the Choptank River dates prior to 1690 and is still in use. In the wooded cemetery are graves of Revolutionary War heroes and members of the Carroll family.

Cumberland

Cumberland City Hall (mem)

City Hall Plaza, Centre and Bedgord streets; Mon–Fri, 8–4. Free.

A mural inside City Hall depicts Washington and British general Edward Braddock, who assembled 2,000 men here in 1755 for his march to disaster at the Forks of Ohio.

Washington's Headquarters (site)

Riverside Park, Greene Street, 301-777-5905; Open by appointment. Free.

A 21-year-old George Washington built the first fort in the Western frontier in 1754, on a hill overlooking Washington and Green streets. The only building remaining from Fort Cumberland, built a year later, is the one-room headquarters of Washington's first command. He was commander at Fort Cumberland for two years, drilling for an attack in the French and Indian War that never came. Washington made a final visit here in 1794 when the fort was reoccupied during the Whiskey Rebellion.

Frederick

Hessian Barracks (site)

101 Clarke Place, 301-662-4159; Open by appointment. Free.

The stone structure was put up in 1777 to serve as an arsenal and barracks during the Revolutionary War. Hessian mercenaries were imprisoned here. Nearby is Mount Olivet Cemetery, where Thomas Johnson — Maryland's first elected governor in 1777 — is buried.

Georgetown

Colonial Supply Base (site)

Route 213, historical marker.

The town on the Sassafras River was an important base for the flow of supplies to the Continental Army.

Grantsville

Braddocks' Trail (site)

Route 40; Open daily, 24 hours. Free.

Following the Nemacolin Indian Trail, British commander Braddock built this trail under the direction of his aide-de-camp George Washington. The site can be viewed from a historical marker along Route 40.

Ironside

Durham Parish Church (site)

8700 Ironside Road, Route 425, 301-743-7099; Open by appointment. Free.

The simple brick parish church was established in 1666. Among the Revolutionary War–era worshippers was General William Smallwood, commander of the crack Maryland and Delaware Continental troops.

Kennedyville

Shrewsbury Episcopal Church (site)

Route 213; Open daily, dawn to dusk.

The parish was established in 1692 but the church only dates to the 1840s, constructed with the bricks of the 1772 church that stood here. The graveyard contains graves of Revolutionary War soldiers, including the final resting place of General John Cadwalder.

Marbury

Smallwood's Retreat (site)

Smallwood State Park, Route 224, 800-784-5380; May–Sept: Sat–Sun, 12–5. Admission charged.

William Smallwood's Maryland Regiment was noticed immediately by its fine uniforms and excellent equipment. Once in action they quickly became recognized as one of the most capable military units of the Revolution, seeing action in major battles from New York to South Carolina. Smallwood himself was wounded in leading the regiment at White Plains, New York. By the time his unit had marched south Smallwood was a major general.

In the twilight of the war, however, Smallwood was temporarily subordinated to General von Steuben and he refused to serve under a foreigner. Smallwood was sent home and put to work raising men and supplies. So successful were his efforts, he gained still more recognition as an administrator. After the war Smallwood became Maryland's fourth governor, serving three one-year terms beginning in 1785.

Smallwood's small brick home on the eastern shore of the Potomac was resuscitated by the state of Maryland in the 1950s. It is now the centerpiece of a 629-acre state park.

Oldtown

Michael Cresap Museum (site)

Main Street at Green Spring Road, 301-478-5154; Jun–Oct by appointment. Free.

Michael Cresap was a legend on Maryland's western frontier, where he gobbled up land as a speculator and defended his property with ferocious zeal. When the Revolution erupted he sought a commission with the Continental Congress and quickly signed up 130 men to lead. The Maryland men, outfitted in hunting shirts and moccasins and brandishing Indian war paint, marched to Boston in scarcely more than three weeks and made an immediate impression on Washington's army, both for their fighting ability and their lack of discipline. Ill before the march, Cresap attempted to return home in the fall of 1775 but died in New York City.

His two-and-a-half story stone house dates to 1764 and is Allegany County's oldest. Artifacts and historical remnants are featured inside.

Oxford

Robert Morris Inn (site)

314 North Morris Street, 410-226-5111; Daily, 8–9. Free.

The corner building was the eighteenth century boyhood home of Robert Morris, Jr., a signer of the Declaration of Independence and the finance minister for the first government of the Continental Congress. The inn was constructed by a ship's carpenter using wooden peg paneling, ship nails and hand-hewn beams. Across the street is the Oxford-Bellevue Ferry, established in 1683 and considered the oldest privately owned ferry in continuous operation in the country. The ferry was powered by oars for over 200 years.

Tilghman Monument (site)

Oxford Cemetery, Route 333, east of town; Open daily, 24 hours. Free.

Lt. Col. Tench Tilghman served as aide-de-camp for George Washington through much of the Revolution and carried the news on horseback of General Charles Cornwallis' surrender from Yorktown, Virginia, to the Continental Congress in Philadelphia. When Tilghman died in 1786 at the age of 42, Washington said, "He was in every action in which the main army was concerned. A great part of the time he refused to receive pay. While living no man could be more esteemed and since dead none more lamented than Colonel Tilghman. No one had imbibed sentiments of greater friendship for him than I had done. He left as fair a reputation as ever belonged to a human character."

Tilghman was buried in Old St. Paul's in Baltimore before his remains were brought to this place of honor in 1977. The cemetery itself was established in 1808.

Port Tobacco

Thomas Stone National Historic Site (site)

6655 Rosehill Road, 301-934-6027; summer: daily, 9–5; other times: Wed–Sun, 9–5. Free.

Port Tobacco thrived in the seventeenth century, becoming the second largest river port in Maryland. Much of the tobacco sent to England was loaded on its city dock. After the Revolution the harbor began silting up and the railroad passed it by. Port Tobacco devolved from county seat to ghost town.

Parts of the historic area have been restored, including a Federal-style courthouse bordering a small village green. The plantation home of Thomas Stone, a signer of the Declaration of Independence, features a tour, exhibits and a video program.

Thurmont

Catoctin Furnace (site)

Route 806 South, off Route 15; Open daily, dawn to dusk.

The foundry was built in 1774 and operated until 1903. It produced iron for the Continental Army and later, for Civil War arms. Catoctin Furnace was built by the family of Thomas Johnson, a lifelong friend of George Washington. After a career in the colonial assembly Johnson was elected to the First Continental Congress, and on June 15, 1775, he nominated Washington as commander-in-chief of the Continental Army.

He prodded his Maryland colleagues to support independence and after a brief service as the state's first brigadier general he returned to serve three one-year terms as governor during the Revolution from 1777 to 1779. He continued to agitate in local politics until his appointment as an associate justice to the U.S. Supreme Court in 1791. He retired in 1793 and lived in retirement at Rose Hill on North Market Street in Frederick until his death in 1819 at the age of 86.

Wye Mills

Wye Grist Mill (site)

Route 662, just north of village, 410-827-6909; Mid-Apr–Mid-Nov: Mon–Fri, 10–1, Sat–Sun, 10–4.

The first mill ground flour on this spot in 1682, and the mill is known to have produced flour for Washington's troops at Valley Forge. The restored mill still operates today with demonstrations on the first and third Saturday of each month. Up the hill on Route 662 is the Wye Oak, a massive white oak estimated at over 450 years old. The tree is 96 feet high and measures 119 feet across at its crown; a branch which fell from the tree in 1984 weighed over 70,000 pounds. The Wye Oak is the Maryland state tree.

Massachusetts

Revolutionary Status: Original Colony
Estimated Colonial Population: 338,000
Colonial Capital: Boston
Last Colonial Governor None
Troops Provided: 15 Continental regiments

Revolutionary Timeline

October 1, 1768: Seventeen hundred British soldiers land in Boston to protect British customs officers

March 5, 1770: British soldiers fire into a threatening mob, killing five and wounding six in the Boston Massacre

December 16, 1773: Rebels heave 45 tons of East India tea into the harbor to protest import taxes in the Boston Tea Party

March 31, 1774: George III closes Boston Harbor with the Intolerable Acts

April 19, 1775: The first shots of the Revolution are fired at Lexington and Concord

June 17, 1775: New England militia withstand three assaults from British regulars before surrendering Breed's Hill in the Battle of Bunker Hill

March 17, 1776: The British evacuate Boston

January 25, 1787: Massachusetts militia disperse Shay's Rebellion at Petersham

Arlington

Jason Russell House (site)

7 Jason Street, off Massachusetts Avenue, 617-648-4300; Tue–Sat, 1–5. Admission charged.

The British retreat from Concord had been a march of terror with rebel potshots coming at them, seemingly from every post and barn along the route. By late in the day the British retreat had regained order and the redcoats were in no mood to endure the sniping any longer. The land closer to Boston was covered with flat fields and the British moved efficiently through the terrain. Near the Russell House a flanking patrol flushed out some Essex militia, who fled to the two-story house.

The frustrating events of the day for the British would spell doom for the men in the Russell House, as they did for homes elsewhere on the retreat path. Jason Russell was shot down in his doorway and 11 more militia were killed in the house. Eight Americans brandishing muskets from the basement were spared as the angry British moved on.

Now restored and converted into a museum, the Jason Russell House features artifacts and exhibits dealing with the Revolutionary War era. Bullet holes still scar the walls in the 1740 house.

Boston

Alexander Hamilton (mem)

Commonwealth Avenue between Arlington and Berkeley streets.

A native of the West Indies, Alexander Hamilton joined the Revolution as an aide and private secretary to George Washington. He capped his military career by leading a charge against a critical British position at Yorktown. This larger-than-life rendering of Hamilton in granite, by Dr. William Rimmer, was unveiled in 1865.

Boston Bricks (mem)

Winthrop Lane between Arch and Otis streets.

A series of pavement inserts celebrate the city, its present character and its past history. One hundred bronze reliefs commemorate such events as the Boston Tea Party and Boston Massacre and such heroes as George Washington and Paul Revere.

Boston Common (site)

Beacon, Charles, Boylston, Tremont and Park streets.

The oldest public park in the country was set aside in 1634 for the grazing of cows and goats and sheep. It was also a military training ground for Colonial militia and British soldiers. On the evening of April 18, 1775, 700 of the best British troops, grenadiers and light infantry assembled on the Common for a march to Concord. They would suffer a casualty rate over 40 percent before they returned to Boston.

The British continued to use the Common while in Boston during the Revolution. In 1824, at the Lafayette Mall on the Common, the French hero was given the honor of laying the cornerstone for the Bunker Hill Monument. The Boston Massacre Monument on Tremont Street is an 1888 sculpture of freedom by Robert Kraus that features a flag, broken chain, eagle and a trod-upon British crown.

Boston Massacre Site (site)

Intersection of State and Congress streets.

Since the enactment of the Townshend Revenue Acts of 1767, and its duties on glass, paint, paper and other staples, there had been periodic clashes between Royal soldiers and the citizenry of Boston. On March 5, 1770, a gathering Colonial mob roamed Boston, hurling insults and the occasional snowball at the redcoats patrolling the streets. Outside the Old State House the mob had grown to about 60 men who successfully provoked the British guard into opening fire. Five Boston men died.

It is probable, although not proven, that the mob did not materialize by accident and that Boston radicals orchestrated the day's tragic events. The murdered men were quickly martyred and the incident could always be counted on to be brought up at any Revolutionary meeting, especially as Colonial discontent subsided when London repealed the Townshend Acts a month later. Five of the seven British regulars brought up for trial, defended by John Adams and Josiah Quincy, were acquitted. The other two received slight punishment for manslaughter.

The site where British soldiers killed five colonists is marked by a circle of cobblestones in the middle of the intersection at the east end of the Old State House.

Boston Tea Party Ship and Museum (site)

Congress Street Bridge, 617-338-1773; Mar–Nov: daily, 9–5. Admission charged.

The Tea Act of May 10, 1773, was a particularly heinous law to Bostonians because it favored tea imported to America from the East India Company. By late November protest meetings about British taxation in the colonies were drawing thousands to meetinghouses around Boston. A meeting on December 16, 1773, drew an overflow crowd to the Old South Meeting House. The rabble demanded the governor send the *Dartmouth* and two other tea ships back to sea.

Late in the afternoon, after no Royal action had been taken, a band of thinly disguised Indians bolted from the meeting and boarded the three ships in the harbor. The raiders deposited 342 chests of tea into the water. King George III punished the people of Boston by closing the port with a series of Intolerable Acts in the spring of 1774. Rather than isolate Boston, however, the crown had simply further united the colonies, pushing them closer to full revolt.

The museum features a full-size working replica of the *Brig Beaver II*, one of the three original "Tea Party" ships. Exhibits and films delineate the political and economic conditions precipitating the raid. A reenactment ceremony is staged each December.

Bunker Hill Monument (site)

Monument Square in Charlestown, 617-242-5641; Daily, 9–4:30. Free.

Massachusetts governor Lt. Gen. Thomas Gage seemed not to be overtly concerned when his beaten troops returned from Lexington and Concord. He did nothing, except write letters to London. The Americans at Cambridge were busily sealing off Boston before Gage decided to occupy Dorchester Heights, south of Boston, and Breed's Hill in Charlestown across the Charles River.

The Americans learned of Gage's scheme on June 13, 1775, and laid plans to fortify Bunker Hill, next to Breed's Hill. The Americans under Colonel Richard Gridley, engineer of the Provincial Army of New England, began their defenses the night of June 16 mistakenly, however, on Breed's Hill. This is where the battle would be joined the next morning. A British mapmaker had mislabeled the hill "Bunker Hill" and so the battle would always be called.

Colonel William Prescott commanded the Massachusetts Militia and positioned his troops behind a stone wall all the way to the Mystic River to his north as well as in the hastily constructed redoubt. General William Howe was chosen by the British to charge the hill with four infantry regiments and an artillery company. There was little doubt that Howe had been given enough firepower to dispatch a thousand farmers in a crude fort.

The main assault began at 3:00 in the afternoon. Word had spread around Boston and most of the city was perched on rooftops to see what would happen. A first charge by the British was unsupported by artillery as they had brought the wrong size ammunition. The ferocity of the defensive fire stunned the redcoats, who fell back and regrouped. A second charge was turned back in similar fashion.

The Americans knew the disciplined British troops would come up the hill a third time and they knew there was not enough powder to sustain another defense. Yet they held the hill. The British, supported by full artillery now, finally overran the redoubt and were met by bayonets in desperate hand-to-hand combat. Just before 5:00 P.M. the Americans abandoned Breed's Hill and Boston to the British.

From an army of 2,200 men the British had over 1,000 casualties, including 140 dead. Although over 400 American men were dead or wounded, Nathanael Greene was moved to say, "I wish we could sell them another hill at the same price."

The Bunker Hill Monument Association was formed in 1823 to create one of America's earliest memorials to the Revolution. A proposal by Horatio Greenough for an obelisk, an ancient Egyptian architectural form to honor war heroes and dead, was accepted and the cornerstone laid in 1825. A newly invented derrick, which would soon be in general use in construction, lifted large granite blocks into place. The 221-foot high memorial was completed in 1842; 294 steps lead visitors to the observation deck. There is no elevator. Also on the site is a statue of Colonel Prescott. The visitor center features battle dioramas and exhibits on the Battle of Bunker Hill at Breed's Hill.

Bunker Hill Pavilion (col)

55 Constitution Road, 617-241-7575; Jun–Aug: daily, 9:30–5; Apr–May and Sept–Nov: 9:30–4. Admission charged.

"The Whites of Their Eyes" is a multimedia reenactment of the Battle of Bunker Hill, using sound and visual effects to create the sensation of being in the midst of the first planned battle of the Revolutionary War.

Charlestown Square (site)

Park and Chelsea streets

Charlestown was a thriving port, competing with Boston through much of the early eighteenth century. The heart of Charlestown, on this site, disappeared on June 17, 1775, as British cannon fired on the rebels at Breed's Hill. The recently refurbished park features interpretations of how Charlestown appeared on that day.

Commodore Barry (mem)
Park Street, on the Boston Common.
Commodore John Barry received his first commission on the *Lexington* in 1775. He was appointed to plan and construct the U.S. Navy by President Washington in 1798. The "Father of the United States Navy" died in Philadelphia in 1803.

Copp's Burying Ground (site)
Hull Street.
Boston's second burying ground, it is the final resting place of thousands of merchants, artisans and free blacks. The elevated site was used by the British to rain down cannon fire during the Battle of Bunker Hill in 1775. Cannonballs from Copp's Hill, directed by Maj. Gen. John Burgoyne, destroyed Charlestown. The Old North Church Sexton Robert Newman is buried here.

Delahanty Square (mem)
Mt. Vernon and Bowdoin streets.
Behind the State House on Beacon Hill is a memorial that honors the train of events — all listed — leading to the independence of the United States of America. The beacon, from which the hill derives its name and was cut down in 1811, is symbolized by an eagle.

Ebeneezer Hancock House (site)
10 Marshall Street, Private residence.
This brick building, circa 1764, is the only remaining house in Boston associated with John Hancock. The patriot statesman did not live here but owned it. His brother Ebeneezer, the Deputy Paymaster General of the Continental Army, lived in the house. Hancock is best known for his flamboyant signature at the bottom of the Declaration of Independence, which he affixed as the president of the Second Continental Congress. By consensus the best leader of the Congress in its brief history, Hancock resigned his office in 1777. Returning to Massachusetts, he was elected the first governor of the state, and between 1780 and 1793 he served nine terms. Hancock died in office in 1793.

The house on Marshall Street is a private office building. From 1798 until 1963 the country's oldest continuously run shoe store operated on the first floor of the three-story building.

Faneuil Hall (site)
Faneuil Hall Square, 617-523-1300; Mon–Fri, 9–5. Free.
Peter Faneuil built this still-operating marketplace for the city of Boston in 1742. As was English custom, a public meeting hall was placed on top of the market. So many protests against British policy were voiced here that it became known as "The Cradle of Liberty." During the British occupation the building was used as a playhouse. The top floor of the four-story brick building is home to the Ancient and Honorable Artillery Company, America's oldest surviving military organization. They first quartered here in 1746.

Franklin Statue (mem)

Old City Hall, School Street.

Benjamin Franklin, although forever associated with Philadelphia, was born in Boston and attended the Boston Public Latin School, the oldest in the country, at this site. John Hancock and John Adams were also graduates. The portrait statue of Franklin, designed by Richard S. Greenough, features bronze depictions around the pedestal representing a small portion of his career: printer, scientist, and signer of the Declaration of Independence and the Peace Treaty with Great Britain.

General John Glover (mem)

Between Berkeley and Clarendon streets.

John Glover led a most unusual regiment in the Revolution — an "amphibious" regiment composed of Marblehead fishermen who supplied aquatic transportation for Washington's army. Born in Salem in 1732, Glover became one of the "codfish aristocracy" as a fish merchant and owner of a fishing fleet. His flotilla of small boats saved Washington after the Battle of Long Island by ferrying 9,000 men away from British guns. It was Glover and his men who rowed the Continental Army across the Delaware River for the surprise attack on Trenton. The bronze depiction of John Glover was executed by Martin Milmore in 1875.

Granary Burying Ground (site)

Tremont Street at Bromfield Street; Daily, 8–4. Free.

The cemetery took its name from a nearby grain storehouse. About 2,300 early Bostonians are buried here, including three signers of the Declaration of Independence — John Hancock (died 1783), Samuel Adams (died 1803) and Robert Trent Paine (died 1818). Also interred here are patriots James Otis and Paul Revere.

A Franklin family obelisk in the center is for Benjamin's parents and 16 other relatives. Ten thousand patriots marched to these grounds in March 1770 to bury four of the five victims of the Boston Massacre. The last body was placed here in 1879.

The grounds are typical for an eighteenth century burial yard, with the tombs around the edge and the grave plots in the center. Unfortunately the slate headstones bear little relation to the bodies below. The actual grave sites were ignored when the markers were rearranged in the common nineteenth century fashion of placing the stones in tidy rows.

King's Chapel and Burying Ground (site)

Tremont and School streets, 617-523-1749; Apr–Jun and Sep–Oct: Thur–Sat, 9:30–4, Sun, 1–3; Aug and Nov–Mar: Sat, 10–2. Free.

The fortress-like church designed by Peter Harrison in 1754 has been designated one of the 500 most important buildings in America and the light-filled sanctuary is considered by many to be the most beautiful Georgian church in the United States. As the headquarters for all the Colonial Anglican churches it was particularly detested by the Puritans of Boston. Antiloyalists called it the "Stone Chapel" rather than King's Chapel. In the adjacent burying ground is the grave of William Dawes, Jr., the messenger who rode the countryside the same night as Paul Revere but didn't have a mellifluous enough name for Henry Wadsworth Longfellow, so there was never a "midnight ride of William Dawes."

Old North Church (site)

193 Salem Street, 617-523-6676; Daily, 9–5. Free.

Christ Church, familiarly known as Old North Church, is Boston's oldest standing house of worship, built in 1723. America's first peal of bells rang from the church in 1744. On the night of April 18, 1775, the church sextant Robert Newman, acting on instructions from Paul Revere, climbed to the top of the 191-foot steeple to light two lanterns. Across the countryside the Patriots now knew the redcoats would be crossing the Charles River that night as they marched to Concord.

The steeple has been destroyed twice in fierce storms; the present steeple dates to 1954. Major John Pitcairn, who led the British troops against Concord, was killed in the Battle of Bunker Hill and buried in the building's cellar. When Westminster Abbey requested that his body be sent to London, the wrong bones were shipped and so Pitcairn is still buried in Boston.

Old South Meeting House (site)

310 Washington Street, 617-482-6439; Apr–Oct: daily, 9:30–5; Nov–Mar: Mon–Fri, 10–4, Sat–Sun, 10–5. Admission charged.

"Old South," built in 1729 as the third Congregational Church in Boston, was the largest meeting space in the colony and often served as a town meeting site whenever attendance grew too large for Faneuil Hall, as it commonly did in the days leading to the American Revolution. The most famous of these rabble-rousing meetings launched the Boston Tea Party on December 16, 1773. Old South remained a church for another 100 years. A multimedia presentation chronicles three centuries of Boston history. Also displayed is a scale model of Colonial Boston.

Old State House (site)

Washington Street at the head of State Street, 617-720-3290; Daily, 9:30–5. Admission charged.

The first town house was constructed on this location in 1657. It did not survive a city-wide conflagration in 1711 and the second town house, to be more popularly known as the Old State House, rose in 1713. Royal governors and provincial representatives debated laws and policy in its chambers. The fiery speeches of James Otis against the Writs of Assistance in 1761 and other oratories were so entertaining that the assembly built the English-speaking world's first gallery from which the public could watch government in action. Thereafter the Royal governor complained that assemblymen were less interested in arguing with their fellow members than playing favorably to the crowd.

The Declaration of Independence was read to the Boston people from the East Balcony on July 18, 1776, and in November the new state government convened here. In 1780 John Hancock was inaugurated here as the first governor of the commonwealth of Massachusetts. The Old State House remained in use as the state capitol until 1798.

The Bostonian Society maintains the Boston History Museum in the Old State House. Included in the wide range of city memorabilia is tea salvaged from the Boston Tea Party, a coat belonging to John Hancock and Paul Revere's original engraving of the Boston Massacre. On the second floor is the Council Chamber and Representatives Hall, which includes the spectators' gallery.

Paul Revere (mem)

Paul Revere Mall, Hanover Street.

The rendering of Paul Revere, dedicated in 1940, places him on horseback. It stands in a memorial plaza near Old North Church, where Revere designed the warning system to alert patriots of British troop movements on the night of April 18, 1775. The larger-than-life equestrian statue is the work of Cyrus E. Dallin.

Paul Revere House (site)

19 North Square, 617-523-2338; Apr–Oct: daily, 9:30–5:15; Nov–Dec: daily, 9:30–4:15; Jan–Mar: Tue–Sun, 9:30–4:15. Admission charged.

A fashionable town house was built in this location after a fire in 1676, with wealthy merchant Robert Howard moving in first. Paul Revere, a prospering 35-year-old silversmith, bought the house in 1770. He became increasingly involved in the agitation for liberty, going so far as to place hand-drawn pictures of the Boston Massacre in his window. He became a trusted courier and joined 49 fellow patriots in dumping tea in Boston Harbor.

He had hoped to receive substantial military assignments in the subsequent war but instead designed Continental money; his design of the Massachusetts state seal is still in use. One foray into the field as an artillery commander, at Castine, Maine, proved disastrous for both Revere and the Americans.

Revere prospered in his varied business interests after the Revolution and sold his house in 1800. He operated bell and cannon foundries in Boston and established the first successful copper rolling mill in America in Canton, Massachusetts, in 1801. He died in 1818 at the age of 83, having contributed in the political and industrial revolutions of America.

The building was a cigar factory, grocery store and then tenement housing for much of the nineteenth century and quivered in front of a wrecking ball in 1905 when Revere's great-grandson, John P. Reynolds, initiated a movement to save the building. Today it is Boston's oldest house.

Samuel Adams (mem)

Dock Square Park, Concord Street at Faneuil Hall.

The memorial to Samuel Adams honors the Boston leader as "a patriot; he organized the Revolution." It was in Faneuil Hall that Adams held his public meeting on November 2, 1772, to approve the Boston Committee of Correspondence to "state the rights of the Colonists." The statue of a reflective Adams was erected in 1880. It is the vision of Anne Whitney.

Soldiers' Monument (mem)

Thomas Park, Dorchester Heights.

By the beginning of 1776 the British had long decided to evacuate Boston, but the amazing work done by Washington and his men convinced them to withdraw with alacrity. On the night of March 4 the British retired for the evening, having noted some scattered activity on Dorchester Heights in South Boston. When they awoke they stared in disbelief at three score cannon that Washington had now trained on them. General Howe is said to have remarked that the rebels had done more work in one night than his troops could have done in months. He therefore overestimated the strength of Washington's force by tenfold and canceled plans for a counterattack. By March 17 the city was evacuated.

How had Washington done it? Months earlier Henry Knox had proposed moving captured cannon from Fort Ticonderoga 300 miles overland to Boston, and his "Noble Train of Artillery" had arrived and was ready for deployment. Rufus Putnam solved the problem of positioning the weaponry on the hilltops with a series of precut heavy timbers for fortification. Working quickly, the Continental Army had fortified the high ground with no opposition from the enemy. After foul weather delayed a counterattack, Howe saw no reason to challenge this initiative.

The marble monument was dedicated in 1902 on the 126th anniversary of the British withdrawal from Boston. It stands 115 feet high in Thomas Park, named for General John Thomas, who commanded the operations on Dorchester Heights.

State House (col)

Beacon Street, opposite Boston Common, 617-727-3676; Mon–Fri, 9–5. Free.

Designed by Charles Bullfinch, the Massachusetts State House was completed in 1798 and measured only 65 feet wide. The cornerstone was laid July 4, 1795, by Governor Samuel Adams and Paul Revere. The State House occupies the former site of John Hancock's cow pasture.

The State House features several halls of exhibits pertaining to Massachusetts. The Hall of Flags features a mural of the battle of Concord Bridge and the Doric Hall has a display on the sometimes cantankerous words of John Adams. A bronze bust of Hancock, the first governor of the state, is on the west wall. On the north wall is a statue of George Washington, the first piece of artwork to grace the room. The replica of the Liberty Bell on the front steps was one of 53 cast in France in 1950 and presented to the state of Massachusetts.

Thaddeus Kosciuszko (mem)

Boylston Street Mall.

This larger-than-life bronze of military engineer Thaddeus Kosciuszko by Theo Alice Ruggles Kitson was commissioned in 1927 by Boston Polish organizations to honor the 150th anniversary of his joining the American Revolution.

War Memorial (mem)

Winthrop Square, Adams and Winthrop streets in Charlestown.

The stone gates at the north entrance to the square list the American soldiers killed in the Battle of Bunker Hill on June 17, 1775. It was dedicated on June 17, 1889. Also a brief description of the British loss is engraved.

Cambridge

Christ Church (site)

Garden Street, 617-876-0200; Daily, 7:30–5. Free.

The congregation of this one-story gray frame church, completed in 1761, was largely sympathetic to the mother country, and the Tory rector fled in 1774. No regular services were held for 16 years and local militia used the building as barracks. The organ pipes were melted down for lead shot and other damage was caused during the Revolution.

James Otis (mem)

Harvard Square, Memorial Hall.

James Otis served as advocate general of Massachusetts until 1760, when he resigned in protest of King George III's Writs of Assistance, laws which enabled customs officials to search any house for smuggled goods. Thereafter Otis became a most vocal leader of opposition to the crown and his entertaining speeches won many converts to the rebel cause. He served as a volunteer at Bunker Hill but was suffering from a deteriorating mental state. He was killed by lightning in 1783, a death wish he had often expressed. Thomas Crawford sculpted this memorial to James Otis in 1857.

John Adams (mem)

Harvard Square, Memorial Hall.

This depiction of Revolutionary leader John Adams was the first public commission for Michigan frontier artist Randolph Rogers. It was dedicated in 1857.

Longfellow National Historic Site (site)

105 Brattle Street, 617-876-4491; May–Oct: Wed–Sun, 10–4:30. Admission charged.

George Washington used this Georgian home, built in 1759 by Tory Major John Vassall, as his headquarters during the siege of Boston from 1775 to 1776. Henry Wadsworth Longfellow, who immortalized Paul Revere with his stanzas in "The Midnight Ride of Paul Revere," lived in this house for 45 years beginning in 1837.

Revolutionary Figures (mem)

Fort Washington Park, Waverly Street.

Fighting was narrowly averted in Cambridge during the "Powder Alarm" on September 1, 1774, when hundreds of armed colonists confronted British soldiers helping themselves to arms and ammunition in a local militia depot.

Madeleine Lord sculpted a group of four Cambridge minuteman encamped around a seated Victorian woman, contemplating the Revolution. The life-size steel monument was installed in 1987.

Concord

Concord Museum (col)

200 Lexington Road, 508-369-9609; Apr–Dec: Mon–Sat, 9–5, Sun, 12–5; Jan–Mar: Mon–Sat, 11–4, Sun, 1–4. Admission charged.

Among the 19 period rooms are Revolutionary War interpretations. Included in the collection is the lantern that signaled Paul Revere's historic ride.

First Parish Meeting House (site)

Lexington Street.

The First Provincial Congress of delegates from the towns of Massachusetts first met here on October 11, 1774. President John Hancock would eventually preside over 300 delegates, "called together to maintain the rights of the people." The present white building was put up in 1901 and is the third meetinghouse near the site; the first was on the ridge across the way; the Revolutionary house, built in 1712, stood here until a fire in 1900.

Merriams Corner (site)

Lexington Road at Old Bedford Road.

As the British force of 700 retreated to Boston Harbor there was a running battle all along the 20-mile route. The house at this corner, being restored at present, witnessed some of the toughest skirmishing on the first day of fighting in the Revolution. The original building dates to 1639.

North Bridge (site)

Monument Street, 508-369-6993; Open daily, dawn to dusk.

The Provincial Congress directed the formation of "Minutemen" in Massachusetts towns, and by April 1775 most towns, including Concord, had companies. Concord's was more important than most since the Americans had converted Colonel James Barrett's farm into an arsenal of sorts. Bullets, flints and cartridges were stuffed in barrels and cannon were submerged in furrowed fields. It was this stash that Maj. Gen. Thomas Gage ordered his men to discover and destroy. Before the march on Concord, however, he warned his troops to "take care not to plunder inhabitants or hurt private property." News of the British departure from Boston reached Concord early on April 19 and minutemen rushed to the town.

Upon reaching Concord the British fanned out to search for the hidden cache of weapons. Meanwhile, Americans massed a mile west of the North Bridge over the Concord River and near Barrett's farm. In the town of Concord the British raiding party burned some tools and barrels of flour. Seeing smoke coming from the town and thinking it burning, some 400 American militia, marching in formation, approached three British regiments — totaling 96 men — on the bridge.

The groups faced each other across the wooden bridge, not 60 yards apart, when shots rang out — from the British or the Americans, it will never be known. Two patriots, Isaac Davis and Abner Hosmer, fell dead. Major John Buttrick shouted at his fellow Colonials, "Fire, fellow soldiers! For God's sake, fire!" Two British soldiers died and nine were wounded, including four of the eight regimental officers. The redcoats fled to join their main force and were not pursued by the Americans. England now had an armed revolt in their American colonies.

The historic North Bridge was a tourist attraction as early as the 1780s but it floated down the Concord River in 1793. The current arched wooden bridge is the fourth span at this spot and it dates from 1956. A short interpretive trail explains the positions of each side on April 19, 1775. On the eastern side, where the redcoats made their stand, is an obelisk where the first men fell and the graves of the British soldiers lay — "They came three thousand miles and died to keep the past upon its throne."

On the western bank is a Minuteman Statue created by Daniel Chester French for the centennial of the skirmish in 1875. It bears the words of Ralph Waldo Emerson's *Concord Hymn*: "By the rude bridge that arched the flood, their flag to April's breeze unfurled. Here once the embattled farmers stood, and fired the shot heard round the world." Continuing up the trail to the west is the North Bridge visitor center, a 1911 house built by militia leader Buttrick's descendants. The center features artifacts and a short film. The formal garden overlooks the North Bridge.

Old Burying Ground (site)

Lexington Road.

Although the headstones date back to 1677, their slate composition makes them easily read. The Revolutionary War graves are near the summit, where the Liberty Pole stood.

Old Manse (site)

Monument Street, 508-369-3909; Apr–Oct: Mon, Wed, Fri, 10–5, Sun, 11–5. Admission charged.

Near the North Bridge the Reverend William Emerson built this house in

1770. The Emerson family watched the events of the morning of April 19, 1775, from an upstairs bedroom. Decades later his grandson Ralph Waldo would pen the *Concord Hymn*.

Wright Tavern (site)
  2 Lexington Road, 508-369-3120. Private offices.
  Built in 1747, Amos Wright was operating a public house here by 1775. The next door meetinghouse, now gone, entertained committees of the Provincial Congress when they became too large to just meet in the two-story, red frame tavern. When the redcoats marched from Lexington on April 19, 1775, their commanders Colonel Francis Smith and Major John Pitcairn set up headquarters here.

Framingham

Minuteman Statue (mem)
  Union and Main streets.
  Theo Alice Ruggles Kitson created the Colonial blacksmith, still with apron, forge and hammer loading ammunition into his rifle. The statue reflects the popular theme of minutemen leaving everyday life to fight. The *Minuteman* was dedicated in 1905 on the drill field of the town's militia.

Hinsdale

Israel Bissell Gravesite (site)
  Hinsdale Cemetery, off Route 8.
  The small town in western Massachusetts is the final resting place of Isaac Bissell, a post rider with Paul Revere who delivered the news of fighting in Lexington and Concord to Philadelphia and the Continental Congress in 1775 after Revere was arrested.

Lexington

Buckman Tavern (site)
  1 Bedford Street, 617-862-5598; Apr–Oct: Sat, 10–5, Sun, 1–5. Admission charged.
  Built in 1709, John Muzzey started a "publique house of entertainment " in the yellow clapboard building in 1714. Later owner John Buckman was a minuteman who often hosted gatherings after training on the Green, which is across the street. It came to be headquarters for the Lexington Minutemen at the beginning of the Revolution. The interior of Buckman Tavern appears much as it did in 1775, including an old front door with a bullet hole from a British musket ball. In the yard is a memorial with a frieze of six minutemen.

Hancock-Clarke House (site)
  36 Hancock Street, 617-861-0928; Apr–Oct: Mon–Sat, 10–5, Sun, 1–5. Admission charged.

The Reverend John Hancock built the original home on this site as a small parsonage in 1698. On the evening of April 18, 1775, two Colonial agitators, Samuel Adams and Hancock's grandson John, were guests of the Reverend Jonas Clarke in the parsonage. Two alert riders, William Dawes and Paul Revere, arrived on different occasions that night to warn Adams and Hancock that British soldiers had departed Boston and were on their way to Lexington. The warning could not be delivered often enough as both houseguests were considered particularly notorious by the British. Hancock wanted to line up with the Lexington minutemen, but when Revere arrived after being captured on his way to Concord the three men headed out of town.

The house, expanded by John Hancock's father in 1734, contains furnishings and portraits of the Hancock family. Among the interesting relics are pistols of Major John Pitcairn, who led the British advance that day. John Hancock lived in the house during his early school years from 1744 until 1750.

Harrington House (site)

Bedford and Harrington streets, private residence.

Jonathan Harrington owned this house on the west end of Lexington Green in 1775. He answered the call to arms early on the morning of April 19 and fell in the volley fired by the British regulars. Mortally wounded, he dragged himself across the street and died at his wife's feet on his doorstep.

Lexington Battle Green (site)

Massachusetts Avenue, Bedford Street and Hancock Street.

The Lexington of 1775, originally called Cambridge Farms, consisted of about 30 families. The public area was a triangular green which was laid out at the town's founding in 1640. It was the meeting place for the Lexington Minutemen since their organization on December 13, 1773. They were alerted to formation by a ringing of a bell on the green.

Shortly after two o'clock in the morning on April 19, 1775, the bell pealed and about 130 men assembled to hear the news that 700 elite British troops were marching up the road from Boston. By 4:30 A.M. no redcoats had appeared and many minutemen had returned home when a rider dashed onto the green with the news that the British were a half-mile from Lexington.

Captain John Parker assembled his remaining 77 farmers and artisans in two parallel lines as the British approached. He told his men not to fire unless fired upon but reputedly admonished them that "if they mean to have a war let it begin here." Major John Pitcairn spoke briefly to the minutemen and ordered them to disperse. Parker, seeing the size of the British force, ordered them to do just that. But as the Colonials scattered a shot rang out — from which side is not known — and a general British volley exploded into the crowd. The Americans returned intermittent fire as they fled the green.

Eight Lexington men were dead and another ten wounded. Only two British soldiers were slightly hurt. The redcoats continued marching to Concord, the flurry that turned a political revolt into war having lasted less than 30 minutes. The spirit of the Lexington Minutemen was not broken, however. Parker placed his militia on bluffs along the road and killed several British soldiers on their return march to Boston.

Despite the significance of the Lexington Green nothing was done to note it until General Ulysses S. Grant made a Centennial observance visit in 1875. More than 100,000 visitors came with him and it suddenly became obvious to town officials that their common ground was of considerable importance to Americans.

A boulder with Parker's immortal words marks the line of the Lexington militia, roughly through the middle of the green. A tablet has been placed on the site where the Old Belfry containing the alarm bell once stood.

Reenactment: The Lexington Minutemen Company, the seventh oldest military organization in the Americas, is the only company that has remained in continuous existence since the Revolutionary War. Each year, the Lexington Minutemen and his Majesty's Tenth Regiment of Foot recreate the Battle of Lexington on Patriots Day, April 19th.

Lexington Visitor Center (mem)

1875 Massachusetts Avenue, 617-862-1450; Daily, 9–5. Free.

Adjacent to the visitor center is a memorial to the five ships named *Lexington*, including the first, a 16-gun brig originally named *Wild Duck*, purchased by Congress in 1776. The *Lexington* captured three British ships off the Virginia coast before being taken by an enemy frigate in the West Indies. The *Lexington* crew overpowered their captors and brought the prize into Baltimore. In 1777 while in European waters with the *Dolphin* and *Reprisal*, the trio took 18 ships before running out of ammunition in September. The *Lexington* was captured off of France. Inside the center is a diorama and other information pertaining to the clash on the green.

Minuteman Statue (mem)

Bedford Street and Massachusetts Avenue, on Green.

This rendering of an American patriot represents Captain John Parker as he appeared on the morning of April 19, 1775, as commander of the Lexington militia. It faces the line of the British approach. The monument by Henry Hudson Kitson was dedicated on April 19, 1900.

Munroe Tavern (site)

1332 Massachusetts Avenue, 617-647-9238; Apr–Oct: Mon–Sat, 10–5, Sun, 1–5. Admission charged.

The British had already had a full, and not uneventful, day when they reached Munroe Tavern for the second time on the afternoon of April 19, 1775. They had marched past the public house, one mile east of the Lexington Green, in the predawn hours on their way from Boston to Concord. The first shots of the Revolution had been fired in Lexington at 5:00 A.M. and skirmishing had taken place in Concord until noon. Enduring constant pressure from Colonial snipers on their march back to Boston, the British ranks were in danger of breaking when they met up with Brig. Gen. Earl Percy's reinforcements —1,100 strong — at William Munroe's tavern.

The British stayed for about 90 minutes, resting and nursing wounds while Percy organized an orderly retreat. At 3:45 P.M. the British moved out for the 12-mile march to Charlestown, resisting rebel fire for the entire four hours. Percy had seen enough of the Colonial militia to assert that the Americans should not be dismissed as "an irregular mob." They were, he concluded, ready to see a rebellion through.

The earliest part of the tavern dates to the 1690s. Munroe, an orderly sergeant of Captain Parker's minuteman company in 1775, purchased the tavern in 1770. He remained proprietor until 1827. Among the souvenirs from the Revolution are articles pertaining to George Washington, who dined at the Munroe Tavern during a visit to Lexington in 1789.

Museum of Our National Heritage (col)
33 Marrett Road, 617-861-6559; Mon–Sat, 10–5, Sun, 12–5. Free.

The "Lexington Alarm'd" exhibit examines small-town life when the first military encounter of the War for Independence took place. There are dioramas and relics of the first days of the Revolution.

The Old Belfry (mem)
Massachusetts Avenue and Clark Street.

This is a reproduction of the original belfry whose bell sounded the alarm that summoned the Minutemen to the Green. The original stood here until moved to the green in 1768; it was destroyed in 1909.

Old Burying Ground (site)
Unitarian Church, beyond the Green.

The oldest stone in the burial ground is dated 1690. Among the graves are those of the Reverend John Hancock and Captain John Parker.

Revolutionary Monument (mem)
Massachusetts Avenue, on the Green.

Perhaps the first monument erected to the Revolution, the memorial was dedicated in 1799 to those "who fell on this field, the first victims to the sword of British tyranny and oppression ... they nobly dared to be free!" The remains of the eight men — Robert Munroe, Jonas Parker, Samuel Hadley, Jonathan Harrington, John Brown, Asabel Porter, Isaac Muzzey and Caleb Harrington — were brought from the Old Cemetery and reinterred on this spot on April 20, 1835.

Lincoln

Minute Man National Historical Park (site)
Battle Road visitor center, Airport Road off Route 2A, 617-862-7753; Apr–Oct, 9–5. Free.

Many of the sites in Concord, Lincoln and Lexington have been melded into the Historical Park, commemorating the battle that began the War for Independence. Much of the park is on either side of Battle Road, Route 2A, as it stretches four miles from the Battle Road visitor center to the North Bridge visitor center in Concord.

On April 19, 1775, the column of disciplined British regulars marched down the Battle Road back to Boston as the Colonial militia sniped at them from behind barns and stone walls. By nightfall the British had suffered 73 deaths. Another 174 were wounded and many more missing. Forty-nine Americans were killed.

Orientation programs at the visitor center feature exhibits and relics from the opening day of the Revolution. A film, *To Keep Our Liberty*, explains the causes of the rebellion.

Paul Revere Capture Site (site)

Route 2A; open daily, 24 hours.

Paul Revere was one of a system of alert riders that had long existed in the colonies, and on the night of Revere's famous ride scores were active. Revere, William Dawes and Samuel Prescott had been riding since 2:00 A.M. when they were halted on this spot by a British patrol. Dawes turned back and escaped. Prescott hopped a wall and used his local knowledge of the area to escape. Revere was arrested, returned to Lexington and released that morning. A stone tablet and interpretive sign are at the pull-off along Battle Road.

Marblehead

Abbot Hall (col)

Washington Street; Mon–Fri, 9–5. Free.

The original 18' by 12' canvas of "Spirit of '76" by Archibald Willard resides in Marblehead. Willard was a wheelwright and wagon painter who broke into commercial painting by producing humorous homespun paintings for mass reproduction. He conceived the work of a Revolutionary fife-and-drum corps as a moneymaker to be marketed for the 1876 Centennial. Willard called the painting "Yankee Doodle" and intended it as a lighthearted remembrance, but after his father, who was the model for the central figure of the trio, died, the project assumed a more somber tone. When completed, "Spirit of '76" became the most reproduced painting of the nineteenth century.

Powder House (site)

37 Green Street.

Muskets and powder were stored in the brick magazine during the French and Indian War, the Revolutionary War and the War of 1812. It was built in 1755.

St. Michael's Church (site)

26 Pleasant Street.

The bell at the 1714 Episcopal Church, one of the oldest in America, rang so persistently at the news of the Declaration of Independence that it cracked. It was recast by Paul Revere and still rings today.

Newburyport

George Washington (mem)
High and Pond streets.
John Quincy Adams Ward, the preeminent sculptor of his day, completed this larger-than-life bronze of a standing George Washington in 1878, in the middle of his prolific career.

Quincy

John Adams Birthplace (site)
133 Franklin Street, 617-773-1177; Apr–Nov: daily, 9–5. Admission charged.
Radical rebel and second president of the United States, John Adams was born in a salt box house in 1735. He lived here until his marriage in 1764. John and Abigail Adams then moved into the neighboring two-story house, a family inheritance.

John Adams House (site)
135 Adams Street, 617-770-1175; Apr–Nov: daily, 9–5. Free.
John Adams purchased this house in 1788, just before he was about to spend 12 years as vice-president and president of the United States. Adams stayed in the "Old House" until his death on July 4, 1826 — the same day as his longtime friend and sometime foe, Thomas Jefferson, died.

Michigan

Revolutionary Status: Claimed by the Massachusetts colony
and the Connecticut colony

Detroit

Detroit Historical Museum (col)
Woodward and Kirby avenues, 313-833-1805; Wed–Fri, 9:30–5, Sat–Sun, 10–5. Admission charged.
The British used Detroit, long recognized for its strategic location on the 27-mile Detroit River, as its Northwest headquarters during the Revolutionary War. The French first fortified the area in 1701 and strengthened it considerably before turning over the post to British commander Robert Rogers in 1760.

The most feared raiding parties of the Revolution in the West were organized in Fort Detroit. Henry Hamilton led one such army of 200 in late 1778 to occupy Vincennes, Indiana. After a treacherous march that lasted over two months his garrison was captured by George Rogers Clark.

The loss of Hamilton, known as the "Hair Buyer" for his policy of paying for enemy scalps, caused little disruption in the British activity. Major Richard Lernault built a new fort in 1778 and the British continued to harass the Ohio Valley throughout the war. Fort Lernault was not surrendered until 1796, and on its foundations rose the town of Detroit.

Operated by the Detroit Historical Commission, the museum traces the growth of Detroit from 1701 until the present with reconstructions, films and exhibits.

Mackinac Island

Fort Mackinac (site)

Mackinac Island, 906-847-3328; Jun–Labor Day: daily, 9–6; May and Sept–Oct: 9–5. Admission charged.

The American Indians knew the island as the "Great Turtle" and it was to this three-mile-long island that the British, alarmed at George Rogers Clark sweeping through the Ohio Valley, moved in 1780. The French had built the first fortifications in the area on the mainland but the British sought the added security of the island in Lake Huron. The extensive works were still being perfected when the British surrendered the post in 1796.

The restored Fort Mackinac, on the high limestone bluffs overlooking the harbor, features all original buildings. Costumed interpreters reenact the life of an eighteenth century fort.

Niles

Fort St. Joseph Museum (col)

508 East Main Street, 616-683-4702; Wed–Sat, 10–4. Free.

After the British made an enfeebled attack on the Spanish settlement in St. Louis, the Spanish undertook a retaliatory expedition against the British stronghold of Detroit. Captain Eugenio Pourre and a combined force of 120 militia and Indians surprised Fort Joseph, in the southwestern tip of modern-day Michigan, in January 1781. The defenders made no attempt to hold the position and surrendered at the appearance of the Spaniards. Pourre stayed only a day, long enough to establish a Spanish claim in the region, and returned to the Mississippi Valley. The museum features artifacts from the site of Fort St. Joseph.

Mississippi
Revolutionary Status: Spanish territory

Kosciusko

Kosciuszko Museum and visitor center (mem)
Town Square, 601-289-2981; Mon–Fri, 10–5, Sat, 10–4. Free.
The Mississippi town was named for Polish engineer Thaddeus Kosciuszko, whose fortifications did much to aid the American cause in the Revolution. The visitor center features a lifelike wax replica of Kosciuszko and a tabletop display of his fortifications at West Point.

Natchez

Fort Rosalie (site)
South Broadway.
The terminus of the Natchez Trace, the main road through the Old Southwest, is the town of Natchez, on the Mississippi River. The French first built Fort Rosalie in 1716 but it was destroyed by the Natchez Indians, who had helped construct the outpost in happier times, in 1729. The British gained control of the region in 1763 but did not rebuild a fort in Natchez until 1778.

Congress authorized civilians to go privateering against British merchant ships on March 19, 1776. American privateers would capture more than 2,000 merchant vessels and 16,000 crewmen during the war. The southern Mississippi River was not immune.

On January 11, 1778, commanding a keelboat he whimsically christened the *Rattletrap*, Navy captain James Willing set out from Pittsburgh to find Tory ships in the lower Mississippi. Equal parts patriot and pirate, Willing plundered Natchez on February 19 and sacked Manchac, Louisiana, four days later. He captured and sold four British merchant ships.

In 1779, when Spain declared war on Great Britain, Fort Rosalie was seized along with several other Mississippi River forts. On April 22, 1781, the Spanish surrendered the garrison to an attacking force of 200 Tories and Indians.

Fort Rosalie did not long outlast the Revolution. The site of the fort is at Rosalie, one of the fine antebellum homes in Natchez, where once half of America's millionaires lived.

Missouri

Revolutionary Status: Spanish territory

Jefferson City

Thomas Jefferson (mem)
State Capitol, High Street.
The trading post on the Missouri River was chosen as the state capital in 1826, the year of Jefferson's death. A statue of Jefferson commands the front steps of the Capitol.

Kansas City

Valley Forge (mem)
Washington Square, Pershing and Grand streets.
The equestrian statue of Washington is a replica of the work by Henry Merwin Shrady in Brooklyn Plaza in New York. The money was raised from 109,000 people and dedicated in 1932, the bicentennial of Washington's birth.

St. Louis

General Von Steuben (mem)
Tower Grove Park.
The rendering of the resolute drillmaster standing aforefront of the American flag was donated by the German government for the St. Louis World's Fair in 1904.

George Washington (mem)
Lafayette Park.
This monument to the first president is one of six bronze castings executed from the life-size statue of George Washington by Houdon in the capitol rotunda in Richmond.

Jefferson National Expansion Memorial (site)
Riverfront at Market Street, 314-982-1410; Open daily, 6 a.m.–11 p.m. Free.
Pierre Laclede sailed from New Orleans in 1764 to expand the French fur industry. On a high bluff at the confluence of the Missouri and Mississippi rivers he built a small trading post. Its favorable location assured the success of the settlement and shortly the French population approached 500, even though the region was under Spanish control.
The Spanish built Fort San Carlos on this site in 1778, a year before Spain declared war on Great Britain. The British, with their Indian allies, attempted

to eradicate Spanish settlements from the Mississippi Valley. On May 26, 1780, the British moved on Fort San Carlos with a force of over 1,200 men. Captain Don Fernando de Leyba defended the post with a handful of regular troops, several hundred settlers and, most importantly, five cannon.

The British were unprepared for any resistance, let alone the firepower mounted by de Leyba. They quickly withdrew and plundered surrounding farms in their retreat. A Spanish counteroffensive the next year pushed as far as Fort St. Joseph, Michigan.

The 91 acres of the park cover the site of the original St. Louis settlement. The most striking feature at the National Memorial is the Gateway Arch, built where Fort San Carlos stood. The Gateway Arch required 886 tons of steel and specially designed equipment was necessary to reach the top of its 630 feet. Films in the visitor center tell the history of the St. Louis settlement and its role in the expansion to the West.

New Hampshire

Revolutionary Status: Original Colony
Estimated Colonial Population: 73,000
Colonial Capital: Portsmouth
Last Colonial Governor: John Wentworth
Troops Provided: 3 Continental regiments

Revolutionary Timeline:
December 14, 1774: John Sullivan and the New Hampshire militia take Fort William and Mary, the first British military post to fall into American hands

Concord

Constitution Ratification Site (site)
Walker and Bouton streets.

New Hampshire was known for its strong Loyalist tendencies but revolutionary fervor spread quickly when it came. In 1775 New Hampshire rebels forced its colonial governor, Sir John Wentworth, himself native-born, to flee and the following year established an independent provisional government, the first in the 13 colonies. In 1788 New Hampshire became the ninth and deciding state to ratify the U.S. Constitution, creating the United States of America on this spot.

Durham

Old Meeting House Site (site)
Newmarket Road (Route 108).

Durham is the home of Maj. Gen. John Sullivan, a taciturn Irishman whose checkered Revolutionary War experience nonetheless did not prevent him from thrice being elected governor of New Hampshire. He was captured after being routed at Long Island, and Congress demanded his removal after his performance at Brandywine. Washington refused and Sullivan served well in Germantown. His final campaign was in western New York, where Washington sent him to punish the Five Nations of the Iroquois for their support of the British. Sullivan burnt many fields and villages but did not destroy the Indian threat. He resigned his military commission on November 30, 1779.

In a meetinghouse on this site in 1774, Sullivan and a cadre of Durham patriots supposedly stored gunpowder that had been purloined from the British in a raid at Fort William and Mary. Sullivan lived in a house at 23 Newmarket Road and is buried nearby.

Exeter

American Independence Museum (col)

1 Governors Lane, 603-772-2622; May–Oct: Tue–Sat, 10–4, Sun, 12–4. Admission charged.

Exeter was one of the first towns where liberty festered in the colonies; British lords were burned in effigy here and Royal commands openly defied. When the Revolutionary War began the colony capital was moved away from Tory-influenced Portsmouth to receptive Exeter. The museum is housed in the Cincinnati Memorial Hall, once the state treasury from 1775 to 1789.

In addition to furnishings of the era the museum holds one of the three known Purple Hearts awarded during the Revolutionary War; an original copy of the Declaration of Independence; and a working draft of the Constitution with notes made by delegate Nicholas Gilman. Also in the museum complex is the 1775 Folsom Tavern.

Keene

Wyman Tavern Museum (site)

399 Main Street, 603-352-1895; Memorial Day–Labor Day: Thur–Sat, 11–4.

In 1775 Isaac Wyman led 29 minutemen from the tavern to Lexington at the outset of the Revolutionary War. Five years earlier the trustees of Dartmouth College held their first meeting in the popular public house.

Londonderry

Revolutionary War Monument (mem)

Routes 128 and 102.

The "Revolutionary War Monument" was dedicated during the town's Bicentennial celebration in 1976. Using native granite, local artist Patricia Verani crafted three minutemen firing their muskets on a background of the state of New Hampshire ringed by nine stars. The minutemen represent the three major battles in which soldiers from Londonderry participated: New Castle, Bunker Hill and Bennington. The nine stars signify New Hampshire's place as the ninth state to ratify the Constitution.

Manchester

John Stark House (site)

2000 Elm Street, 603-623-0313; Tue–Fri, 9–4, Sat, 10–4. Admission charged.

Manchester's most noted Revolutionary was John Stark, a woodsman who fought the Indian Wars. Nearing 50 when he joined the rebellion, Stark led brilliantly at Bunker Hill but was miffed at being passed over for promotion after Trenton and Princeton. He returned to farm in New Hampshire until the British moved on Albany, and Stark was placed in charge of the state militia. He crushed the Germans at the Battle of Bennington and received the appointment he desired in the Continental Army — brigadier general. He retired on November 3, 1783, to return to the farm and his 11 children. Stark, one of the last surviving Revolutionary War generals, lived until 1822, dying just before his 94th birthday.

The home is a small frame building of his childhood. Stark is buried in land he used to own on North River Road, now Stark Park.

Manchester Historic Association (col)

129 Amherst Street, 603-622-7531; Tue–Fri, 9–4, Sat, 10–4. Free.

The library and museum features artifacts and material relating to the Revolutionary War, including Stark's storied military career.

New Castle

Fort Constitution Historic Site (site)

Route 18 at United States Coast Guard Station; Open daily, 24 hours.

Four months before his famous ride to Lexington and Concord, Paul Revere mounted his horse and rode north to Portsmouth with a different warning: The British had banned the importation of military stores by the colonies. Wasting little time, John Sullivan and Patriot politicians organized 400 men and on December 14, 1774, presented themselves at Fort William and Mary, garrisoned by only four men. Captain John Cochran surrendered the fort. Its stores of 60 muskets, 16 cannon and 100 barrels of gunpowder were hauled away, some to be later used against the British at Bunker Hill. Although no fighting occurred the incident is remembered as one of the earliest overt acts of aggression against the British. Interpretive panels explain the remnants of Fort Constitution, as it was renamed, in the small park.

Portsmouth

Governor John Langdon House (site)

143 Pleasant Street, 603-436-3205; Jun–Oct: Wed–Sun, 11–5. Admission charged.

A wealthy merchant, John Langdon first took an active role in the Revolution when he helped lead the raid on Fort William and Mary. He served in Congress during the First Continental Congress and when the British threatened the Lake Champlain area he personally pledged funds to finance the defense by local militia. Later, Langdon took the field to command units at Bennington and Saratoga.

After the war Langdon returned to Philadelphia to again serve in Congress. He signed the Constitution and went on to become the first president of the Senate. In the early 1800s Langdon served three terms as governor of New Hampshire and respectfully declined a Republican nomination for vice-president in 1812.

Langdon's magnificent balustraded house was built between 1783 and 1785 and reflected his status as New Hampshire's leading citizen. Langdon and his wife, Elizabeth, hosted many prominent visitors here, including President George Washington in 1789. Washington described the white clapboard Georgian mansion as "the finest house in Portsmouth."

John Paul Jones House (site)

43 Middle Street, 603-436-8420; Jun–Oct: Mon–Sat, 10–4, Sun, 12–4. Admission charged.

Jones stayed in Portsmouth twice supervising the outfitting of warships at the Langdon shipyards. In 1777 he oversaw the construction of *Ranger*, his first commission, and on October 4, 1782, he returned for the rigging of the *America*. He never set sail on *America*, however, as it was used as reparation to France for a French ship wrecked by a careless pilot off the Boston shore. It was during his second stay, lasting just over a month, that Jones boarded at the pale yellow clapboard house of the Widow Purcell.

Liberty Pole (site)

Prescott Park, 105 Marcy Street; Open daily, 24 hours.

Rescued from decaying wharves and warehouses by the largesse of two local residents — the Prescott sisters — the park, adorned with thousands of flowers, was the site in 1766 where the Portsmouth citizenry first raised a liberty pole to protest the Stamp Act. In 1824, this act of revolutionary defiance was permanently commemorated by the installation and dedication of a new liberty pole, which continues to be replaced as necessary.

Also in Prescott Park is the 1705 Sheafe Warehouse, where John Paul Jones outfitted the *Ranger*. It was designed so that gundalows — flat-bottomed river boats — could easily transfer their goods. A reproduction gundalow is seasonally docked adjacent to the building which houses a small boat-building museum.

Moffatt-Ladd House (site)

154 Market Street, 603-436-8221; Mid-Jun–Mid-Oct: Mon–Sat, 10–4, Sun, 2–5. Admission charged.

William Whipple, born in 1730, took to the sea in his early teens and was captaining a ship by 1755, engaging in the profitable slave trade of the times. By 1775 he was a successful Portsmouth merchant seduced by the growing Revolutionary movement. He was elected to the Second Continental Congress and affixed his name to the bottom of the Declaration of Independence.

Whipple worked vigorously in Congress at Philadelphia, excusing himself only to serve with his state militia at Saratoga in 1777 and Newport in 1778. Returning to New Hampshire, Whipple served as an associate justice of the state superior court from 1782 until his death in 1785.

This striking blue three-story frame home overlooking the water was built by Whipple's father-in-law, a successful merchant in 1763. Whipple married his daughter Katherine in 1768 and lived here until he died. He is buried in North Cemetery on Maplewood Avenue. Prince Whipple, his slave, is buried here, too.

Peirce Island (site)

Across Mechanic Street Bridge.

At the far end of the island are overgrown remains of earthen ramparts of Fort Washington, built to protect Portsmouth during the Revolutionary War. The British never did invade the seaside town. Across the water from Peirce Island, named for Portsmouth's wealthiest merchant, is the Portsmouth Naval Shipyard, the first of six public shipyards founded by Congress on June 12, 1800.

Thomas Thompson House (site)

145 Pleasant Street, private residence.

This white frame house was built next door to John Langdon's house in 1784 for his friend and business partner, Captain Thomas Thompson. Thompson was master of the frigate *Raleigh*, which was built in Langdon's shipyard on Badger's Island and is known as the first ship of the American Navy. The *Raleigh* is depicted under construction on the New Hampshire state flag and seal.

Tobias Lear House (site)

49 Hunking Street, private residence.

Built around 1740, this mustard-colored frame building was the childhood home of the fifth Tobias Lear. He later became secretary to George Washington and tutor to Washington's adopted grandchildren. The president visited Lear's mother here when he came to Portsmouth in 1789.

New Jersey

Revolutionary Status: Original Colony
Estimated Colonial Population: 133,000
Colonial Capital: Rotated between Perth Amboy and Burlington
Last Colonial Governor: William Franklin
Troops Provided: 4 Continental regiments

Revolutionary Timeline:

November 18, 1776: George Washington evacuates Fort Lee ahead of a British invasionary force led by Lord Charles Cornwallis

December 26, 1776: Washington captures 918 Hessians at the Battle of Trenton

January 3, 1777: Washington caps "The Nine Days' Wonder" with a stunning victory over the British at Princeton

Winter, 1776-1777: Continental Army camps at Morristown

March 21, 1777: British slaughter American foraging party at Hancock's Bridge

October 22, 1777: Nathanael Greene stops 2,000 Hessians in defending Fort Mercer, which is evacuated a month later

June 28, 1778: Continental Army comes of age in decisive victory in Battle of Monmouth Courthouse

September 28, 1778: Charles Grey ambushes American outpost at River Vale in Baylor Massacre

Winter, 1778-1779: Continental Army camps at Middle Brook

Winter, 1779-1780: Continental Army camps at Morristown

June 23, 1780: Americans repulse British in Battle of Springfield for a second time

June 26, 1783: Continental Congress assembles in Princeton

Alpine

Cornwallis Landing Site (site)

Palisades Interstate Park, Route 9W.

In the summer of 1776 Sir William Howe piled up a succession of impressive victories over Washington's amateur army around New York and desperately wanted to end the American revolt. He overran Fort Washington in Yonkers and sent Lord Cornwallis across the Hudson to finish the American Army at Fort Lee. On November 19 Cornwallis and 6,000 men landed in Alpine, six miles north of Fort Lee, and began an arduous climb up a twisting path to the top of the Palisades. Some sailors dragged artillery up the 300-foot cliffs. It was a remarkable march but the British force narrowly missed catching the demoralized Americans. Still there was no doubt in the British camp that the Americans had little fight left in them.

A historical marker notes Cornwallis' accomplishment at Alpine. The Blackledge-Kearney House served as a stopover for General Lord Cornwallis. Four rooms in the 1750 house have been restored to reflect three major periods in its existence.

Batsto

Batsto Village (site)

Route 542, 609-561-3262; grounds: daily dawn to dusk; visitor center: 9–4:30. Admission charge for parking on weekends and holidays.

Batsto was founded in 1766 by Charles Read of Burlington, New Jersey, who was the most noted ironmaster in West Jersey prior to the Revolution. He built the Batsto Iron Works near the mouth of the Batsto River. It was the first known bog iron furnace to be established here.

Bog ore is impure, formed from decayed vegetable matter interacting with iron salts in the stream beds. Along the banks it mixes with mud and hardens into thick, rocky beds, which are harvested. The New Jersey Pine Barrens around Batsto provided rivers to power the mills and provide transportation to New York and Philadelphia and abundant wood to fire the charcoal furnaces.

By 1773, John Cox, a Philadelphia merchant and trader, became owner of the Batsto Iron Works. During his ownership, and that of Joseph Ball to whom he sold Batsto in 1779, the Works became an important supplier to the Continental Army during the American Revolution. Such wartime products as munitions; camp kettles; iron fastenings; and fittings for artillery caissons, wagons and ships were manufactured here. A British spy on the shore of Batsto Lake reported the daily production of the remote site to the British.

The ironworks disappeared when cheap, mineable iron ore was discovered in the West. The restored village features a bog ore exhibit, charcoal kilns, farm buildings and a working sawmill demonstration. The visitor center details the history of Batsto and includes Revolutionary War cannonballs produced here and iron pans which were used to evaporate sea water for salt for Continental troops.

Bound Brook

Middlebrook Encampment (site)

Middlebrook Road, 908-560-1617; Open daily, dawn to dusk. Free.

With his main army ensconced, more or less, in winter quarters at Morristown in the winter of 1776-1777, General Washington established a forward outpost in this location, covering the passes through the Watchung Mountains to prevent a British advance on Philadelphia past his southern flank. It was a strong defensive position from which General Sir William Howe hoped to lure the Continentals, split and destroy the army. But Washington was able to counter Howe's strategic maneuvers, frustrating the British leader and sending him to sea to launch his Philadelphia offensive.

Washington returned his army to Middlebrook in the winter of 1778. With the lessons of past winter camps well learned Washington now directed the soldier huts to be built in parallel lines, above ground and roofed with timber rather than damp sod. Still the boredom of camp life spawned the usual desertions and pilfering of local farms. Worse, the declining value of Continental money made recruiting bounties worthless and food shortages were legion. Still, with northern operations at an end and with the winter a mild one, the Continental Army, now a professional fighting machine wielded under Baron von Steuben, marched from Middlebrook in June 1779 with pride.

The site of Washington's Revolutionary War encampment is undeveloped and open for visiting. Ceremonies take place here every Independence Day.

Bridgeton

Liberty Bell (site)
Cumberland County Courthouse, Broad Street; Mon–Fri, 9–5. Free.

Bridgeton was founded in 1686 and earned its name in 1716 when a bridge was built across the Cohansey River. By the Revolution the town population had grown to 200 and was the county seat. This celebrated bell rang out the news of the Declaration of Independence on July 7, 1776.

Caldwell

Old Cannon (mem)
Roseland Avenue.

Skirmishing took place through Caldwell along Bloomfield Avenue. The cannon, used in the war, sits in the center of town as tribute to those who participated. An interpretive plaque on the base details Caldwell and the Revolution.

Elizabeth

Boxwood Hall State Historic Site (site)
1073 East Jersey Street, 201-648-4540; Wed–Sat, 10–12 and 1–6, Sun, 1–6. Free.

Elizabethtown, as it was known during the Revolution, was the site of many attacks and skirmishes in the war years, but many pre–Revolutionary buildings remain. Boxwood Hall, built by the mayor in 1750, is one of the finest. Its most prominent resident was Elias Boudinot, a president of the Continental Congress and later, as acting secretary of foreign affairs, a signer of the Paris Peace Treaty with Great Britain. The body of martyred James Caldwell was displayed in front of Boxwood Hall in 1782 and Elias Boudinot spoke in tribute.

Boudinot later sold the red clapboard building to Jonathan Dayton, youngest signer of the Constitution. Subsequent owners drastically altered the appearance of the house, which is now maintained and designated as a national landmark.

Englishtown

Village Street (site)
Water Street and Main Street, 908-463-3090; Open by appointment. Free.

There is no definitive record that this attractive red clapboard inn was used during the Revolutionary War, but it can be safely assumed that it was too pleasing a shelter to have been left vacant by visiting officers. It was built in 1726 as a home and tailor shop but was in use as an inn and tavern by 1760. Daniel Herbert purchased the building in 1777 and was taxed on the property in 1779, but there are no records from 1778, when the Battle of Monmouth was fought nearby. Tradition has it that Washington drew up Charles Lee's court-martial papers here, charged with disobeying direct orders.

Fort Lee

Fort Lee Historic Park (site)

Hudson Terrace, just south of the George Washington Bridge, 201-461-1776; Mar–Dec: Wed–Sun, 10–5. Free; parking fee from Apr–Nov.

Construction of a fortress on the Palisades Cliffs 300 feet above the Hudson River began hastily in September 1776 as Washington tried futilely to protect the nation's interior. But its twin bastion, Fort Washington, collapsed to the British on November 16 and Lord Cornwallis wasted little time in clearing the entire Hudson River fortifications. He ferried 6,000 men across the water and landed six miles north of Fort Lee. The forewarned Americans were able to evacuate but sacrificed critical supplies in their flight. Fort Lee was the final in an unbroken string of disasters for the Continental Army following the Battle of Long Island, and Washington's troops limped in retreat to the Delaware River.

Cannon batteries have been reconstructed on the cliffsides, reached by two short interpretive trails. While the cannons were trained on the Hudson River, the earthen fort was protected by wooden abatises to the rear. Opposite the southern overlook is a reconstructed eighteenth century soldier's hut with a well, woodshed and baking oven. The 11,000-foot visitor center contains two floors of audiovisual displays, detailed exhibits and a 12-minute film presenting the story of Fort Lee in the American Revolution.

Freehold

Covenhoven House (site)

West Main Street and Barkalow Avenue, 908-462-1466; May–Oct: Tue–Thur, Sun, 1–4, Sat, 10–4. Free.

Sir Henry Clinton used this 1706 Dutch house as headquarters just before the Battle of Monmouth Court House, staying with Mrs. Elizabeth Covenhoven, a 74-year-old widow. The building has been restored to circa 1740 and period furnishings have been installed.

Monmouth Battlefield State Park (site)

Route 33, 908-462-9616; park open daily, dawn to dusk; visitor center, daily 9–4. Free.

Word reached General Washington shortly before noon on June 18, 1778, that the British Army was evacuating Philadelphia. Within 24 hours he had his newly drilled army on the move, hoping to engage the enemy before they reached New York. The first days of summer 1778 were oppressively hot, and many British soldiers died of heat exhaustion trudging along sandy roads in the airless woods of central New Jersey. Washington indeed caught up with his quarry.

Washington placed General Charles Lee in charge of a 5,000-man advance force to move on Monmouth Court House. Washington would remain eight miles to the west in Cranbury, preparing to deliver a crushing blow that could not have been imagined in the shadow of New York City two years earlier. But he had given command to a general with no taste for battle on this day.

Lee outlined no plan of action for his fellow generals, and when the order came from Washington to attack at 5 A.M. he dallied until 7:00. When finally in motion he approached tentatively against the British rear guard. When the battle was finally joined confusion reigned and the Americans soon scattered in retreat. Coming up in support, Washington met Lee on the road with 5,000 of his best troops rushing around him.

A stunned Washington immediately took personal command of the battle and stopped the retreat. Eagerly his troops, hardened from their experience at Valley Forge, rallied to check the British attack and forced their foe from the field. Washington ordered a counterattack but the record heat had sapped the energy of his troops. It was the last major battle of the Revolution in the north.

Washington did not get the complete annihilation of the British force that he had sought but it had probably been his finest hour in the field. His important victories at Trenton and Princeton had been accomplished with detachments, but at Monmouth he had led an entire army in decisive and imaginative fashion. Furthermore he had battled the elite troops of the British Army with now equally professional men in his Continental Army. With the British in retreat to New York all that remained for the moment was to draw up court-martial papers for Lee.

The only interpretation of the Battle of Monmouth is in the visitor center, which features exhibits tracing the troop movements of what evolved into the longest battle of the Revolution. On display are 3 of the 62 pages of Charles Lee's court-martial, including charges for disobedience of orders, leading a disorderly retreat and disrespecting the commander-in-chief. Artifacts recovered from the field are displayed as well. Trails, unadorned with historical markers, traverse the scene of some of the most desperate fighting.

Reenactment: The Battle of Monmouth is relived through both days of the weekend closest to June 28.

Greenwich

Gibbon House (site)

Ye Greate Street, 609-872-5970; Apr–Dec: Tue–Sat, 12–4, Sun, 2–5. Free.

Greenwich, on the Cohansey River, was the site of New Jersey's Tea Party.

The Gibbon House was built in 1730 by wealthy merchant Nicholas Gibbon and is patterned after a London townhouse.

Haddonfield

Indian King Tavern Museum (site)
233 Kings Highway East, 609-429-6792; Wed–Sat, 10–12 and 1–4, Sun, 1–4. Free.

Built in 1750, this early American public house and tavern was an important social, political and military stop along the King's Highway. The New Jersey Assembly adopted the Great Seal in the three-story brick building. It was New Jersey's first state historic site. Guided tours examine the historical displays and period artifacts.

Hancock's Bridge

Hancock House (site)
New Street and Locust Island Road, 609-935-4373; not currently open.

After failing to annihilate the entire Patriot foraging party at Quinton's Bridge, Colonel Charles Mawhood rededicated his efforts to eliminating the Rebel raiders at Hancock's Bridge, south of British-occupied Salem. Operating under intelligence that a large Rebel force was using the house of staunch Loyalist William Hancock, the Queen's Rangers under Major John Simcoe marched through the stormy darkness of March 21, 1778, against the position.

Instead of happening upon a force equal to his own 400 troops, which he expected, Simcoe's men circled a house with only 30 Americans sleeping inside. Simultaneously, the British forced their way in the front and rear doors, bayoneting the guards and stabbing the Rebel soldiers, some of whom had been their friends and neighbors before the war. The only retreat was to the attic, where the men were slain or severely wounded. No gun was ever fired. No sound of ammunition exploding alarmed the little village. In all 20 were killed and the rest sustained serious wounds.

Included in the carnage was Loyalist Hancock, who had the ill fortune to return from the village unbeknownst to Simcoe. After the attack, the British departed from New Jersey with the few cattle and other forage they had garnered.

Labeled by the Americans as a "massacre" and "murder," the atrocities can be placed not at the feet of the British regular army but the vitriolic Tories, long considered unprincipled in the conduct of war. The brick Hancock House was constructed in 1734 of Flemish bond and is decorated on its west end with a herringbone pattern of glazed bricks marking the initials of the builders.

Jefferson

Picatinny Arsenal (site)
Off Route 15, 201-724-2797; Open daily, dawn to dusk.

On this site a Colonial forge operated during the Revolutionary War, producing cannonballs and solid shot for Washington's Colonial Army.

Morristown

Fort Nonsense (site)
Off Ann Street, from Western Avenue; Open daily, 24 hours.

High on a hill, southwest of Morristown, Washington ordered an earthen fort constructed, with cannon facing the Watchung Mountains and the British in New York City beyond. The redoubt was sufficient for about 30 men. The origin of the fort's name is unknown, although local legend maintained that the soldiers had dubbed it so ingloriously because they assumed their duty was Washington's way of keeping them busy. But Washington valued the high ground and surely this location, with its sweeping views of the mountains and valley between the Americans and the enemy, afforded that.

Fort Nonsense is part of the Morristown National Historical Park. It can be visited anytime and features interpretive signs and a stone outline of the redoubt.

Jockey Hollow Encampment (site)
Western Avenue, 201-539-2016; Daily, 9–5. Admission charged.

The main soldiers' camp during the winter of 1779-1780 was constructed in Jockey Hollow, five miles southwest of Morristown and Washington's headquarters at Ford Mansion. Washington's men were experienced camp builders by this point in the war and felled 600 acres of hardwood forest to build carefully arranged lines of hillside huts.

But nothing could have prepared the Continental Army for the worst winter of the eighteenth century. Twenty-eight blizzards pounded the slopes and whipped through the wooden huts. The quartermaster could not keep the army clothed, and many times the sun came up and went down without any food being issued to the men. The Continental Congress, beleaguered by unchecked inflation, was unable to provide for the army and survived only through the largesse of local governments.

Even battle-tested veterans, survivors of Valley Forge, were on the precipice of mutiny at Morristown. Washington managed to hold his force together but his pleas in Philadelphia for help went unheeded. A year later, the Pennsylvania Line, comprising ten regiments, indeed mutinied during another winter at Morristown, killing an officer and marching on Philadelphia to demand supplies and back pay. Only then did Congress appreciate the extent of the dissatisfaction of its men in the field.

A tour road explores the hollows that were home to 10,000 suffering soldiers in 1779-1780. On a hillside cleared by the Pennsylvania Brigade, near the Grand Parade Field, are five reconstructed soldier huts. The headquarters of General Arthur St. Clair, the Wick family home, is open behind the visitor center. In the center is a cross-section of a timber hut, designed to sleep 12 men. A short film is presented.

Morristown National Historical Park (site)
Historical Museum and Library; Washington Place, off I-287, 201-539-2016; Daily, 9–5. Admission charged for museum.
Morristown, a village of 250, was a center of iron supply for the American Revolution. Even though it lay only 30 miles west of the main British force in New York it was protected by a series of parallel mountain ranges. It was these twin luxuries of a defensible position in close proximity to the enemy which twice brought General Washington to camp his main army here, first in 1777 and again in 1779–1780.
After the Battle of Princeton in January 3, 1777, Washington's army was too worn down to continue an offensive and trudged into winter quarters at Morristown. The 5,000 soldiers swarmed the tiny town seeking shelter in the few public buildings, private homes, barns and stables then in existence. Steadily Washington rebuilt his flagging troops, overcoming desertion and incipient food shortages. His greatest foe, however, was disease. An outbreak of smallpox threatened to decimate the small army and Washington ordered the little known and, to many, horrifying procedure of inoculation. Some indeed died but most of his troops did not contract the deadly pox.
Washington again brought his army to Morristown at the end of 1779, having successfully driven the British back to New York. He accepted the hospitality of Mrs. Jacob Ford, Jr., a widow with four young children, to stay in her home, the finest in Morristown. Washington made his headquarters in the Ford Mansion, behind the park visitor center. The museum describes the encampments through historical objects and exhibits. A 20-minute film is screened every half-hour.

Schuyler Hamilton House Museum (site)
5 Olyphant Place, 201-267-4039; Open by appointment. Admission charged.
The Colonial mansion, built in the 1760s, was the home of Dr. Jabez Campfield and was used by General Washington's personal physician, Dr. John Cochrane. An aide of Washington in Morristown, Colonel Alexander Hamilton, courted a houseguest, Betsy Schuyler, the daughter of General Philip Schuyler.

Thomas Paine (mem)
Burnham Park, Washington Street.
The monument depicts Thomas Paine seated at the winter camp of 1776-1777 in Morristown. He is using a drum as a desk and is writing his famous pamphlet *The Crisis*. His line "these are the times that try men's souls" can be clearly read on the sculpted piece of paper. The bronze on a marble base was sculpted by Georg Lober and dedicated on July 4, 1950.

Newark

Wars of America (mem)
Military Park.

Amos Van Horn provided $100,000 for this memorial and Gutzon Borglum won the commission. Dedicated in 1926, the monument features a colossal group of 42 figures and 2 horses, set at the end of a reflecting pool. It depicts all the wars of America up to World War I.

Paramus

Washington Spring Garden (site)
Van Saun Park, Forest Avenue, 201-262-2627; Daily, 9–dusk. Free.

Washington Spring was used as the primary source of pure water for the American Continental Army as it encamped on the west side of the Hackensack River between September 4 and September 20, 1778. The spring was likely the center of the camp in the area known as Steenrapie.

Local legend has it that George Washington drank from the spring while reviewing his troops on parade. Washington had established headquarters in present-day Mahwah at the Hopper House, destroyed in 1890. The Continental Army moved from its Steenrapie encampment on September 20 to go to Tappan, New York.

Paulsboro

Fort Billings (site)
Northwest section of town on Delaware River.

Fort Billings was built during the Revolution to prevent the British fleet from communicating with Philadelphia. It has the distinction of being purchased by Continental Congress on July 4, 1776, the first land purchase of the new government. The next day it was deeded to the 13 united colonies. Nothing remains of the fort, which was garrisoned again in the War of 1812. A stone monument honoring Fort Billings marks it site on the Delaware River.

Perth Amboy

Proprietary House/Royal Governor's Mansion (site)
149 Kearney Avenue, 908-826-5527; Sunday, 1–4. Admission charged.

Built between 1762 and 1764, the building was the home to William Franklin, the last royal governor of New Jersey and illegitimate son of Benjamin Franklin. Franklin was arrested by order of the Provincial Congress of New Jersey in June 1776. General Sir William Howe moved in during the British occupation of Perth Amboy. It is the only remaining official governor's residence in the original 13 colonies.

Plainfield

Drake House Museum (site)

602 West Front Street, 908-755-5831; Sunday, 2–4. Admission charged.
Washington used the Drake family home as headquarters in 1777. The
museum presents two centuries of Plainfield history through the lives of the
Drakes and the families that followed.

Port Monmouth

The Spy House Museum (site)

119 Port Monmouth Road, 908-787-1807; Sunday, 12–5. Free.
The now-expansive house began life as a small one-room cabin in 1663. During the Revolution it served as an inn and was the headquarters for raids against
the British fleet anchored in New York Harbor. The museum explores the heritage of the entire shore region, not just its surreptitious side.

Princeton

Morven (site)

55 Stockton Street, 609-683-4495; Wednesday, 11–2. Admission charged.
A tragic figure of the Revolution, successful lawyer Richard Stockton lived
in this grand Georgian mansion beginning in the 1750s. Stockton was a moderate with mostly a cursory involvement in politics at the local level. He was
elected to the Second Continental Congress on June 22, 1776, and arrived in
Philadelphia just in time to vote for separation. He signed the Declaration of
Independence on August 2.
That winter the British seized Stockton. When it was revealed that their prisoner had signed the Declaration of Independence he was subjected to such cruelty in his New York prison that the Continental Congress protested to General
Sir William Howe. Stockton was freed, but not before being forced to swear his
allegiance to King George III and sign the amnesty proclamation. He returned
to Princeton to discover his estate pillaged and most of his wealth drained. An
untreated lip wound, a souvenir from his prison days, festered into a tumor
which spread to his throat and he died a broken man in 1781 at the age of 50.
The yellow brick house set back from Stockton Street was twice devastated
by fires but restored. Morven served as the official residence of New Jersey governors from 1953 until 1981. The house and gardens are now open for tours on
a limited schedule.

Nassau Hall (site)

Princeton University, facing Nassau Street, opposite Witherspoon Street,
609-258-3000; campus tours: Mon–Sat, 10, 11, 1:30 and 3:30, Sun, 1:30,
3:30. Tours free, admission to museum in Nassau Hall.
Nassau Hall *was* the College of New Jersey — Princeton University since

1896 — when it was completed in 1756. The 170-foot long four-story brownstone — the most impressive college building in the middle colonies — contained classrooms, eating and sleeping areas, and a chapel for the entire student body of 70. The British occupied Princeton in 1776 and used Nassau Hall as barracks. During the Battle of Princeton some redcoats took refuge here and were driven away by artillery fire. Americans treated wounded soldiers in Nassau Hall.

Princeton became the nation's capital in 1783 when mutineers surrounded Independence Hall to receive backpay. Congress adjourned in Philadelphia and assembled in Nassau Hall on June 26, 1783, remaining in session until November. A small museum is maintained on the first floor of Nassau Hall; a monument to American wars graces the entrance foyer. Ten names are listed for the Revolution.

Princeton Battle Monument (mem)

Monument Drive.

The imposing stone sculpture by Frederic MacMonnies celebrates Washington's victory. Unveiled in 1922 by President Warren Harding, it is an unrealized copy of the Arc de Triomphé in Paris. It depicts Washington on horseback, sternly refusing defeat at the Battle of Princeton and inspiring his troops to final victory. Nearby is a two-foot high stone and slate monument bearing a frieze that honors the marines of Washington's troops.

Princeton Battlefield State Park (site)

500 Mercer Road, south of town; Open daily, 24 hours.

Having finally achieved an important victory at Trenton in late December 1776, Washington was in no mood to remain back on the western side of the Delaware River. He came across just before the new year in hopes of surprising the British at Princeton. For his part, Maj. Gen. Charles Lord Cornwallis avowed to drive the enemy back across the Delaware and reestablish control of New Jersey. He amassed 5,500 men and set out to meet Washington in Trenton.

Washington was not waiting for such a clash. He put his ragged troops on the march, planning to outflank the British, destroy a rear guard at Princeton and capture a vital supply depot in Brunswick. Little matter that his troops had little food and some lacked shoes. Moving swiftly along a little known road through the frozen night, Washington was on the way to achieving his objective when an alert British rear guard spotted his army at daybreak through the leafless trees.

Lt. Col. Charles Mawhood quickly retraced his steps and smashed into a detachment under Brig. Gen. Hugh Mercer. Mercer's men were pushed back up a field of frozen cornhusks. Mercer himself was bayoneted seven times near the Thomas Clark House, but according to legend he refused to be taken from the field and was laid under a still-standing white oak tree. He would die of his wounds nine days later in the Clark House. A crushing defeat seemed certain but Washington had ridden back upon hearing the musket fire and arrived to take command of the battle. Joined by reinforcements from his main army, the Americans chased the British down the road to the town of Princeton.

Washington could carry his brilliant counteroffensive no further. He moved his worn-out army to Morristown, and the British skulked back to New Brunswick. Cornwallis had hoped to have all of New Jersey — and soon Philadelphia — under his control. Instead, Washington's "Nine Days' Wonder" had left him with just the ports around New York City.

When Cornwallis surrendered to Washington in Yorktown he told him, "When the illustrious part that your Excellency has borne in this long and arduous contest becomes a matter of history, fame will gather your brightest laurels rather from the banks of the Delaware than from those of the Chesapeake." The American Revolution was saved at Trenton and Princeton but little has been done to develop the sites historically. The terrain of the main fighting of the Battle of Princeton has remained virtually unchanged since the Revolution. Only a tile map is on-site for interpretation. The Clark House still stands at the crest of the grounds and in the distance are British and American graves, marked by the Ionic columns from the portico of an 1836 Philadelphia mansion.

Princeton Cemetery (site)
Entrance on Greenview Street; Open daily, dawn to dusk.

The historic burial ground contains the graves of Jonathan Edwards, Aaron Burr and John Witherspoon — New Jersey College president and signer of the Declaration of Independence.

Rockingham Historic Site (site)
Route 518, 609-921-8835; Wed–Sat, 10–12, Sun, 1–4. Free.

Washington traveled to Princeton in August 1783 at the bequest of Congress to discuss the establishment of a peacetime army. He settled in Rockingham, built in 1734 and owned by John Berrien since 1764. As debate in Congress droned on, Washington's short stay elongated, and in October the British indicated they would be abandoning New York in November. Within the week Congress discharged all soldiers who were already at home for the summer. Washington had an aide prepare a "Farewell Orders to the Armies" for the small detachment still at West Point, New York — the remaining Continental Army. Congress never did achieve a voting quorum in Princeton, and Washington returned to West Point in early November. The restored house is adorned with period furnishings and has been periodically open to the public since 1897.

Quinton

Quinton's Bridge (site)
Route 49, historical marker only.

After General Anthony Wayne rustled 150 head of cattle from the Salem area to herd back to Washington's troops at Valley Forge in February 1778, the British landed 1,500 troops in the region to restore order. At Quinton's Bridge on

March 18 the raiders blundered into a British trap, losing nearly half their force of 100 men. The original bridge, and scene of many American drownings and deaths, is about 100 yards upstream from the current bridge. No structures from that time remain. Historical markers interpret the engagement.

Rahway

Merchants and Drovers Tavern (site)
1632 St. Georges Avenue, 908-381-0441; Open by appointment.

This four-story eighteenth-century tavern was an important stagecoach stop on the King's Highway between New York and Philadelphia and host to famous Revolutionary War figures. It is open through appointment with the Rahway Historical Society.

Ringwood

Ringwood Manor (site)
Ringwood State Park, 1304 Sloatsburg Road, 201-962-7031; May–Oct: Wed–Sun, 10–4. Admission charged.

Iron was unearthed in the Ramapo Mountains in the early 1700s, and the first forge appeared in 1739. By 1771 the lucrative London-based American Iron Company controlled the considerable output for the forge when Scottish engineer Robert Erskine arrived to manage the operation. Erskine proved an excellent ironmaster but was unable to keep working capital flowing from the home office. When the Revolution broke out Erskine lined up with the Patriot cause and formed his workers into a local militia. This not only afforded his forge protection but kept his workers from being displaced into the Continental Army.

Iron from Ringwood wound up in army camps as stoves and on the battlefield as ordnance. Erskine manufactured most of the huge chain that would be stretched across the Hudson River to impede British ships. As important as that contribution was, Erskine was even more valuable in another arena — mapmaking. Trained in topography and possessing a rare talent as a draftsman, Erskine made 129 maps — some having as many as 20 sheets — in just 30 months as surveyor general for the Continental Army. Unfortunately, Robert Erskine caught cold during a field expedition and rapidly deteriorated, passing away on October 2, 1780, at the age of 45.

The land around Ringwood in the eighteenth century was dotted with the magnificent mansions of the wealthy mine and forge owners. Erskine's was no exception; his first home burned during the Revolution but was replaced with an even grander one, in which General Washington and his associates were often entertained. The Ringwood iron mine produced steadily until 1931, and subsequent owners expanded the manor until it eventually reached 78 rooms. Twenty-one have been restored. The grave of versatile American patriot Robert Erskine is on the grounds.

River Edge

Steuben House State Historic Site (site)
Historic New Bridge Landing Park, 1209 Main Street, 201-487-1739; Wed–Sat, 10–12 and 1–5, Sun, 2–5. Free.

This Dutch home, the oldest section of which dates to 1695, was used by both American and British forces during the Revolution. In 1780 Washington briefly made it his headquarters. After the war the house — then confiscated Tory property — was purchased by the state of New Jersey and presented, with gratitude for services rendered, to General Friedrich von Steuben. The Baron never lived here, however, preferring the 16,000 upstate New York acres that he was also given. The Steuben House is now part of a complex in the park that features three Dutch Colonial homes.

River Vale

Baylor Massacre Burial Site (site)
Red Oak Drive, River Vale and Old Tappan roads, 201-646-2780; Open daily, dawn to dusk.

In September 1778 the British under Maj. Gen. Charles Grey — known as "No-flint Grey" for his part in the earlier Paoli Massacre — once again destroyed an American outpost under cover of darkness. Led by Tory guides, Grey's men ambushed and annihilated a 12-man security picket at the bridge across the Hackensack River at this point and caught 104 Continental dragoons asleep in three barns nearby. Only 37 men escaped unhurt.

Colonel George Baylor and his second-in-command, Major Alexander Clough, hid in a chimney, were discovered and severely wounded. Clough died of his wounds; Baylor never recovered, dying two years later. He was widely criticized by his peers for leaving his troops in such a lightly defended position.

As with many routs by the British, cries of "massacre" were shrieked by rebel propagandists. But bodies of Colonial soldiers uncovered in tanning vats decades later appeared to support the claims of ghastly treatment of the inexperienced troops by the seasoned British.

The remains of six dragoons were found in 1967 during an archaeological dig and reinterred in 1970 in this small park by the Hackensack River. Commemorative plaques and gravesites detail the bloody events of September 28, 1778.

Roselle

Abraham Clark House (site)
West Ninth Avenue and Chestnut Street, 908-486-1783; Open by appointment.

This replica home belonged to Abraham Clark, the "poor man's counselor" and signer of the Declaration of Independence as a Continental congressman. Colonial artifacts are on display.

Salem

Friend's Burial Ground (site)
West Broadway; Open daily, dawn to dusk.
On this site in 1675 John Fenwick signed the treaty to create Salem with the Lenni Lenape Indians. The bargaining took place under the Salem Oak, which the locals estimate has stood for 600 years; its foliage covers one-quarter acre. In the burying ground are graves of Revolutionary veterans.

St. John's Episcopal Church (site)
Grant and Market streets; Open daily, dawn to dusk.
Founded in 1722, the first church on this location was built in 1728. It was used by the British when they occupied Salem during the Revolution. The present church dates to 1838; graves of Revolution soldiers are in the cemetery to the rear.

Scotch Plains

Osborn-Cannonball House (site)
1840 East Front Street, 908-232-1199; Open for special events.
The 1700s saltbox farmhouse was hit by an American cannonball during a skirmish with the British here. Period clothing and furnishings can be viewed at the house, operated by the Historical Society of Scotch Plains.

Somerville

Wallace House (site)
38 Washington Place, 908-725-1015; Wed–Sat, 10–12 and 1–4, Sun, 1–4. Free.
During his winter camp from December 11, 1778, until June 3, 1779, General Washington used this two-story clapboard house as a headquarters. It was the second camp for the Continental Army at Middle Brook, Washington having used this strong position to check any British designs on Philadelphia a year earlier in May 1777. The General and Mrs. Washington also spent time in the Old Dutch Parsonage, a distinguished brick home across the street.

Springfield

Battle of Springfield (site)
Cannonball House, 126 Morris Avenue, 201-379-2634; Open by appointment.
As the summer of 1780 approached Washington had contained the British in New York and made camp in Morristown while the main of the enemy army shifted its attentions to the American South. Unexpectedly, on June 7, the British, under General Wilhelm von Knyphausen, landed an assault force at

De Hart's Point near Elizabethtown and pushed through gaps in the Watchung Mountains towards Morristown. His advance was halted by a spirited American defense led by Colonel Elias Dayton, in complete contradiction to British intelligence that American morale in New Jersey was flagging.

Knyphausen, who had acted on his own in the absence of commander Sir Henry Clinton, made an embarrassed retreat to his beach head at De Hart's Point. Clinton returned on June 17 to find his force split across the river, but fearing Washington's joining with the arriving French force, he ordered another attack. The Second Battle of Springfield commenced on June 23, with both sides considerably reinforced.

The Colonials' well-organized defense forced the British to withdraw once again. Before retreating, however, Knyphausen burned all but four of the buildings in Springfield.

The Cannonball House, a simple 1750 farmhouse, is one of the four survivors. It was struck in the side by a cannonball, which is among the exhibits on display.

Tennent

Old Tennent Church (site)
Tennent Road, north of Route 522; Open daily, dawn to dusk.

The 1751 frame church stands adjacent to the battlefield; spectators clamored onto the roof and steeple to observe the Battle of Monmouth on June 28, 1778. Buried in the graveyard is British Lt. Col. Henry Monckton, who died leading a third desperate assault on the American center. The grenadier was cut down so close to the American lines that his body was dragged behind the rebel lines. He was buried with full military honors at Old Tennent Church after the battle.

Titusville

Washington Crossing State Park (site)
Route 29 and Route 546, entrance to park on Route 546, 609-737-0623; Memorial Day–Labor Day: 8–8; Sep–May: 8–4:30. Admission charged to park.

On December 26, the last of Washington's troops and supplies came ashore here at 3:00 in the morning, more than three hours after he had hoped. He marched his troops seven miles south from this point to surprise the Hessians at Trenton. The Continentals killed some 100 enemy and captured another 900, including their arms and artillery.

That afternoon the Hessians were marched back through the snow to Washington's Crossing and rowed back across the Delaware River to Pennsylvania. On New Year's Day the captives were marched through the streets of Philadelphia, boosting morale and convincing many that the Revolution was indeed viable.

The park, separated from the shoreline by Route 29, features the Ferry House, which Washington used as a command post, out of the snow and hail, during the seven-hour crossing. He then assembled his troops, including Colonel Alexander Hamilton and Lieutenant James Monroe, in an adjoining field. The visitor center contains a large collection of Revolutionary War artifacts.

Down by the banks of the Delaware River, with a separate parking area, is the stone Nelson House where the ferries disembarked. In the yard is a replica flat-bottomed ferry of the kind which were critical in transporting Washington's horses and 18 cannon.

Toms River

Huddy-Asgill Affair (mem)
Huddy Park.

Toms River, behind a long barrier island, was a haven for privateers feasting on British shipping in the Revolutionary War, but it gained prominence by an incident that occurred just after the cessation of hostilities. A band of Tories, seeking prized saltworks, surprised Captain Joshua Huddy on March 24, 1782, as he defended the blockhouse. The blockhouse was burned and Huddy hanged on April 12, apparently in retribution for his having killed a Tory leader.

Angry Patriots demanded the surrender of Loyalist captain Richard Lippincott, the leader of the hanging party. When the band refused to produce him another British captain was selected by lot by the Americans. The sacrifice was 20-year-old Sir Charles Asgill. Back in England, Lady Asgill sailed to France to plead for the life of her only son, and indeed Congress finally ordered him released.

A replica of the blockhouse and Hubby Park, both on the waterfront in downtown Toms River, remember this affair.

Trenton

Old Barracks Museum (site)
Barrack Street, 609-396-1776; Daily, 10–5. Admission charged.

The two-story stone barracks are the only surviving Colonial barracks in the United States. Constructed in 1758 for the French and Indian War because New Jersey citizens refused to put British soldiers up in their houses, it was occupied by British, Hessian and American troops during the Revolution. It was these barracks that Washington targeted in the Battle of Trenton.

Trenton Battle Monument (site)
Intersection of North Broad Street and Pennington Avenue, Tue–Sat, 10–12 and 1–5. Admission charged.

The British battered the Continental Army across New York and New Jersey throughout 1776, and by Christmas Howe had stretched a line of pickets from Perth Amboy in the east to Trenton in the west. The British Army enjoyed an understandably restful Christmas in 1776, most certain that the war would be over come spring.

Colonel Johan Gottleib Rall and his Hessian troops commanded the post in Trenton, a hamlet of about 100 dwellings in the Revolution. Rall held the "country clowns" of the American fighting machine in such low regard that he did not bother to erect defenses around his position, in direct defiance of superior orders. He received but ignored warnings that an American army was threatening Trenton. When Washington struck he crushed the Hessians swiftly and paraded his prisoners out of town with similar alacrity. The Americans had not only gained respect and rejuvenated morale at Trenton, but proved that Washington was the man who could successfully lead this revolt.

The 150-foot column, dedicated on October 19, 1893, rises on the site where Washington placed his artillery on December 26, 1776. Thomas Eakins created the bas-relief scenes around the base of the column. An elevator rises to the observation deck in the monument, which is capped with a statue of George Washington. Inscribed are the words of Henry Clinton: "All our hopes were blasted by that unhappy affair at Trenton."

Union

Caldwell Parsonage (site)
909 Caldwell Avenue, 908-687-8129; Open by appointment.

Presbyterian minister James Caldwell was known as the "Fighting Parson" to his admirers and the "high priest of the Revolution" to Tory detractors. On June 7, 1780, as the British invaded northern New Jersey from Staten Island, Hannah Caldwell and her children took refuge in the parsonage at Connecticut Farms (now Union). She was later found dead — killed, says the inscription on her monument, "by a shot from a British soldier, June 25th [incorrect date], 1780, cruelly sacrificed by the enemies of her husband and of her country." There is no evidence that the fiery rhetoric of patriots eager to martyr Mrs. Caldwell is correct and, in fact, there is a suspicion that her death came at the hands of a former servant seeking revenge.

Some 17 months later the Reverend Caldwell was also slain under suspicious circumstances after an argument with a sentinel in Elizabethtown. The soldier was hanged for murder and later evidence revealed he may have been bribed to kill Caldwell at his first opportunity. The British burned the Caldwell home on this site.

The death of Hannah Caldwell is depicted on the official Union County seal. The Union Township Historical Society administers the property.

Wayne

Dey Mansion (site)
199 Totowa Road, 201-696-1776; Wed–Fri, 1–4, Sat–Sun, 10–12 and 1–4. Admission charged.

George Washington made this two-story Georgian house his headquarters in July of 1780 while the army camped nearby. He returned in the fall that year, supposedly under threat of a British plot to kidnap him. The manor house was constructed around 1740 for Colonel Theunis Dey.

Woodbury

Fort Mercer (site)

Red Bank Battlefield, 100 Hessian Avenue, two miles west at Delaware River, 609-853-5120; Open daily, dawn to dusk. Free.

Fort Mercer — named for Scottish Brig. Gen. Hugh Mercer, who died at Princeton — teamed with Fort Mifflin across the Delaware River to form a considerable detriment to any force planning a water approach to Philadelphia. Thaddeus Kosciuszko fortified this bluff above the river with nine-foot high earthen walls embedded with an abatis (sharpened tree branches). In command of the garrison was Colonel Christopher Greene and 400 of his fellow Rhode Islanders with 14 cannons.

After using a land route from the south and west to take Philadelphia on September 26, 1777, it immediately became imperative to open the Delaware River to keep supplies to the British Army flowing. The inevitable attack on Fort Mercer was not a month in coming. On October 21, 1,200 Hessians under Colonel Carl Emil Ulrich von Dolop ferried from Philadelphia and landed north of the fort at Cooper's Ferry, now Camden. After camping for the night in Haddonfield the Germans pressed on.

During the night a young apprentice blacksmith named Jonas Cattell ran the five miles from Haddonfield to Fort Mercer to warn Greene that a large enemy force was camped to his north, a lightly protected side of Fort Mercer. Greene redeployed his men away from the river to the northern face as von Donop arrived and demanded surrender.

Greene chose to fight and repulsed two German advances up the steep slopes. The fire from the American defenders was withering and the Hessian ranks were thinned by nearly half before leaving the field. They returned to Philadelphia the next day without von Donop, who was a battlefield casualty. He died at the Whitall House in the fort. He was interred on the battlefield on October 28.

Five days earlier, the 64-gun British warship *Augusta* exploded and sank under heavy American fire. Two Americans were captured and hanged for guiding the Hessians down the New Jersey side of the river to Fort Mercer, which was soon abandoned. The British stormed Fort Mifflin on November 16 and rather than face the overpowering force now across the river, the Americans destroyed Fort Mercer as they surrendered Philadelphia completely to the British.

Parts of Fort Mercer have been reconstructed, affording sweeping views of the Delaware River and the strength of its position. A soaring monument surmounted by a sentry was dedicated near the center of the former works in 1905. An exhibit rarely seen at battlefield sites is a cheveaux-de-frise, used as underwater obstructions. This one, salvaged from the Delaware River, is a large coffer filled with long heavy poles into which iron-tipped spikes project out at 45-degree angles. The coffer was floated in the river, filled with rocks and sunk just below the waterline to impale enemy ships.

James and Ann Whithall, whose house was used as a field hospital during the Battle of Red Bank and is open to the public, suffered a fate typical of Quaker families in the Philadelphia area during the Revolution. The Whithall farm was commandeered by the Continental Army in April 1777 and their apple orchard destroyed to build Fort Mercer. As their son Job remembered, "They turned us out of our kitchen, ye largest room upstairs, ye shop and took our hay to feed the horses." When the Hessians attacked, Ann refused to leave the house and legend maintains that after a cannonball crashed through the north wall she simply carried her wheel to the basement and kept on spinning.

Reenactment: The third weekend in October remembers the defense of Fort Mercer with an Eighteenth Century Day. The warning run of Jonas Cattell is celebrated with a 10-kilometer road race from Haddonfield to Fort Mercer.

New York

Revolutionary Status: Original Colony
Estimated Colonial Population: 168,000
Colonial Capital: New York City
Last Colonial Governor: William Tryon
Troops Provided: 5 Continental regiments

Revolutionary Timeline:

January 19, 1770: Forty British troops draw bayonets against club-wielding New Yorkers in the Battle of Golden Hill after soldiers destroy "Liberty Pole"

May 10, 1775: Ethan Allen, Benedict Arnold and 83 Vermont Green Mountain Boys capture Fort Ticonderoga

August 27, 1776: British overwhelm Americans in Battle of Long Island; Washington escapes only with a nighttime flotilla to Manhattan

September 15, 1776: British move into Kip's Bay and enter New York City

September 16, 1776: Americans score rare, albeit minor, victory in Battle of Harlem Heights

September 22, 1776: Nathan Hale is hung as a spy in New York City

October 11, 1776: Arnold successfully delays British invasion of Hudson River in Battle of Valcour Bay

October 28, 1776: British narrowly miss destroying the Continental Army at the Battle of White Plains

November 15, 1776: The Americans lose nearly 3,000 men as William Howe forces the surrender of Fort Washington

June 17, 1777: John Burgoyne launches British invasion of New York from Canada, hoping to split the colonies along the Hudson River with a force of more than 8,000 men

August 3, 1777: British begin costly and unsuccessful siege of Fort Stanwix
August 6, 1777: Battle of Oriskany weakens invading British ties with Indians
August 14, 1777: American militia destroy Hessian foragers at Battle of Bennington
October 6, 1777: Henry Clinton captures Fort Montgomery
October 17, 1777: Burgoyne's invasion ends when he surrenders 6,300 troops after two climatic battles near Saratoga
July 15, 1779: Anthony Wayne's daring victory at Stony Brook energizes the Patriot cause in America
July 19, 1779: Indian raider Joseph Brant burns the village of Minisink
August 29, 1779: John Sullivan defeats the Iroquois in the Battle of Newtown
September 22, 1780: John André, British spy and Benedict Arnold contact, is captured in Tarrytown
September 25, 1780: General Benedict Arnold deserts the Continental Army
October 2, 1780: Major John André executed at Tappan
October 25, 1781: Battle of Johnstown takes place six days after the British lay down arms in Yorktown
April 1782–August 1783: Continental Army makes its final camp at New Windsor
November 25, 1783: After seven years of occupation, the British leave New York

Albany

Albany Institute of History and Art (col)
125 Washington Avenue, 518-463-4478; Wed–Sun, 12–5. Admission charged.

The museum presents exhibits on the culture and history of the Hudson Valley. One of its historic documents is a "declaration of independence" signed by 225 villagers in Coxsackie on January 27, 1775. The Coxsackie residents, almost all with Dutch names, called for opposition to "the execution of several arbitrary and oppressive acts of the British Parliament." The action by the Dutch in the Hudson River Valley predated the rest of the colonies by almost 18 months.

Schuyler Mansion State Historic Site (site)
32 Catherine Street, 518-434-0834; Apr–Oct: Wed–Sat, 10–5, Sun, 1–5. Admission charged.

When Philip Schuyler was born in 1733, three generations of Schuylers had already settled in upstate New York before John Philip. After serving as a captain in the French and Indian War, Schuyler returned to Albany, heir to thousands of Mohawk and Hudson Valley acres. He oversaw their development personally and began construction of this magnificent rose-red brick mansion in 1761. He called his imposing home "The Pastures" when it was completed in 1762.

With the Revolutionary stirring in America he was drawn away from his agrarian dealings in 1768 and sought election in the colonial assembly. Schuyler was elected in 1768, serving seven years until going to Philadelphia as a member of the First Continental Congress. He spurned his appointment to the Second Continental Congress, however, in favor of resuming his military career. Respected for his ability to move men and supplies, Schuyler was commissioned a major general on June 15, 1775, and placed in charge of an invasion of Canada.

Falling ill, Schuyler had to stay behind in September 1775 as the ill-fated invasion progressed without him. He attempted to keep munitions and supplies flowing northward, but when the mission failed in June 1776 he was held responsible by many fellow officers and members in Congress. Still, he was placed in command of the Northern Department of the war and laid the groundwork for the ultimate defeat of Lt. Gen. John Burgoyne's invaders in 1777. But his detractors in Congress had him removed from command on August 4, even though he earned the accolades on the field, he did not reap rewards in the halls of Congress. He did not, however, allow petty slights to turn him from the Revolutionary cause. He returned to Congress in 1779 and was elected as one of the first two U.S. senators from New York in 1789.

The Pastures remained Schuyler's primary home among several. Every major luminary of the Revolution was entertained here, including "Gentleman Johnny" Burgoyne, who was a prisoner-guest. In 1780 Schuyler's daughter Betsy married Alexander Hamilton in the parlor. When Philip Schuyler died in 1804 he was eulogized by Daniel Webster as "second only to Washington in the services he performed for the country."

Ten Broeck Mansion (site)

9 Ten Broeck Place, 518-436-9826; Apr–Dec: Wed–Fri, 2–4, Sat–Sun, 1–4. Admission charged.

The mansion is a Federal-style home built in 1798 for General Abraham Ten Broeck, a locally prominent politician, businessman and patriot who served in the American Revolution. In 1779 he became the third generation Ten Broeck to serve as mayor of Albany. In the Dutch tradition, the construction date and initials of the owners are inscribed in wrought iron on the north and south gables. The collection includes mementos of his career.

Beacon

Mount Gilian Historic Site (site)

145 Sterling Street, 914-831-8172; Apr–Dec: Wed–Sun, 1–5. Admission charged.

During the Revolutionary War, fires burning on the summit of Mount Beacon to warn General George Washington of British movements up the Hudson River gave the mountain and the city their names. The historic site includes Verplanck Homestead, headquarters of General Baron Friedrich von Steuben, inspector general of the Continental Army in 1783. On May 13, 1783, several of Washington's senior officers formed the Society of Cincinnati on this site, the nation's first veterans group.

Buffalo

General Casimir Pulaski (mem)
Main and Division streets.
The rendering of Pulaski, hero of Poland and the United States, was a gift from the Polish people to the citizens of the United States in 1979. Pulaski is sculpted from dark brown bronze with his hands resting on the pommel of a sword bearing the crest of Poland. The work by Kazamierz Daniewicz rests on a polished black granite base.

Cherry Valley

Cherry Valley Museum (col)
49 Main Street, 607-264-3303; Memorial Day–Columbus Day: daily, 10–5. Admission charged.
Notorious British raiders Walter Butler and Joseph Brant melded their military talents against this strategic, but ineptly defended, settlement on November 11, 1778. In four hours a merciless band of 700 raiders killed 15 militia and perhaps twice as many innocent townspeople. The rest of the residents were captured but released the next day. The museum maintains the local history and a large stone memorial to the victims of the Massacre of 1778 is in the village cemetery.

Croton-on Hudson

Van Cortlandt Manor (site)
South Riverside Avenue, off Route 9, 914-631-8200; Apr–Dec: Wed–Mon, 10–5. Admission charged.
The restored eighteenth century Dutch-English manor house was the home of Patriot leader Pierre Van Cortlandt, who later went on to become New York's first lieutenant governor. His son Philip commanded American troops during the war. Benjamin Franklin, John Jay and the Marquis de Lafayette and others stayed here during the Revolution.

Crown Point

Crown Point State Historic Site (site)
At the Lake Champlain Bridge, four miles east of Routes 9N and 22, 518-597-3666; May–Oct: Wed–Sat, 10–5, Sunday, 1–5. Admission charged.
Save for an occasional short portage, it is almost possible to travel from Montreal to New York by canoe, thanks in large part to the more than one hundred miles of water passage through Lake Champlain. Clearly, Lake Champlain was a vital highway linking two diverse regions of British North America. Not only did the lake narrow to a quarter-mile at Crown Point, but it was roughly halfway between Montreal and Albany. Whoever controlled Crown Point would control the entire water passage.

The French claimed Crown Point first, in 1731. At the waterside sprouted an irregular-shaped limestone bastion, Fort St. Frederic, in 1734. For the next quarter-century the French ruled the Champlain Valley and a not insignificant community grew up on the peninsula. This combined military and civilian presence thwarted British expansion in the region, and during the French and Indian War four campaigns were mounted to take the fort. Finally, in 1759, a combined force of British Regulars and Provincial troops numbering over 12,000 finally captured Fort St. Frederic.

The British immediately began construction of "His Majesty's Fort of Crown Point," 200 yards west of the French post. Three redoubts and a series of blockhouses and redans were interconnected by a network of roads. The earthen walls were 25 feet thick, fronted by a trench 30 feet wide and 14 feet deep. There were 105 gunmounts and casements for 4,000 men. Storehouses held four months of provisions. The fortification complex covered over 3½ miles, making it one of the most ambitious military engineering projects undertaken by the British in Colonial North America.

A fire in April 1773 caused a powder magazine to explode, and the outpost nearly burned to the ground. A small garrison was left on the site as most of its firepower was transferred to Fort Ticonderoga, 12 miles south. At the outbreak of the Revolution a skeleton force of nine British defenders surrendered the fort to Colonel Seth Warner. During the remainder of the Revolution Fort Crown Point changed hands several times — never in serious fighting — and was tactically important only as a satellite for Fort Ticonderoga.

Ruins of both forts remain as they have always been. The French, who never fully developed Fort St. Frederic, were much more thorough when they abandoned the position and blew it into Lake Champlain. The ramparts are still extant and can be explored from the inside of the fort by footpath.

The interpretive footpath also covers the perimeter of the expansive British Fort Crown Point, traversing the top of the tremendous earthworks. In the interior of the fort, standing stark against the level grass, are two magnificent remains of Georgian-style stone barracks. An orientation film is offered in the visitor center.

Elmira

Newtown Battlefield (site)

Route 17, three miles east of town, 607-732-6067; Memorial Day–Columbus Day: daily, dawn to dusk. Free.

Throughout the Revolution, American settlers from the Hudson River to Lake Erie were terrorized by Indian and Tory raids. Washington long wanted to squelch enemy activity in the region but was otherwise occupied in winning the war from Boston to Philadelphia. With his successes in the summer of 1778 Washington had fought his final battle in the North and was only supervising the trapped British Army in New York City. By 1779 he was ready to invade the Iroquois.

He selected Maj. Gen. John Sullivan to lead 4,000 seasoned Continentals into the Six Nations' lands. To Washington this was a punitive expedition and he did not want to hear about any more Indian problems. His instructions to Sullivan called for "the total destruction and devastation of their settlements." And he wanted prisoners, including women and children, to be brought back and held as hostages to insure future cooperative behavior from the Iroquois.

Sullivan approached his assignment with glacial enthusiasm. He organized his troops in Easton, Pennsylvania, on May 7 but did not set out for western New York until six weeks later. By late August he was approaching the Iroquois. With a force of some 800 Indians, 250 Tories and a handful of British regulars, the Iroquois decided their best chance was a surprise attack. Walter Butler, a despised Mohawk Valley Tory, violently objected to the strategy but the Indians were determined to destroy this mighty column before it gained momentum. They fortified the mountain pass along the Chemung River, just south of Elmira, and lay in wait as Sullivan approached on August 29.

Despite their elaborate preparations, three companies of Daniel Morgan's Virginia riflemen, leading the advance, spotted the trap. The Americans skillfully negotiated the difficult terrain around the pass and destroyed the defensive breastworks with artillery. Many of the Indians deserted immediately but those who remained fought bravely. Outnumbered five to one, the British and Indian forces retreated over the mountains with much difficulty.

Sullivan did not pursue. He kept marching for the next six weeks and never met as much resistance again. He destroyed 40 towns but scarcely carried out Washington's orders. He returned few prisoners, and the Iroquois renewed their raiding in 1780 and 1781 with unprecedented ferocity.

The land around the battle site, near the Chemung River, remains in private hands and is largely undeveloped. In the park is a monument to General Sullivan, a 60-foot obelisk commemorating the only real skirmish of his 1779 expedition.

Fort Edward

McCrae Burial Site (site)

Route 4, two miles south of town.

Jane McCrae, a local girl, was kidnapped and murdered by an Indian patrol while on her way to see her fiancé, a Tory soldier in the British camp. The exact details of the atrocity are muddled but American propagandists seized on the tragedy to inflame the local citizenry and swell the roles of the militia. This is her original grave, at the site of an American camp. Her remains were later moved to the Union Cemetery on Broadway Street, where her most recent grave can still be seen.

Old Fort House Museum (site)

29 Lower Broadway (Route 4), 518-747-9600; Jun–Labor Day: daily, 1–5; Nov–Dec: daily, 1–4; Sep–Oct, Sat–Sun, 1–5. Admission charged.

On the portage trail between the Hudson River and Lake Champlain, Fort Edward was fortified through the French and Indian War and the Revolutionary War. The Smythe House was built in 1772 and served the British as a tavern and courthouse. During the Revolution it was the headquarters for American generals Philip Schuyler and John Stark, and British general John Burgoyne. Washington and Benedict Arnold also used the building for brief periods. The house is now part of an historical complex.

Fort Johnson

Fort Johnson (site)
   Route 67, west of town, 518-843-0300; May 15–Oct 15: Wed–Sun, 1–5. Admission charged.
   This is the third home of Sir William Johnson, who arrived in America as an Indian agent and was so successful he won a baronetcy. It was largely through his efforts that the Indians sided with the British during the Revolution. The two-story stone house was built in 1749 and was confiscated during the Revolution. It was later sold at auction.

Fort Plain

Fort Plain Museum (site)
   389 Upper Canal Street, 518-993-2527; Mid-May–Mid-Sept: Wed–Sun, 12–5. Free.
   After the British surrender in Yorktown, most of the remaining fighting of the Revolutionary War took place on the frontier of New York. From this post, built originally as a fortification around a stone house, Colonel Marinus conducted many successful American operations in 1782–1783. Guided tours of archaeological remains and museum exhibits are offered.

Germantown

Clermont State Historic Site (site)
   1 Clermont Avenue, off Route 6, 518-537-4240; grounds open year-round; house open Memorial Day–Oct: Tue–Sun, 11–4. Admission charged.
   The first Robert Livingston to emigrate to America arrived in 1673 and within a dozen years had acquired by grant and purchase 160,000 acres on the east side of the Hudson River. His third son, Robert II, built Clermont around 1730. Seven generations of Livingstons would follow into the mansion. The British burned the building in 1777, and Robert III's wife Margaret rebuilt Clermont from 1779 until 1782.
   In 1804, Robert Livingston IV moved in to begin a very active retirement. Livingston was a delegate to the Second Continental Congress and was a member of the committee to draft the Declaration of Independence. In 1803, as minister to France, he negotiated the Louisiana Purchase. In his stay at Clermont

he experimented extensively on his farm and helped Robert Fulton produce the first practical steamboat. The *Clermont II*, named for the Livingston home, made a record-setting run from New York up the river to the estate.

Herkimer

General Herkimer at Oriskany (mem)
Myers Park.
General Nicholas Herkimer began his march to liberate Fort Stanwix from Herkimer, departing a stone house called Fort Dayton in August 1777. The bronze memorial depicts Herkimer, wounded in the leg, directing his troops at Oriskany, where they were ambushed.

Huntington

Nathan Hale Memorial Monument (mem)
Mill Dam Road and Route 110.
A large boulder facing Long Island Sound has been placed on the spot where it is believed the British captured Nathan Hale in September 1776, a few days after he had volunteered as a spy. He was executed in New York on September 22.

Johnstown

Fulton County Court House (site)
North William and East Main Street, 518-725-0473; Daily, 9–5. Free.
Sir William Johnson founded the town that bears his name after a dozen houses sprung up near his home at Johnson Hall. In short order the town became county seat and Sir William erected the low brick courthouse in 1772. It remains in use today, the only Colonial courthouse still standing in New York. A large iron bar was bent into a triangle and used as a bell to announce the sessions of court. Still in the belfry, it was rung in honor of the Declaration of Independence.

Johnson Hall State Historic Site (site)
Hall Avenue, west of Route 29, 518-762-8712; May–Oct: Wed–Sat, 10–5, Sun, 1–5. Admission charged.
Built in 1763, the white clapboard Georgian house was the last home of Sir William Johnson, superintendent of Indian affairs for the northern colonies. His son, Tory leader Sir John Johnson, inherited the estate in 1774, and it was confiscated during the Revolution. Johnson was not left wanting, however. He was given thousands of acres in Canada as gratitude from the British.
On October 25, 1781, militia Colonel Marinus Willett, with a force of 416 men, overtook a Tory and Indian raiding party near Johnson Hall. The Patriots attacked from the southeast but the superior British numbers under Major

John Ross withstood the assault and threw the Americans back. Willett and his men retreated and fled to Fort Johnstown (the old jail located on Montgomery and South Perry streets). The Battle of Johnstown took place six days after Lord Cornwallis had laid down his arms in Yorktown, Virginia.

St. John's Episcopal Church (site)

North Market Street; Open daily, dawn to dusk.

Sir William Johnson built St. John's in 1772 and was buried under the chancel two years later. The church burned in 1836 and a second rose on the site in 1840, but it was built in a slightly different location and Johnson's grave was "lost." It was discovered later that year and Johnson's body, including the lead ball he carried in his hip as a souvenir from his victory at Lake George, was placed in the rear of the church. It is marked by four simple cornerstones.

Katonah

John Jay Homestead State Historic Site (site)

400 Jay Street, 914-232-5651; Apr–Oct: Wed–Sat, 10–4, Sun, 12–4. Free.

John Jay began his political career as a delegate to the First Continental Congress, and he eventually became president of the Congress. He later attained great prominence as a coauthor of the Federalist Papers. He became an early advocate of a strong central government and served as first chief justice of the U.S. Supreme Court. He also served two terms as governor of New York. This two-story frame house was built as his retirement home in 1801; he lived until 1829 and is buried in a private cemetery in Rye, New York.

Kingston

Old Dutch Church and Cemetery (site)

Main Street, between Wall and Fair streets, 914-338-6759; Mon–Fri, 9–4. Free.

The graveyard of the Dutch Reformed Church, established in 1659, contains the grave of George Clinton, the first governor of New York. Also resting in the 1761 burial ground are other Revolutionary War veterans.

Senate House State Historic Site (site)

312 Fair Street, 914-338-2786; Apr–Oct: Wed–Sat, 10–5, Sun, 1–5. Admission charged.

Colonel Wessel Ten Broeck built the one-story limestone house about 1676. A century later the building was used for the first meeting of the newly elected New York State Senate. The session was interrupted on October 16, 1777, when the British plundered and burned the town. The rooms in the Senate House appear as they did in 1777; a museum in the rear features more objects relating to the government's work, including the crafting of the first New York constitution.

Lake George

Fort George Ruins (site)
Off Fort George Road; Open daily, dawn to dusk.

In June 1759 British General Jeffrey Amherst arrived at Lake George and immediately began to fortify the southern end of the lake. The site was on high ground east of the ruins of Fort William Henry, which had been destroyed by the French in 1757. A provincial officer described the fort walls as being "about 14 Feet thick Built of Stone & Lime." The fort, however, was never finished.

In May 1775, Fort George was captured by Patriot forces under Captain Bernard Romans. It was not a difficult prize — the British fort was held by one man, a 65-year-old caretaker named Captain John Nordberg. On July 16, 1777, American Major Christopher Yates set fire to Fort George as the British approached. The fort did not burn completely and the British used it as a supply link to General Burgoyne's invading forces in 1777. After the British surrender at Saratoga the Redcoats evacuated the Lake Champlain area.

By 1780 the British were back again at Fort George. This time when they retreated they burned it. Eventually the local people used the fort as a quarry and it disappeared. A 15-foot wall is all that remains of Fort George.

Knox Cannon (mem)
Fort George Road.

A Revolutionary War cannon commemorates one of the great feats of the Revolution: Henry Knox transporting 119,000 pounds of artillery from Fort Ticonderoga to Boston in the winter of 1776. Knox's supply train passed along this road on his 300-mile journey to liberate Boston.

Little Falls

Herkimer Home State Historic Site (site)
Route 169, three miles east of town, 315-823-0398; May–Oct: Wed–Sat, 10–5. Admission charged.

Nicholas Herkimer built the most successful empire in the Mohawk Valley during the middle part of the eighteenth century. He aligned himself with the rebel cause and when his powerful Loyalist neighbors the Johnsons and Butlers took refuge in Canada, Herkimer assumed the leadership of the Whig party in the valley. A veteran of the French and Indian War, he led the militia in an attempt to break the British stranglehold at Fort Stanwix, near present-day Rome. His force was ambushed at Oriskany on August 6, 1777, and General Herkimer, despite a thigh shattered from a musket ball, personally directed a successful retreat from the field. Carried home, he died 11 days later, just short of his fiftieth birthday, after a botched amputation.

The two-story brick house on a stone foundation was built in 1764. The building has been changed considerably since Herkimer's ownership. The Erie Canal was dug through the backyard, and various nineteenth century owners made haphazard additions and conversions. It was even a tavern for one period. Nicholas Herkimer is buried in the family cemetery adjoining the house; his grave is marked by a tall stone monument erected by New York state in 1896.

Mastic Beach

William Floyd Estate (site)
245 Park Drive, 516-399-2030; Memorial Day–Sept: Fri–Sun, 10–4. Free.

William Floyd, Long Island's only signer of the Declaration of Independence, was forced to flee his mansion, built by his father in 1724, during the Revolution. During the war British troops were housed here. After the war, both Jefferson and Madison visited, more interested, it was said, in Floyd's comely daughter than their fellow Continental congressman. The estate remained in the Floyd family for eight generations, expanding from the original 6-room farmhouse to a 25-room mansion.

Minisink Ford

Minisink Battleground (site)
Route 168, 914-794-3000; Open daily, dawn to dusk. Free.

Mohawk Chief Thayendanegea was well known to American settlers during the Revolution as the murderous Joseph Brant. On one of his many raids against towns on the frontier, Brant burned and looted Minisink on the night of July 19, 1779. Local militia totaling nearly 150 set off after Brant, who trapped and ambushed the Americans at a well-known fording place on the Delaware River.

Roughly a third of the militia force was killed, including 17 wounded who were being tended to by their leader, Lt. Col. Benjamin Tusten, a physician. Tusten was also slaughtered in the massacre, at a place that came to be known as Hospital Rock.

Hospital Rock is reached by a short path, 100 yards from a battle monument. Also nearby is Sentinel Rock, where Brant stormed through the Colonial defenses.

Mohawk

Fort Herkimer Church (site)
Route 5, two miles east of town.

German Palantines settled this region beginning in the 1720s and this stone church was started in the 1730s. Construction proceeded at a leisurely pace and the walls formed the center of Colonial Fort Herkimer in the French and Indian War. The building was completed in 1767 and during the Revolution the church was part of a stockaded fort.

The most dramatic day of the war for Fort Herkimer Church took place on a Sunday in September 1778, when settlers were able to avoid a raiding party of Tories and Indians by gathering inside its walls. They had been alerted by Adam

Helmer, who learned of the raid and raced 22 miles to Herkimer, barely staying ahead of the invaders.

New Rochelle

Thomas Paine Museum and Cottage (site)
20 Sicard Avenue, 914-632-5376; Spring–Fall: Fri–Sun, 2–5. Admission charged.

Few arrived so late or played such an important role in the Revolution as Thomas Paine. An outcast, radical thinking Englishman, Paine sailed to America in 1774 at the age of 37. Within four months he had published an attack on slavery in the colonies and in January 1776 produced a 47-page pamphlet that would galvanize the Revolutionary movement, *Common Sense.*

Common Sense sold 100,000 copies in three months, convincing much of the American populace that independence was the only future course. The success of *Common Sense* caused Congress to push for approval of a final breaking of relations with England in June and July of 1776. Paine remained in America during the Revolution and continued to inspire the people with his impassioned writings.

When the disorganized Continental Army suffered repeated defeats in the wake of the Declaration of Independence he assured his readers that "these are the times that try men's souls. This summer soldier and the sunshine patriot will, in this crisis, shrink from the service of their country; but he that stands it *now*, deserves the love and thanks of man and woman.... What we obtain too cheap, we esteem too lightly; it is dearness only that gives everything its value."

Paine eventually returned to Europe and defended the French Revolution in *The Rights of Man.* In 1794 he published a collection of atheist writings in *The Age of Reason,* which helped ostracize him in the United States, to which he returned in 1802. The influential political theorist and fighter for human rights lived the final seven years of his life in abject poverty.

Paine lived in this small cottage from 1802 until 1806. It had been presented to him in 1784 in gratitude for his service in the Revolution by the state of New York. It is maintained, near its original location, as part of a cultural complex.

New York (City)

City Hall (site)
City Hall Park, Chambers Street and Broadway, Manhattan, 212-788-4636; Mon–Fri, 10–3:30. Free.

Near this spot, with George Washington in attendance, the Declaration of Independence was read to the Continental Army on July 9, 1776.

Conference House (site)
7455 Hylan Boulevard, Staten Island, 718-984-2086. Admission charged.

With Washington's army bottled up on Manhattan in the summer of 1776, the British sent word to the Continental Congress that they would be willing to discuss peace. Benjamin Franklin, John Adams and Edward Rutledge went to meet Admiral Richard Howe, his brother General William Howe having declined to join the conference.

On September 11, the two sides met in the Billopp House, a 1680 stone manor. Howe would not recognize American independence and the Congressional delegation was not about to consider anything less. The war's only peace conference was cordial, meaningless, and necessarily brief. The Congressmen returned to Philadelphia.

Federal Hall National Memorial (site)

Wall and Nassau streets, Manhattan, 212-825-6888; Mon–Fri, 9–5. Free.

The present building, of Greek Revival design, was erected in 1842 on the site of New York's old City Hall. Demolished in 1812, City Hall hosted the Stamp Act Congress in 1765 and the first Congress under the Constitution in 1789. It was the nation's Capitol until August 31, 1790. George Washington took the oath of office as the first president of the United States on its balcony and the Bill of Rights was adopted after debate in its chambers.

The museum in Federal Hall contains material pertaining to Washington's inauguration, the Bill of Rights and the history of City Hall.

Fort Greene Park (site)

Myrtle and DeKalb avenues and St. Edwards and Cumberland streets, Brooklyn; Open daily, dawn to dusk.

After destroying the Continental advance line in the Battle of Long Island, Sir William Howe hesitated in moving against the main army on Brooklyn Heights. He settled for entrenchments which became the earthen star fort, Fort Putnam. Fearing an entrapment, Washington sailed his army away to Manhattan on the night of August 29, 1776. Although surprised at the disappearance of his quarry Howe and his fellow officers were not overly concerned. They were certain this insurgency was just about over.

Fort Putnam remains no more. The site became a park in 1815, named for Maj. Gen. Nathanael Greene. The "Martyrs' Monument," designed by Stanford White, is dedicated to the Continental soldiers who died on British prison ships in Wallabout Bay. Such ships as the *Jersey* were virtually floating tombs — filthy, disease-ridden and crowded with Patriot supporters. The deceased were often thrown into shallow graves on the shores of the bay. The remains of many were collected and placed in the crypt marked by the 145-foot granite column, dedicated in 1908.

Fort Tryon Park (site)

192nd Street between Broadway and Riverside Drive, Manhattan; Open daily, dawn to dusk.

This 250-foot hill was manned by American troops, north of Fort Washington. Colonel Moses Rawlings directed Maryland and Virginian riflemen from this vantage point and provided the most effective resistance to the British as they overran the fort. The site is undeveloped.

It was during an attack on Rawlings by 3,000 Hessian troops that Margaret "Molly" Corbin, Revolutionary War heroine, took the place of her mortally wounded cannoneer husband. She was severely wounded in the onslaught. For her gallantry she was awarded a pension by General Washington. Recognition of Corbin's heroism and service came in 1926, when the Daughters of the American Revolution verified her records and had her remains transferred to the West Point Cemetery.

Fort Washington Park (site)

Fort Washington Avenue and 183rd Street, Manhattan; Open daily, dawn to dusk.

Since August 27, 1776, the British had sent Washington's troops reeling from Long Island across Manhattan and finally to Fort Washington and Fort Lee on the Hudson River. Fort Washington, the earthworks on the New York side, stood 200 feet above the water and appeared impregnable to American officers who voted to defend it against the marauding troops of Sir William Howe. Colonel Robert McGaw convinced the American council of war that he could hold Fort Washington until the end of the year. Washington was not so sure.

On November 13 a combined British and German force prepared for an assault on Fort Washington. Howe coordinated attacks on four fronts and when in position demanded that McGaw surrender on November 15. The ultimatum was refused and bombardment began on the morning of November 16. Washington sailed across the Hudson River from Fort Lee to meet with McGaw. He decided to allow McGaw to fight until dark, when the fort should be evacuated.

McGaw could not make it to nightfall. Howe's blistering attack forced capitulation by 3:00 P.M. Washington watched from across the river at Fort Lee as 2,818 of his best men were taken prisoner. Another 59 had been killed. It was another dispiriting setback for the Americans, but the army survived.

The site is undeveloped but marked at a rock outcropping which, at 265 feet, is the highest natural point on Manhattan Island.

Fraunces Tavern Museum (site)

54 Pearl Street at Broad Street, Manhattan, 212-425-1778; Mon–Fri, 10–4:45, Sat, 12–4. Admission charged.

Etienne de Lancey, a wealthy merchant, built an elegant townhouse here in 1719. The family moved on in 1737 and used the building as a warehouse. Samuel Fraunces, a West Indian of African and French extraction, bought the property in 1762 for about $260. "Black Sam" converted the space into the Queen's Head Tavern, which he leased, and devoted himself to operating a wax museum.

The Queen's Head, with a spacious meeting room known as the Long Room, was a popular gathering place and it was here, on December 4, 1783, that George Washington bade an emotional farewell to his senior officers in the Continental

Army. Fraunces was rewarded by Congress for his kindness to Patriot prisoners entombed in the city's notorious jails during the long British occupation and he became Washington's steward when he returned to New York as president in 1789. He followed the chief executive to Philadelphia, where he died in 1795.

Hamilton Grange National Museum (site)

287 Convent Avenue, Manhattan, 212-283-5154; Wed–Sun, 9–5. Free.

Alexander Hamilton strode across the Revolutionary landscape with an insatiable desire for glory that was known in the eighteenth century as "a craving for distinction." He rose from illegitimate beginnings in the West Indies on the strength of his towering intellect and unwavering ambition, which won him enemies and admirers alike.

Hamilton broke off his schooling at King's College — later Columbia University — in 1775 and was commissioned an artillery captain in March 1776. Although scarcely 21 years of age, his writings and clear intellect soon attracted attention within the Continental Army. Washington made Hamilton an aide-de-camp on March 1, 1777, and for four years he served the commander. As Hamilton's influence in the inner circle increased, he lobbied successfully for the participation of blacks in the revolution, both slave and free. Eager for glory on the battlefield, Washington gave him a regiment under Lafayette in Virginia and Hamilton indeed earned accolades in subduing the British at Yorktown.

After the war Hamilton was a leading voice in the creation of the Constitution and molded American fiscal policy as secretary of the treasury from 1789 until 1795. Even his longtime adversary Thomas Jefferson mourned when Hamilton was fatally wounded by a bullet from Aaron Burr in a duel on July 11, 1804.

The Grange was Hamilton's last home, built in 1801–1802 on 16 acres of land. The Federal-style house was Hamilton's country home; today it is in the busy Harlem district. The house is interpreted as the horticultural retreat it was for Hamilton in the early nineteenth century.

Inwood Hill Park (site)

Seaman Avenue, Manhattan; Open daily, dusk to dawn.

The high ground in this park was known as Cock Hill during the Revolution and served as an outpost for Fort Washington. The site is undeveloped.

Morris-Jumel Mansion (site)

65 Jumel Terrace, between 160th and 162nd streets, Manhattan, 212-923-8008; Wed–Sun, 10–4. Admission charged.

The two-story brick house, one of Manhattan's oldest surviving residences, was a British and Hessian quarters during the Revolution. More importantly, George Washington lived in a small suite of rooms on the second floor from September 14 to October 18, 1776. The commander-in-chief directed the Battle of Harlem Heights from this position on September 16.

The British landed troops at Kip's Bay on September 15 and marched north to Washington's fortifications in the high ground at Harlem Heights. The next day they were spotted by an American reconnaissance patrol led by Lt. Col. Thomas Knowlton, one of Washington's brightest young officers, at dawn. He fought a successful delaying action as Washington left the mansion to observe the action from American advance posts.

General Washington ordered an offensive and in heavy skirmishing the British were pushed back. Washington, fearing a major showdown, did not press the action and was satisfied to return to the Morris-Jumel house with a rare, morale-boosting victory. It had come at a price; Knowlton was one of the 30 American dead.

The Battle of Harlem Heights took place near the present day Grant Memorial and Columbia University, off 120th Street.

Museum of the City of New York (col)

Fifth Avenue and 103rd to 104th streets, Manhattan, 212-534-1672; Wed–Sat, 10–5, Sun, 1–5. Admission charged.

Period rooms include the Colonial and Revolutionary War eras. There are dioramas and exhibits to explain the battle for Manhattan and subsequent British occupation of the city for seven years.

Prospect Park (site)

Prospect Park W. and Prospect Park S.W. and Flatbush and Parkside avenues, Brooklyn; Open daily, dawn to dusk.

The urban sprawl of Brooklyn has swallowed up the original sites of the Battle of Long Island, one of the most important tactical struggles of the Revolution. But much of the action took place in the passes through this park.

After losing Boston in March 1776, Sir William Howe retreated to Canada. He sailed to Staten Island on July 2–3 and waited for reinforcements. By August 20 he had a force of over 30,000 men, a quarter of which were German mercenaries. It was the largest British army yet assembled in the New World. Washington, already in New York with the Continental Army, knew an attack would be forthcoming. He chose to establish fortifications along the Brooklyn Heights on the western end of Long Island.

On the morning of August 26, 1776, Howe's assault began. The British and Germans soon routed the American left and center. Desperate fighting ensued at the stone Cortelyou House, which guarded the main American escape route from the field. Brig. Gen. William Stirling attacked the house six times to divert British musket fire, while colonials attempted to scamper away through the stream by the house. British reinforcements were required to drive the dogged Stirling away.

As was his pattern, the overconfident Howe failed to follow up on his rout and finish American military resistance, and the Continental Army survived, albeit in disorderly retreat. Almost all of Stirling's 250 Maryland troops were dead. The Maryland Monument near Lookout Hill in the park stands as testament to their heroics.

The Battle Pass Marker is a work of Frederic Wellington Ruckstull. Installed in 1923, the granite marker with a bronze eagle is located at the site of a strategic road during the Battle of Long Island. It is also the site where General John Sullivan was captured. Near the Grand Army Plaza entrance is a semicircular tablet on a boulder commemorating the Battle of Long Island.

St. Paul's Chapel (site)

Broadway and Fulton streets, Manhattan, 212-602-0800; Mon–Fri, 9–3, Sun, 7–3. Free.

The 1766 church is the only remaining Colonial church in New York City and possibly the oldest public building still standing in Manhattan. Governor George Clinton had a designated pew and British officers worshipped here during the occupation. Several are buried in the churchyard, as is General Richard Montgomery, whose body was moved here in 1818 from Quebec where he fell in 1775. George Washington also attended services at St. Paul's, including a special service conducted on April 30, 1789, after his inauguration as first president of the United States.

Trinity Church (site)

Broadway at Wall Street, Manhattan, 212-602-0800; Mon–Fri, 9–11:45 and 1–3:45, Sat, 10–3:45, Sun, 1–3:45. Free.

Trinity Church was originally built in 1696–1697 but burned in the great fire of September 1776. The present building, which for 50 years was the tallest in New York, was completed in 1846. Alexander Hamilton, officer in the Continental Army and U.S. treasurer, is buried in the church.

Valley Forge (mem)

Brooklyn Plaza, Brooklyn.

Henry Merwin Shrady won the competition to create a memorial likeness of George Washington and considered his achievements at Valley Forge to be the manifestation of his greatness. He sculpted Washington atop a horse with bowed head.

Washington Arch (mem)

Foot of Fifth Avenue, Manhattan.

Standing at the head of the square is the Washington Arch, designed by Stanford White.

Newburgh

Washington's Headquarters State Historic Site (site)

84 Liberty Street, 914-562-1195; Wed–Sat, 10–5, Sun, 1–5. Admission charged.

George Washington used the house of the Widow Hasbrouck as his headquarters longer (almost 17 months) than any other building during the Revolution. Jonathan Hasbrouck, a prosperous merchant and colonel in the local militia, had finished the 1725 family home with a commanding view of the Hudson River in 1770. Hasbrouck died in 1780.

Washington arrived in April 1782 and created a significant amount of American history here before leaving in August 1783. He flatly refused the suggestion that he ascend to the head of an American monarchy in the coming new nation; he stemmed a budding mutiny at the American camp at New Windsor; he celebrated the formal treaty ending the war on April 19, 1783; and he created the first American military award — the Order of the Purple Heart. Only three were known to be given out before the long-ignored order was revived in 1932.

The Hasbrouck House became the first historic property ever purchased by a state when New York acquired the building in 1850. Constructed of fieldstone, it has been restored and furnished as a military headquarters. The 1908 adjoining brick building is a museum with artifacts from the Continental Army, including a piece of the boom used to protect the great chain that stretched across the Hudson River to protect West Point.

On the grounds, in front of the house is a 1924 rendering of "The Minuteman," a bronze on a stacked stone pedestal. The grave of Uzal Knapp, the last of the Life Guards (1759–1856), is marked by a fence with small shields of eight Revolutionary generals. Overlooking the river is the massive 1887 Tower of Victory monument. Erected with four stone arches, the monument commemorates the disbandment of the army, under proclamation of the Continental Congress on October 18, 1783. It is nearly the size of General Washington's headquarters.

North Hoosick

Bennington Battlefield State Historic Site (site)

Route 67, three miles east of town, 518-686-7109; May–Labor Day: daily, 10–7; Sept–Oct: Sat–Sun, 10–7. Free.

British General John Burgoyne's plan to split the colonies by swooping down from Canada to capture Albany and join with British forces in New York City was proceeding swiftly and with better results than expected by the end of July 1777. Burgoyne realized that he was outpacing his supply lines, now stretched some 185 miles. He especially needed horses for his German dragoons.

Tory intelligence told him of beef, horses and draft animals cramming the fields around Bennington, Vermont. Further, the American storehouse was lightly defended. Burgoyne gave Lt. Col. Friedrich Baum, a Brunswick commander who spoke no English, the assignment to capture the supplies. Baum would lead 800 men, mostly the Germans who needed the horses, on the mission.

Marching east on August 11, Baum found his 40-mile trek slow going, mostly because his cavalrymen in cumbersome uniforms were on foot. Five miles from Bennington, Baum encountered an unexpected American scouting party. The Americans were driven off but Baum was certain of further American resistance. He sent word to Burgoyne for reinforcements and entrenched on high ground between the Walloomsac River and Little White Creek.

The American militia were under the leadership of headstrong John Stark of

New Hampshire. A hero at Bunker Hill, Stark was miffed at not being promoted and left the Continental Army. He took command of 1,500 troops for the Vermont Council of Safety with the understanding that he would not in any way answer to Congress.

A day of stifling rain gave both sides a chance to consider their positions. Baum had fatally scattered his forces about the hillside, and Stark decided to split his force into three columns and envelop the enemy. The first volleys covered the hill at 3:00 P.M. on August 16th, and within two hours the American militia had taken the field in hot fighting. The British reinforcements now arrived but were chased away by Seth Warner's Green Mountain Boys.

The Battle of Bennington cost the British Army over 900 of its best soldiers, 200 of them being killed. The victory by New England militiamen was one of the earliest decisive Colonial victories of the Revolution and showed Burgoyne he would not be able to live off the land as he marched deeper into enemy territory. He would not again underestimate the resources of his foes. After Bennington he wrote to his superiors that Vermont contained "the most rebellious race of the continent and hangs like a gathering storm on my left."

As for Colonel Baum, he suffered a mortal wound and died, not knowing there never were any horses in Bennington.

The 200-acre park is undeveloped and features only interpretive signs and maps at the top of the hill defended by Baum and his men. There are memorials to each of the three states — Vermont, New Hampshire and Massachusetts — that sent men to protect Bennington.

Oriskany

Oriskany Battlefield (site)

Route 69, two miles west of town, 315-768-7224; Memorial Day–Labor Day: Wed–Sat, 10–5, Sun, 1–5. Free.

While other settlers in the Mohawk Valley were reluctant to defend their remote villages, Nicholas Herkimer was not intimidated by the British presence in the region. With Lt. Col. Barry St. Leger marching on the American position at Fort Stanwix, Herkimer assembled a force of 800 men and boys — all males in the valley between 16 and 60.

On the morning of August 4, 1777, with St. Leger now surrounding Fort Stanwix, Herkimer's militia set out on the 30-mile march north to relieve the fort. He sent the fort's commander a message to fire three cannon when the letter was received and to follow up with a diversionary attack on the British siege line. Two days later, Herkimer had still heard no cannon and was only ten miles from St. Leger's troops.

Herkimer's impulse, grounded in his military training in the French and Indian War, was to halt the advance. His regimental commanders pressed him to continue the assault and two openly impugned his loyalty and bravery. Herkimer relented and restarted the expedition, unaware that his position had been revealed to St. Leger the night before.

At Oriskany, six miles below the fort, the militia and 400 accompanying oxcarts would have to cross a gully that ran between steep slopes — an ideal spot for an ambush. Herkimer's 60 Oneida Indian scouts detected nothing as the mile-long American column descended into Oriskany. The bulk of his advance force of 600 men were deep into the slash in the hills when musket fire from Tories and Indians engulfed them from the trees. More than a dozen officers, including Herkimer, fell in the initial volley.

Demanding to be propped against a tree, blood gushing from a gaping thigh wound, Herkimer directed his band of farmers to form a circle against the snipers. Unfortunately his rear guard of 200 had fled down the road. A heavy rainstorm rendered weapons unusable for about an hour and Herkimer took good advantage of this blessed respite. He ordered his men to fight in pairs, allowing one man to load his musket free of Indian tomahawk charges.

Fighting like trained regulars, Herkimer's troops' fierce resistance began to dispirit the Indians. They had signed on for an ambush and were now in a protracted hand-to-hand battle. They began to desert the field and the Tories were forced to withdraw as well. The American militia were able to march out of their deadly trap.

The Battle of Oriskany weakened St. Leger's alliance with the Indians and he was never able to break through at Fort Stanwix. His failure in the Western theater proved disastrous to Lt. Gen. John Burgoyne's plan to split the colonies along the Hudson River, and he would eventually surrender his entire army. The exact number of casualties at Oriskany has never been determined with certainty but has been called "the bloodiest battle of the Revolution" with one of the highest casualty rates of the war. One who died, 11 days after being wounded, was Nicholas Herkimer.

The terrain remains as unspoiled as it was over 200 years ago and the Tories' lethal trap in the ravine can easily be envisioned. The visitor center features an audiovisual presentation of the battle and offers tours of the grounds. A large obelisk memorial lists the names of the militia killed at Oriskany and a small stone monument marks the spot where Herkimer is believed to have orchestrated the Americans' successful defense.

Oswego

Fort Ontario State Historic Site (site)
East 7th Street, north of Route 104, 315-343-4711; May–Sept: Wed–Sat, 10–5, Sun, 1–5. Admission charged.

The frontier post overlooking Oswego Harbor and Lake Ontario was first fortified by the French in 1755. Tory refugees from the Mohawk Valley fled to Fort Ontario and launched raids back into central New York, including St. Leger's failed invasion, throughout 1777. The Continental Army torched and partially destroyed a vacant Fort Ontario in 1778. The British returned in 1782 and held the post until the Jay Treaty of 1796 finally forced them to leave. Fort Ontario remained active until World War II and today is interpreted as the star-shaped fortress appeared in 1868–1869, although there are exhibits on the Revolution.

Oyster Bay

Raynham Hall Museum (site)

20 West Main Street, 516-922-6808; Jul–Aug: Tue–Sun, 12–5; Sept–Jun: Tue–Sun, 1–5. Admission charged.

Raynham Hall was used as an officers' quarters during the British occupation of Long Island, which lasted from 1776 until the end of the war. John Graves Simcoe, commander of the Queen's Rangers, lived here while his troops raided New York and New Jersey coastal towns in 1778 and 1779. An infamous visitor to Raynham was John André, who had begun covert meetings with Benedict Arnold in May 1779, 16 months before Arnold went over to the British.

Pawling

John Kane House (site)

126 East Main Street, 914-855-1448; May–Oct: Sat–Sun, 2–4. Free.

The house of Tory John Kane was used as headquarters by General Washington for two months in the fall of 1778. Nearby, the Oblong Meeting House was pressed into service as a hospital for Continental Army troops.

The house serves as a museum for Pawling history, which includes "Prendergast's Rebellion." In 1766 a group of embattled farmers skirmished briefly with British troops over land rents in the Hudson Valley.

Plattsburgh

Clinton County Historical Museum (col)

48 Court Street, 518-561-0340; Tue–Fri, 12–4, Sat, 1–4. Admission charged.

Off the west shore of Lake Champlain, Brig. Gen. Benedict Arnold engaged the British in the Battle of Valcour on October 11, 1776. The action, which delayed the British invasion of the Hudson Valley by more than six months, is depicted in a diorama and other exhibits in the museum.

Poughkeepsie

Clinton House (site)

549 Main Street, 914-471-1630; Tue–Fri, 10–3. Admission charged.

George Clinton's remarkable career began in 1768, when he was elected to the Colonial assembly at the age of 29. Caught up in the revolutionary fervor, Clinton went to the Second Continental Congress and spoke passionately for independence. He missed signing the Declaration of Independence after voting for liberty on July 2 because of military duty back in New York, where he was a brigadier general in the militia.

In the first elections held under New York's new constitution in 1777, Clinton won both the contest for governor and lieutenant governor. Not allowed to fill both offices he chose to be governor — the first of six consecutive terms and 18 years in office. He opposed the ratification of the Constitution, fearing it would infringe on his power. He won two terms as vice-president of the United States under Jefferson in 1804 and Madison in 1808 to end 44 years of public service.

The two-story fieldstone building that was the governor's home dates to 1767.

Remsen

Steuben Memorial (site)

Starr Hill Road; two and one-half miles west of routes 12 and 28, 315-831-3737; Apr–Sep: Wed–Sat, 10–5, Sunday 1–5. Free.

Friedrich Wilhelm Augustin von Stueben arrived in the United States early in 1778, speaking no English and bearing only a letter of introduction from Benjamin Franklin. He was put in charge of drilling the troops at Valley Forge and credited with creating the professional army necessary to win the war. He was promoted to major general and commanded a division at Yorktown.

After the Revolution, von Steuben settled in New York City, where he became an American citizen and was feted around town. In 1786 New York presented the general with 16,000 acres of land in the Mohawk Valley. He built a cabin and lived in the remote hills as a lifelong bachelor until his death at the age of 64 in 1794.

A replica of Baron von Steuben's cabin was reconstructed in the park in the 1930s and contains personal effects of the general. Sacred Grove, a short walk from the house, contains the tomb under which the Revolutionary drillmaster rests.

Rome

Fort Stanwix National Monument (site)

Route 26, north of town, 315-336-2090; Apr–Dec: daily, 9–5. Admission charged.

Mohawk travelers and later English settlers could travel by canoe from the Great Lakes to the Atlantic Ocean if their transport could be picked up and carried across a short, level stretch of ground between the Mohawk River and the Wood Creek, near present day Rome. The British built Fort Stanwix here in 1758 to replace three smaller forts that protected the Oneida Carry during the early years of the French and Indian War. The fort, named for its builder Brig. Gen. John Stanwix, never saw action and was abandoned when the British won Canada in 1763.

In June 1776, Colonel Elias Dayton began rebuilding an old frontier fort on the strategic portage between the headwaters of the Mohawk River and Wood Creek. By July 1777, Fort Stanwix was garrisoned with 750 troops. It was eventually fortified.

Fort Stanwix was a prime objective in General Burgoyne's New York campaign of 1777. Needing a western diversion to draw troops away from Albany, he sent Lt. Col. Barry St. Leger against Fort Stanwix to clear the western approach to Albany in late July. St. Leger, reinforced with Tories and Indians, arrived at the fort on August 3 and quickly decided against a frontal assault. American defender Colonel Peter Gansevoort "rejected with disdain" the British demand for surrender.

St. Leger and his 1,700 men settled into a siege. He was first distracted by a relief column of Nicholas Herkimer three days later at Oriskany, but the Americans were forced into retreat with severe casualties. Three weeks into the action Brig. Gen. Benedict Arnold began another relief mission from Fort Dayton, 30 miles to the south. As Arnold approached with 800 Continentals, St. Leger's Indian allies deserted and he soon retreated. The British never conquered Fort Stanwix; the American defenders in Albany never turned away from Burgoyne's army; and the British initiative to win the upper Hudson River was over.

Fort Stanwix was manned until 1781 but never tested again. In October 1784, American and Iroquois representatives met here to negotiate the Treaty of Fort Stanwix, which set terms for a separate peace with the Indians and forced the Iroquois Confederacy to cede large tracts of their ancestral lands to the United States.

A blockhouse was constructed at Fort Stanwix to store ammunition, but it disappeared sometime after 1815. By 1830 the fort was leveled. It has been completely reconstructed to its 1777 appearance inside a palisade fence above the glacis. The visitor center is in the West Barracks at the center of the fort's four bastions.

St. Johnsville

Fort Klock Historic Restoration (site)

Route 5, two miles east of town, 518-568-7779; Memorial Day–Columbus Day: Tue–Sun, 9–5. Admission charged.

On October 19, 1780, just east of Fort Klock, Tory and Indian raiders under Sir John Johnson and Joseph Brant temporarily halted their march after another successful raid against the Americans in the Mohawk Valley. Maj. Gen. Robert Van Rennselaer, with a force of 1,500 Americans, caught the raiders and drove them from the field. Despite a two-to-one manpower advantage, Van Rennselaer chose not to take up the chase. He was later charged with incompetence but was acquitted.

Fort Klock began life as a stone farmhouse in 1750 and was fortified with a timber fence in the Revolution. Today, Fort Klock is part of a restored eighteenth century village, including a schoolhouse and blacksmith shop.

Salem

Revolutionary War Cemetery (site)
Archibald Street; Open daily, dawn to dusk.
The remains of approximately 100 identified Revolutionary War soldiers who fell during the Battle of Saratoga are interred here.

Saratoga Springs

The Surrender of General Burgoyne to General Gates (mem)
Urban Cultural Park Visitors Center, 297 Broadway.
The bas-relief of painted concrete depicts General John Burgoyne surrendering his sword to General Horatio Gates. The men are flanked by three subordinates in a wooded setting. It was erected in 1915.

Schoharie

Old Stone Fort Museum Complex (site)
North Main Street, one mile north of town, 518-295-7192; Jul–Aug: Mon–Sat, 10–5, Sun, 1–5; May–June and Sept–Oct: Tue–Sat, 10–5, Sun, 12–5. Admission charged.
The fertile wheat fields in the Schoharie Valley were bountiful targets for Tory raids during the Revolution. A 1772 Dutch Reformed church was stockaded here as a fort. Militia defenders defused a halfhearted Tory effort to capture the fort in 1780.

Schuylerville

Field of Grounded Arms (site)
Ferry Street (Route 29), one block east of Route 4; Open daily, 24 hours.
On October 17, 1777, General John Burgoyne and 6,300 troops laid down their weapons in this field, ending the great British offensive to divide the colonies by capturing the Hudson Valley. While many communities like to anoint their parochial Revolutionary history as "the turning point of the Revolution," this is one claim that rings truest. The site, however, is noted only by a small marker at a city baseball field.

Saratoga Battle Monument (mem)
Burgoyne Street (Route 338), west of Route 4; Open daily, 24 hours; interior closed for renovations.
Horatio Gates accepted Burgoyne's surrender, ending the battle of Saratoga, down the hill from the ornate gray granite obelisk. The area, originally an Indian camping ground, was settled by French refugees in 1688 and named Saratoga. In 1831 it was named Schuylerville after Revolutionary War general Philip Schuyler. Thus it was Saratoga during the Revolution.

The 154-foot, 6-inch monument was started during the Battle of Saratoga Centennial in 1877 and finished six years later. One hundred and eighty-four iron stairs lead to the top where it commands a lofty view of battlefield sites. Decorative life-size bronze statues reside in special niches around the monument: Schuyler faces his home to the east; Daniel Morgan, commander of his celebrated riflemen, faces west; Gates looks to the north; and the fourth niche sits empty, in recognition of the leadership of Benedict Arnold who later turned traitor. A veterans' cemetery sits beyond the memorial.

Saratoga National Historical Park (site)
Route 4, eight miles south of town, 518-664-9821; Apr–Nov: daily, 9–5. Admission charged.

On February 28, 1777, Lt. Gen. John Burgoyne submitted a plan to the British ministry called "Thoughts for Conducting the War from the Side of Canada." The ultimate goal was to sever the American states along the Hudson River by moving on Albany. It became the basis for British military strategy in 1777.

Burgoyne marched out of St. Jean, Canada, in June with nearly 10,000 men. He took Fort Ticonderoga on July 6 and continued to the foot of Lake George with ease, pushing back General Schuyler's northern army. Now Burgoyne's master plan began to disintegrate. In the West, Barry St. Leger was unable to capture Fort Stanwix and would not draw defenders from Albany. In the South, William Howe completely ignored the grand strategy and sailed to the Chesapeake Bay, not the Hudson River; his own progress was being impeded by Schuyler's men felling trees and blocking the trails. His pace slowed to barely a mile a day.

By August, Schuyler was receiving reinforcements from Washington's Continental Army, including two valued generals, Benedict Arnold and Benjamin Lincoln. Arnold led the relief column to Fort Stanwix and Lincoln helped thwart the German brigades at Bennington. Arnold and Thaddeus Kosciuszko had also fortified the Albany Road from the high ground at Bemis Heights with 9,000 men. As the summer ended Burgoyne's assault force was winnowed to 6,000.

On September 19, 1777, Burgoyne threw three columns at the American defenses, now commanded by Horatio Gates after Schuyler had been ousted in political intrigue. But the departed general had the Americans well prepared. The fighting — known as the Battle of Freeman's Farm — where the American middle fought, left the British in command of the field, but it was bought at a terrible price.

Burgoyne wanted to resume his offensive the next day but received word that Sir Henry Clinton was offering to sail from New York City with a diversionary force. Burgoyne busied himself for the next two weeks building an extensive system of field fortifications. His ranks, however, were being depleted by desertion and disease. There was not enough food for both horse and soldier. On the American side, by contrast, Schuyler's groundwork brought not only fresh provisions but fresh men.

On October 7, Burgoyne attempted one more desperate charge to break the

American line and reach Albany. At the Second Battle of Saratoga the British were again driven back, and before they could reassemble, Arnold, who had been relieved of command following a shouting match with Gates, charged on the field against orders and led a charge at the British middle. The British held, secure in their redoubts.

Arnold charged again, this time through a crossfire, and led a storm against the Breymann Redoubt. He received his second bullet in the same leg for the rebel cause, having been hit in Quebec as well. His heroics inspired the Americans to trample the redoubt, and only nightfall saved the British Army from complete annihilation. Burgoyne fell back to camp at Saratoga with a spent army as surrender negotiations began.

The American victory at Saratoga came at a time when Washington's army was being pushed around New York and greatly improved American morale. Politically, it convinced the King of France to ally himself with the rebels. Strategically, the states were not divided for their continuing war effort. Saratoga was one of the decisive battles of American history.

The visitor center sits on Fraser Hill, the highest point in the park. A driving tour of 9.5 miles stops ten times to interpret the action across almost four square miles of land in the two battles of Saratoga. Included in the tour are the key British redoubts and scenes of action. There is a unique monument at the battlefield — to Benedict Arnold's leg. It features a granite boot, epaulets and an inscription documenting Arnold's heroics, but does not mention the traitor's name.

Reenactment: The community based group "Turning Point 77" presents a reenactment to commemorate the anniversary of Saratoga on the weekend closest to September 19.

Schuyler House (site)

Route 4, 518-664-9821; Memorial Day–Labor Day: Wed–Sun, 9–5; Sept: Sat–Sun, 9–5. Free.

The two-story wooden house was built as the Revolutionary War leader's summer house in 1777 after Burgoyne's troops burned much of Schuyler's estate for tactical purposes. It is administered by the National Park Service.

Stony Point

Stony Point Battlefield State Historic Site (site)

Park Road, off Route 9W, 914-786-2521; Apr–Oct: Wed–Sat, 10–5, Sun, 1–5. Free.

The British captured the peninsula of Stony Point in May 1779 and began to fortify it by cutting down trees. An earthen fort, protected by abatis from below, soon occupied the point 150 feet above the Hudson River. Two British ships patrolled the waters. George Washington responded to the British initiative by marching his troops into West Point, to the north. From nearby Buckberg Mountain he personally observed the enemy works at Stony Point and devised a plan for a surprise night attack.

The mission was offered to Brig. Gen. Anthony Wayne, who was eagerly awaiting just such a chance since the debacle in Paoli, Pennsylvania, two years earlier. On July 15, 1779, Wayne led select Light Infantry troops out of Fort Montgomery. For eight hours they struggled over narrow mountain trails, never being told of their mission.

Two miles from Stony Point the plan was revealed for the first time. Three columns would form the Continental force. One column of 300 men would wade through the marshes of the Hudson River from the north. A second column, led by Wayne, would wade through the waters of Haverstraw Bay and approach from the south. Each of these two columns would be further divided into three parts, the most dangerous assignment being drawn by 20 men called "the forlorn hope" who would enter enemy lines first, overcome sentries and sever the sharpened stakes of the abatis. The third column would create a diversion at the fort's front, drawing the British from their posts with musket fire.

The men donned white pieces of paper in their hats to avoid confusion in the dark, unloaded their muskets and affixed their bayonets. Wayne ordered instant death for any man who fired his gun or panicked in the advance. Finally, he told his men there was a $500 prize for the first man into the enemy works.

The assault began shortly after midnight and in 30 minutes was over. The British heavy artillery was not armed at night and, even if it had been ready, could not have been aimed down at the attackers scaling the rocky promontory. The Americans swarmed the position and accepted the British surrender. The assault had cost 15 American lives, mostly from volunteers in the "Forlorn Hope." The British suffered 20 killed and over 500 captured.

It was a complete victory for the now-professional Continental Army, but it carried little tactical importance. Washington could not spare the men to defend the position and destroyed and abandoned it after three days. The British were back the following day but the King's troops were withdrawn in October and the Hudson Highlands were never threatened again.

What the Battle of Stony Point lacked in physical gain it more than compensated as a morale booster in America. The accomplishments of Washington's troops were widely hailed. Congress voted only 11 medals during the Revolution; three were awarded for the action at Stony Point. Wayne, who suffered a head wound but continued to lead the charge, received a gold medal, and the leader of the left flank, Major John Stewart, got a silver medal. Another silver medal, which became a gold when finally awarded in 1783, went to Lt. Col. François Louis de Fleury, a French engineer who won the $500 prize offered to the first man into the upper works. It was the only medal given to a European volunteer during the war.

Through the nineteenth century many visitors had arrived by steamer to view the famous site of Anthony Wayne's surprise attack. In 1902 Stony Point became a public park, and by 1909 an elaborate stone memorial arch was placed over the entrance. A short, excellent interpretive trail of Stony Point features demonstrators in period dress on most days. The small museum in the visitor center is also excellent, packed with artifacts and information pertaining to the battle.

Tappan

André Execution Site (site)
Andre Hill, off Old Tappan Road; Open daily, 24 hours.

British Major John André met his fate as a revealed spy on this hill, marching silently and bravely to the gallows on October 2, 1780. A passionate appeal from General Henry Clinton was ignored, although André had charmed his captors with his intelligence and dignified manner. André's only request was a bullet rather than a noose, but Washington refused.

Major André's body was exchanged for that of General Richard Montgomery, who had died in the Siege of Quebec in 1775. Later, in 1821, André was interred in Westminster Abbey. A polished stone monument marks the location of the original burial site, near where the major was hanged.

DeWint House (site)
20 Livingston Avenue, 914-359-1359; Daily, 10–4. Free.

Daniel DeClark built a small brick and sandstone home in the style of his native Denmark, with wide, sloping eaves, in 1700. During the Revolution George Washington used the house, purchased by Johannes DeWint in 1746, several times as his headquarters. It was during a one-week stay at the DeWint House in the early fall of 1780 that Washington handled the case of British Adjutant John André.

Washington had issued the orders giving Benedict Arnold command of the Hudson Highlands from this house. Arnold had coveted the assignment, already having schemed to betray the garrison to the British. When his contact, Major John André, was intercepted behind American lines he was brought to Tappan and imprisoned. General Washington regarded André as a spy but allowed the young agent to appear before a board of 14 American officers. André confessed to his complicity in the clandestine meeting, including traveling under a false name, and was sentenced to death on September 28.

The replicated Washington's office appears much as it did during the Revolution. A restored 1850 Carriage House is on the grounds and features memorabilia from the commander-in-chief. In the yard is a small bust of George Washington and a replica of his personal 1775 flag.

Tarrytown

Captors' Monument (site)
Patriots' Park, Route 9; Open daily, 24 hours.

On September 22, 1780, British Major John André, envoy for Lt. Gen. Sir Henry Clinton, met with Maj. Gen. Benedict Arnold to discuss the selling of the American post at West Point. André's ship, H.M.S. *Vulture,* was fired on by

West Point batteries and forced to sail two miles down the river. So André had to make his way back overland. Returning to New York on the morning of September 23, a disguised André was detained at this creek by three American patrolmen. André tried to bribe his captors to allow him to move on but he was searched and plans to the fort at West Point were discovered in his boot. When Arnold learned of André's capture he deserted to the British on September 25.

The monument is topped by a bronze figure of John Paulding, one of the American guards. Each of the three men were farmers' sons serving in the militia. Created by William Rudolph O'Donovan, it was dedicated on the centennial anniversary of André's capture.

Ticonderoga

Fort Ticonderoga (site)

Route 74, one mile northeast of town, 518-585-2821; Jul–Aug: daily, 9–6; May–Jun and Sept–Oct: 9–5. Admission charged.

The Indians who lived here called it the place "between the waters." And indeed this was the position to control the two-mile portage from Lake Champlain to Lake George and thus control the entire route between Canada and New York. It would poetically be called "the Key to a Continent" or "America's Gibraltar" during the Revolution.

The French built the first fort on the portage in 1758. They called it Carillon because water fell like a "chime of bells" from Lake George. Just as the fort was being completed the British sent a 15,000 man force — the largest British Army yet fielded in North America — against Carillon. The Marquis de Montcalm did not passively await the massive invasion but ordered wooden fortifications built in the woods three-quarters of a mile west of the fort. The British could not penetrate the defenses and lost 2,000 men killed and wounded in the attack. Despite being outnumbered four-to-one, the French defenders had dealt the British one of their worst defeats ever in North America.

When a return force led by Jeffrey Amherst appeared the next summer, the French knew they were doomed and retreated, destroying part of the fort as they fled. The British renamed the bastion Fort Ticonderoga, but after pushing the French from eastern North America the post held no military importance. It stood like a monument in the wilderness, manned by a few men and falling into disrepair.

When the Revolution began Ethan Allen and Benedict Arnold led an expedition of 83 Green Mountain Boys who surprised the British garrison on May 10, 1775, and captured the fort. The position was not as critical as the cannon and ammunition stored at Fort Ticonderoga. Colonel Henry Knox arrived on December 5 and led the cannon away on a train of 42 heavy sledges pulled by 80 yoke of oxen to Boston, 300 miles away. Knox was able to deliver 43 cannon and 16 mortars.

The British returned in 1777 as General Burgoyne marched down from Canada. They placed cannon on Mount Defiance on the south side of Fort

Ticonderoga, a tactic Arnold had pointed out to General Arthur St. Clair. But the commander did not have enough men to defend the mountain. The cannon did not threaten the fort but would destroy the floating bridge and boats needed for evacuation. As a result the Americans abandoned the fort.

After Burgoyne surrendered, Fort Ticonderoga once again was controlled by the Colonials. Raiding parties were occasionally organized until the end of the war. After the Revolution the fort was never garrisoned again. Its greatest value turned out to be as a quarry for locals who plundered its stone walls for building material.

Fort Ticonderoga was purchased in 1820 by a merchant named William Ferris Pell. It stayed in his family for generations until Stephen Pell decided to privately restore "America's Gibraltar" in 1908. Ten years before there was a national park and twenty years before Williamsburg was reconstructed, Pell undertook the renovation of the historical landmark. Much of the stone walls were rebuilt and two interior barracks have been reconstructed. Scores of cannon line the bastions.

The extensive museum, which fills three floors in the barracks, stems from Pell's private collection and opened in 1909. Among the treasures is a hollow silver bullet that concealed British secret messages and could be swallowed if captured, and General Schuyler's personal flag, made of wool with a ring of circular white linen stars.

Mount Defiance (site)

Off Route 22/74, one mile southeast of town, 518-585-2821; Jul–Aug: daily, 9–5; May–Jun and Sept–Oct: 9–4. Free.

The spot where British general William Phillips placed four 12-pound cannon to force the capitulation of Fort Ticonderoga can be reached by a paved road up the 835-foot mountain. When confronted with the task the commander of the Royal Artillery said simply, "Where a goat can go a man can go, and where a man can go he can drag a gun."

Street Road Cemetery (site)

Route 9N; Open daily, 24 hours.

This cemetery containing the graves of Revolutionary War soldiers is opposite where the original commons in the village of Ticonderoga once stood. The last soldier interred here, a Civil War veteran, was laid to rest in 1936.

Vails Gate

Knox's Headquarters (site)

Forge Hill Road, south of Route 94, 914-561-5498; Memorial Day–Labor Day: Sun and Wed, 1–5. Admission charged.

Colonel Thomas Ellison built a fine stone house for his son John in 1754 attracting the attention of four Revolutionary generals when the Continental Army resided in nearby Newburgh. Henry Knox, the self-taught military tactician and close Washington aide, stayed here four times between 1779 and 1782. Nathanael Greene and Friedrich von Steuben were brief masters in 1779, and after Knox left in 1782 Horatio Gates moved here when commandant of the New Windsor Cantonment. The generals' parties were the social highlights of the American encampments.

A long one-story wooden section is attached to the main two-story stone building. Ruins of the Ellisons' eighteenth century grist mill are visible from paths along the gorge by Silver Stream.

New Windsor Cantonment (site)

Temple Hill Road (Route 300), north of town, 914-561-1765; Apr–Oct: Wed–Sat, 10–5, Sun, 1–5. Admission charged.

The surrender of British general Cornwallis at Yorktown on October 19, 1781, signified only the beginning of the end of the Revolution, not the end of hostilities. The Continental Army continued to watch the British in New York City, and on November 28, 1782, Washington ordered winter quarters to be built at New Windsor. He headquartered six miles away in Newburgh.

Baron von Steuben laid out a village for 7,000 troops, accompanied by 500 women and children or "camp followers." More than 1,600 acres of woodlands were leveled for 600 precisely located huts. The cantonment was dominated by a large public meeting building 110 feet long and 30 feet wide, called the Temple Building.

At New Windsor the army was better housed and better clothed than in previous winter camps. There were still shortages of food, however, and for the most part life remained hard. As peace negotiations in Paris stalled, unrest mounted among officers in the camp as Congress continued to neglect its army. The officers, concerned about back pay, pensions and land bounties connected to their service, issued two unsigned papers which circulated through New Windsor. The first proposed that the officers, without seeking Washington's consent, meet with Congress, and the second went so far as to suggest that the Continental Army seize power from Congress.

With the officers' challenge Washington now faced his greatest personal leadership crisis of the Revolution. He notified Congress and condemned the proposals on March 11, 1783. Four days later the commander addressed the officers in the Temple to denounce the papers. He appealed to their sense of reason and duty as military officers and, when finished, left his stunned audience to mull his words. The officers, their sense of awe for Washington once again inflamed, denounced the resolutions.

The defusing of the Newburgh Conspiracy was the only drama at New Windsor. Washington was able to issue cease-fire orders on April 19, eight years to the day the war's first shots echoed through Lexington and Concord. Most of the soldiers were furloughed during the summer as the peace treaty was signed. The last regulars of the Continental Army marched to West Point. On September 2, 1783, the camp buildings were sold at auction.

Several buildings from the Continental Army's final winter encampment have been recreated at New Windsor's 70 acres. Included on the grounds are a blacksmith shop, a bake oven and the Von Steuben Camp. Dioramas on camp life are featured in the Activities Building and "The Continental Soldier in Camp" exhibit. The Temple Building was reproduced in 1964 and a copy of the "Proclamation of the Cessation of Hostilities" hangs on the door. The visitor center shows an audiovisual presentation on the final phase of the Revolutionary War.

Also at New Windsor is the controversial Mountainville Hut. Local legend insists that the hut was bought at the dispersal auction by Nathaniel Sackett, an area merchant. Sackett moved the hut to his property in Mountainville and attached it to his house. There were many nineteenth century modifications but when the hut was "rediscovered" in 1933 it was acclaimed as the only remaining hut built by Revolutionary War soldiers. The Mountainville Hut has been transported to the cantonment but there is no documentation that it is an authentic New Windsor relic.

West Point

Fort Montgomery (site)

Bear Mountain State Park, Route 9W, five miles south of town; Open daily, dawn to dusk. Free; admission charged for parking.

The works on 1,305-foot Bear Mountain were completed in 1777, before West Point could be fixed of an original faulty design. General Henry Clinton captured the fort on October 6, 1777, as he sailed from New York to assist General Burgoyne's invasion from Canada. Clinton then sailed back to New York rather than Albany, Burgoyne surrendered two weeks later; and the Hudson Highlands were never threatened again.

The site of Fort Montgomery has been covered by a zoo but trails wind past archaeological remains of breastworks and fort structures.

United States Military Academy (site)

Route 218, 914-938-2638; Daily, 9–4:45. Free; admission charged for guided tours.

The Hudson River doubles back on itself as it flows under the promontory of West Point, forcing ships to slow down to drifting speed to negotiate the turn. This geographic feature turned approaching ships into targets for anyone controlling the river at this point.

In 1778 the Continental Army built Fort Arnold (for Benedict) at this spot in the river. The earth and log fortification housed 700 men, 12 cannon and 11 mortars. Fort Putnam was built high on the hills (400 feet above the water) to the west of Fort Arnold to protect against a mountainous overland attack. Downstream, Fort Montgomery covered the water approach to West Point and across the river Fort Constitution stood on the high bluffs of an island in the Hudson. Much of the planning was done by Thaddeus Kosciuszko, who when finished had completed a modern defensive zone that included five forts, seven redoubts and a giant iron chain that stretched across the Hudson River.

The British started to dismantle these defenses a year earlier when forts Washington and Lee fell. The first iron chain at Fort Montgomery broke and the British sailed past. But Sir Henry Clinton still could not move against the main fortification at West Point, where, if he ever could get past that dastardly turn in the river, his biggest warships would be only 46 miles from Albany.

Another way to gain control of West Point presented itself to Clinton in 1779 with the beginnings of a traitorous correspondence with an esteemed American officer, Benedict Arnold. Over the months Arnold provided useful military information to Clinton. Increasingly embittered by perceived snubs by Congress and desperately needing money to fund his high living, Arnold offered to sell West Point, a post to which he had recently been assigned after insistent lobbying of Washington.

The scheme collapsed with the capture of British envoy John André on September 22, 1780. Two nights later, Arnold learned of the capture and boarded the H.M.S. *Vulture* in the Hudson, a great American military career over. The British never fully trusted Arnold and no high command was forthcoming. He was reduced to leading raids along the Connecticut and Virginia coasts. He finally retired on half pay and lived as a merchant in Canada, the West Indies and London. He went to his grave justifying his actions as a way he thought would bring the two sides together in peace sooner.

After the Revolution, Fort Clinton (it was no longer named for Arnold) stayed active as an arsenal. In 1802 it was closed for the creation of the U.S. Military Academy. West Point was never threatened militarily during the war.

The site of Fort Clinton is marked with a monument to the Polish general Thaddeus Kosciuszko. Only a piece of a parapet remains. Fort Putnam — named for Rufus Putnam and his soldiers of the 5th Massachusetts Regiment who built it — has been partially restored. Arnold had this to report to the British on Fort Putnam in 1780: "F.P., stone, wanting great repairs. Wall on the east side broke down, and rebuilding from the foundation. At the west and south side have been a cheveaux-de-frise; on the west side broke in many places. The east side open; two bombproofs and provision magazine in the fort, and a slight wooden barrack."

It was first restored as a war monument in 1909 and then redone for the Bicentennial in 1975–76. A walking path leads around the ramparts with breathtaking views of the Hudson River; an audiovisual program in the McLean Historical Museum describes the defenses built in the Hudson Highlands and the continuous British efforts to penetrate them.

In the Old Cadet Chapel are marble shields on the east wall commemorating the American brigadier and major generals, including Benedict Arnold. Revolutionary War graves are scarce in the cemetery but include heroine Molly Corbin, next to the chapel, and the burial yard's oldest grave, Ensign Dominick Trant. Trant, a native of Cork, Ireland, was a soldier in the 9th Massachusetts Infantry who died at West Point in 1782.

At Trophy Point are displayed captured weapons from every American war, starting with the Revolution. Included at the river overlook are links from the second great chain that was placed across the Hudson River. Each link in the 600-yard chain was two feet across and weighed 114 pounds. The 65-ton chain floated on log rafts to prevent the passage of enemy ships. The ruined walls of Fort Constitution are clearly visible from Trophy Point.

West Point Museum (col)

Olmsted Hall at Pershing Center, Route 9W, 914-938-2203; Daily, 10:30–4:15. Free.

Galleries on two floors feature a large collection of weapons and other military artifacts to tell the story of warfare from ancient times until the present. Other galleries feature the history of West Point and the U.S. Military Academy and the story of the founding of the regular army. The Revolution had been fought as a unique — and often tenuous — collaboration between the Continental Army and the local state militiamen. After the war ended the Continental Army was disbanded and the militia remained. The Articles of Confederation gave no strength for a central government to deal with internal strife or foreign invaders, but it was the former that led to a drive for a stronger form of government, with the power to summon an army. The most dramatic challenge to the new government had been Shay's Rebellion in Springfield, Massachusetts, in 1786 and 1787, which was put down by General Benjamin Lincoln.

White Plains

The Armory (site)

65 Mitchell Place.

An American eagle tops a monument dedicated in 1910 to commemorate the first Westchester County courthouse in White Plains. It was on this spot that the Declaration of Independence was first read in New York, giving White Plains the claim as "the birthplace of the State of New York."

White Plains National Battlefield Site (site)

Two locations: Chatterton Hill and Battle Avenue; Open daily, 24 hours.

Through the summer of 1776 the British had bested Washington in several major skirmishes around New York City but had, by October, still failed to destroy his ragged little band of Continentals and end the Revolution. British general Sir William Howe was determined to do just that before winter fell, hoping to draw Washington into a climatic major battle.

The Americans withdrew from Manhattan on October 18 and marched to White Plains. Washington fortified two hills — Purdy and Hatfield — as his army moved. On October 27 he evaluated his position and determined that Chatterton Hill, which sloped 180 feet up from the Bronx River, should be defended by more than the Massachusetts militia.

He sent two brigades to the hill on October 28, just as the British were massing 13,000 troops across the Bronx River. Howe concentrated his attack on Chatterton Hill, and the only real fighting of the battle took place here. The British and German troops charged valiantly up the hill and pushed the defenders off in 50 minutes of heavy fighting. Washington's main army was now threatened but Howe did not press the attack. Washington fled to rugged hills behind White Plains and the Revolution continued.

The heavily urbanized locale retains three monuments that mark Washington's position during the Battle of White Plains. One is at Chatterton Hill and two are in the neighborhood along Battle Avenue.

White Plains Rural Cemetery (site)

167 North Broadway; Open daily, dawn to dusk.

In this graveyard are the remains of many Revolutionary War soldiers who fell in the Battle of White Plains.

Whitehall

Skenesborough Museum (col)

Route 22, in center of town, 518-499-0716; Jun–Labor Day: Mon–Sat, 10–4, Sun, 12–4; Labor Day–Columbus Day: Sat, 10–3, Sun, 12–3. Admission charged.

Enough boats for the Patriot cause during the Revolution were built here that locals were moved to call Whitehall "the birthplace of the American Navy." The town was settled by 30 British families under Captain Philip Skene in 1759 and called Skenesborough. Captain Skene supported the British during the Revolution, and the town was renamed after the Revolutionary War. The museum features a model of the 1776 shipyard.

Yonkers

Philipse Manor Hall (site)

Warburton Avenue and Dock Street, 914-631-3189; Daily, 9–5. Admission charged.

Frederick Philipse arrived in the American colonies in the 1650s as a carpenter. He prospered in the New World and eventually acquired more than 20 miles of land along the east side of the Hudson River. In 1682 Philipse Manor Hall was started and 11 years later the estate was confirmed as the Manor of Philipsburg.

It is no surprise that a family that rose from such humble beginnings should hesitate to revolt against the political system in which it prospered. Thus, during the Revolution the third lord of the manor remained staunchly loyalist. Philipse Manor was seized by the Patriot government of New York and the land fragmented. At various times the house was occupied by both sides and served as the sometimes headquarters of British general Sir Henry Clinton from 1778 to 1781.

Youngstown

Old Fort Niagara (site)
Fort Niagara State Park, off Route 18F, 716-745-7611; Daily, 9–dusk. Admission charged.

The French fortified Lake Ontario near the mouth of the Niagara River as early as 1726 and it remained in operation, under a host of different flags, until after World War II. The British were in control after the French and Indian War and improved the defenses with redoubt walls built five feet thick. During the Revolution British loyalists used Niagara as a base for bloody raids into the Mohawk Valley. The British, in fact, did not abandon Fort Niagara until 1796, 13 years after the Revolution ended. The site has been restored to its origins as the only fortified French castle in the United States.

North Carolina

Revolutionary Status: Original Colony
Estimated Colonial Population: 204,000
Colonial Capital: New Bern
Last Colonial Governor: Cornelius Harnett
Troops Provided: 9 Continental regiments

Revolutionary Timeline:
May 16, 1771: Royal Governor William Tryon and 1,300 British militia crush an uprising by the western Regulators at the Battle of Alamance
October 25, 1774: Fifty-one women in Edenton protest the use of tea in letter to King George III
February 27, 1776: Scottish Highlanders march to destruction against North Carolina rebels at Moore's Creek
April 12, 1776: North Carolina becomes the first colony to authorize its delegates at the Continental Congress to vote for separation from England when it adopts the Halifax Resolves
May 12, 1776: North Carolina is declared in a state of rebellion and the bombing of Brunswick Town begins shortly thereafter
February 1, 1781: British defeat American militia in Battle at Cowan's Ford
March 15, 1781: Lord Charles Cornwallis wins the battle but loses the Revolution in action at Guilford Courthouse against Nathanael Greene
September 11, 1781: Tory raider David Fanning captures Governor Thomas Burke in Hillsborough

Burlington

Alamance Battleground (site)
Route 62, six miles southwest of town, 910-227-4785; Apr–Oct: Mon–Sat, 9–5, Sun, 1–5; Nov–Mar: Tue–Sat, 10–4, Sun, 1–4. Free.

North Carolina's revolution began with the Regulators, a group of back-country farmers who sought "to assemble ourselves for conference for regulating public grievances and abuses of power." Formed in 1768, the patience of the Regulators grew progressively shorter against a Royal government that ignored the problems of the Piedmont settlers.

In 1770 Regulators violated a British courtroom in Hillsborough and later burned the judge's house. Edmund Fanning, a local government official, was whipped mercilessly before his home was destroyed. Even William Hooper, who would later sign the Declaration of Independence, was brutalized and paraded through the streets. By 1771 the British were forced to raise arms to deal with the rebellion.

Governor William Tyron personally marched from New Bern at the head of 1,100 Royal militia to demand allegiance to the Crown. Approaching Salisbury, he found more than 2,000 Regulators assembled near Alamance Creek. More a mob than an army, many were unarmed. Leadership among the Regulators at Alamance was sorely lacking. Herman Husband, nominal leader of the Regulators, had no stomach for armed battle and rode away when he was unable to convince the Regulators to disperse. A more militant leader, James Hunter, declined command as well.

Although reluctant to attack fellow countrymen, Tryon's militia quickly dispatched the discombobulated Regulators, despite being outnumbered two-to-one. Nine Regulators were killed and dozens wounded. The British Army suffered about 70 casualties.

After executing one prisoner on the battlefield to demonstrate the seriousness with which he regarded the rebellion, Governor Tryon offered pardons for Regulators who would swear allegiance. He then ranged through Regulator farms administering the oath of allegiance with considerable success, but more than 1,500 North Carolinians picked up and moved into the wilderness of Kentucky and Tennessee.

Some 40 acres of the battlefield have been preserved. Walking trails lead to interpretive signs and monuments and the Allen House, a 1780s North Carolina log cabin moved to this park. John Allen was married to Herman Husband's sister. The only leader of the Regulators never pardoned, Husband disappeared into Western Pennsylvania, where he lived under several assumed names and eventually was a leader in the Whiskey Rebellion in 1794. The visitor center offers a multimedia presentation of the battle and the pressures of Colonial policies that precipitated the revolt.

Charlotte

Hezekiah Alexander Homesite (site)
3500 Shamrock Drive, 704-568-1774; Tue–Fri, 10–5; Sat–Sun, 2–5. Admission charged.

Hezekiah Alexander, a member of the Provincial Congress, built this native rock house in 1774. Alexander helped draft the North Carolina Constitution in 1776. The Alexander house is now the centerpiece of a Charlotte history museum.

Signers of the Mecklenburg Resolves (mem)
County Courthouse, 600 East Trade Street.

A village of less than two dozen homes during the Revolution, Charlotte was nonetheless a center of backcountry agitation almost from the time of its chartering in 1768. The Mecklenburg Resolves were adopted here in 1775, and during a one-month occupation of the village in 1780 British general Lord Cornwallis called Charlotte a "hornet's nest of rebellion." Patriot forces sniped at his messengers, hounded his foragers and generally disrupted British activity. When Cornwallis invaded North Carolina a second time in 1781, he passed to the west of Charlotte.

Cornelius

Battle at Cowan's Ford (site)
Route 73 at Lake Norman, eight miles west of town.

As Cornwallis chased Greene through North Carolina his troops became stranded by their guide fording the Catawba River on February 1, 1781. There were two established paths at Cowan's Ford: a shallower, but less direct, route for horses and a straight route for wagons. The Americans naturally defended the easier horse route but when their Tory guide fled under enemy fire the British took the shorter, but harder, route across the river. This happenstance enabled them to scramble up the lightly defended banks and defeat the Patriots. Among the Americans killed was General William Lee Davidson, a hero at Germantown and one of North Carolina's most beloved leaders. A monument remembers the action at Cowan's Ford, which has been covered by Lake Norman.

Currie

Moore's Creek National Battlefield (site)
200 Moore's Creek Road, off Route 210, four miles west of town, 910-283-5591; Daily, 9–5. Free.

North Carolina was distinguished by split loyalties as the rebellion percolated. The Royal government had been forced into exile when British authorities convinced Commander-in-Chief Thomas Gage that strong loyalist support could be roused and order restored. Gage authorized a strong expeditionary force under Lord Cornwallis, Sir Henry Clinton, and Sir Peter Parker to head for Brunswick Town, North Carolina.

A steady stream of Scottish Highlanders had been populating North Carolina for years and the call went out for these Loyalists to assemble in the state's interior and march to join the British Army. Brig. Gen. Donald MacDonald organized some 1,600 men, including some 130 ex–Regulators. On February 20, 1776, MacDonald began his movement toward the coast.

An experienced soldier nearing 70, MacDonald skillfully maneuvered his army past Patriot opposition but lost a race to Moore's Creek Bridge, the only crossing of Moore's Creek — a dark, sluggish stream about 40 miles from Brunswick Town. American Colonel Alexander Lillington quickly erected earthworks on the east side of the bridge and guarded it with 150 men. Another 850 men under Colonel Richard Caswell commanded the western banks. As a further defensive measure, the Patriots removed some planks in the primitive bridge and greased the girders.

The Loyalists now had to decide whether to abandon their march or fight across the bridge. MacDonald had fallen ill and withdrawn, and at a council of war impetuous younger Scots carried the debate. A party of 75 selected broadswordsmen were picked to make an ill-advised assault on the bridge.

An hour before dawn on February 27, the kilted Highlanders charged out of the woods with swords raised and bagpipes squealing. Picking their way over the bridge through the fog, the advance patrol reached the opposite bank, where they met withering fire at the earthworks. What Patriot musketry didn't take care of, a swivel gun and artillery did. The Loyalists lost 30 killed and 40 wounded. Only one Patriot died.

Most of the remaining Tory force scattered and more than 850 were taken prisoner. The victory demonstrated the surprising Patriot strength in the countryside, discouraged the growth of Loyalist sentiment in the Carolinas, and spurred revolutionary feeling throughout the colonies. The British seaborne force moved on and was repulsed off Charleston several months later. It would be years before the British reappeared in the South and their hopes of crushing the rebellion in America were shown to be premature. Big consequences emanated from a small battle in the swamps of North Carolina.

A one-mile history trail visits the key points of the first battle in North Carolina. Remnants of the earthworks can still be viewed and the pivotal bridge has been reconstructed. In the 87-acre park is the Patriot Monument, constructed in 1857 to honor Private John Grady, the only Patriot to die at Moore's Creek.

Reenactment: The park holds an annual celebration and remembrance of the battle. The event is held on the last weekend of February and features a living history encampment, tactical demonstrations, folk singing, a candlelight tour of the battlefield Saturday evening and a formal commemoration program on Sunday.

Edenton

Barker House (site)

108 North Broad Street, 919-482-2637; Apr–Oct: Mon–Sat, 9–5, Sun, 1–5; Nov–Mar: Tue–Sat, 9–5, Sun, 1–4. Admission charged.

In Edenton in 1774, 51 women in town signed a resolution supporting the resolutions passed by the First Provincial Congress. One of the actions the ladies supported was the end of the consumption of tea. The Edenton women mailed their document to England. It attracted enough attention to be satirized in a London newspaper.

As other Colonial towns were staging "tea parties," such an event was invented in Edenton to support the ladies' action. Penelope Barker was chosen to preside over this "tea party." Although the resultant shenanigans were just for show, the Edenton Tea Party is considered the first collective political activity by women in the American colonies.

The Barker House is the departure point for walking tours of historic Edenton. Exhibits pertain to the ladies who would not conform "to that pernicious custom of drinking tea."

Cannons on Edenton Bay (mem)

Courthouse Green at East Water Street.

On display at the Edenton waterfront are three French cannon contracted by Benjamin Franklin that were salvaged from a shipment that went down in Albemarle Sound in 1778. Years later Federal troops put them out of commission and observed that they were a greater danger to the men behind them than to the enemy in front.

James Iredell House (site)

105 East Church Street, 919-482-2637; Apr–Oct: Mon–Sat, 9–5, Sun, 1–5; Nov–Mar: Tue–Sat, 9–5, Sun, 1–4. Admission charged.

Iredell arrived in America in 1768 at the age of 17 to study law. He became attorney general of North Carolina and a Revolutionary leader who was later appointed by George Washington as an associate justice of the first U.S. Supreme Court. With James Wilson, Iredell coauthored the Eleventh Amendment to the Constitution, which was passed into law shortly before his death in 1799.

The Georgian wing of the house was built around 1773, and the Federal wing dates to 1816. The Iredell House is interpreted as a representation of an upper middle-class village home.

Joseph Hewes Monument (mem)

Edenton Green at East Water Street.

The stone monument facing Edenton Bay honors Edentonian Joseph Hewes, who "modestly, but without stint gave his labor and his means to the cause of freedom." In addition to being a signer of the Declaration of Independence, Hewes is notable for winning a commission for John Paul Jones while serving as the chairman of marine, the forerunner of the secretary of the navy. Joseph Hewes died in Philadelphia in 1779, the only signer to do so. Ironically, a Pennsylvania signer, James Wilson, died in Edenton in 1798 while visiting the James Iredell House.

St. Paul's Church (site)

Broad and Church streets.

Built over 30 years, beginning in 1736, St. Paul's is one of the finest Colonial churches in the South. The Episcopal church is unusual in that it does not face the street but instead is directed inward to a churchyard where three Colonial governors — Charles Eden, Henderson Walker and Thomas Pollack — are buried.

Greensboro

Guilford Courthouse National Military Park (site)

New Garden Road, off Route 220 (Battleground Avenue), six miles north of town, 910-288-1776; Daily, 8:30–5. Free.

With the war stalemated in the North in 1778, the British strategy to win the war shifted to the South. Georgia and South Carolina were completely under British control by 1780, and Nathanael Greene, Washington's hand-picked commander of the Southern Department, was determined to keep North Carolina out of British hands. From his base in Virginia, Greene harassed Lord Cornwallis as he spread his attack northward. By early March, Greene was confident enough to face the British in open battle, although scarcely one in five of his 4,000 men had seen battle action.

An ironmaster by trade, Greene was self-taught in the art of war. But he was more than a match for the aristocratic, professional and competent Cornwallis. Pursued by a frenetic Cornwallis, Greene selected sloping ground near Guilford Courthouse to make his stand. He aligned his superior forces in three lines to receive the British assault on March 15, 1781.

The first line, manned by inexperienced North Carolina militia, was quickly brushed aside, and they fled. Breaking through the second Patriot line, however, required savage fighting, and by the time the redcoats reached Greene's last line, Cornwallis was becoming desperate. As the fighting raged Cornwallis directed his artillery to fire grapeshot over his own lines into the melee of friend and foe alike. The harsh directive to fire into his own troops dispersed the Americans and saved his army.

Greene retired from the field. Technically the loser, his losses had been light. Cornwallis kept the field but lost the war at Guilford Courthouse. His army limped on to Wilmington, still convinced that conquering Virginia would collapse the Revolution. Greene let him go and moved southward to reconquer South Carolina and Georgia, confident that American troops assembling in Virginia would destroy Cornwallis — which they did seven months later in Yorktown.

Begun in 1887, the 220-acre park was later established in 1917 as the first battleground of the American Revolution to be preserved as a national military park. A driving tour of more than two miles includes stops at the position of all three of the American lines and the site of Guilford Courthouse, which had been built in 1775. The courthouse was abandoned in 1808, when the county seat was moved six miles south. Nothing remains of either the small wooden courthouse or the community of March 15, 1781.

The grounds are among the most decorated of Revolutionary battlefields, graced by 28 monuments. The Hooper-Penn Monument marks the graves of William Hooper and John Penn, two of North Carolina's signers of the Declaration of Independence. The Cavalry Monument commemorates the dramatic charge of American cavalry against the British Brigade of Guards along the third line. Three names are inscribed on the shaft: Colonel William Washington, also a hero at Cowpens; the Marquis de Bretigny, a French volunteer in America's service; and Peter Francisco.

Francisco was a foundling abandoned near Hopewell, Virginia, in 1760. By the age of 15 Francisco was serving in the 10th Virginia Regiment and was wounded at Brandywine. Meanwhile, he was maturing into a giant of a man who stood 6'6" tall and weighed 260 pounds. Peter Francisco became known as the Continental Army's "Goliath" and his battlefield exploits befitted the size of the man. He was one of the "Forlorn Hope" at Stony Brook and executed a heroic rescue of his colonel at Camden. At Ward's Corner, Virginia, in July 1781, he single-handedly fought through nine mounted Tories, leaving two of the ambushers dead. At Guilford Courthouse, Francisco wielded a 5-foot sword, given to "the strongest man in Virginia" by George Washington, and allegedly killed 11 men. After the Revolution, Francisco worked as a blacksmith and tavern keeper. He died a country squire in Richmond in 1836.

The Stuart Monument honors a British soldier, Colonel James Stuart of the Queen's Guard, who fell here in hand-to-hand fighting, and his sword was found on the grounds in 1866. The most impressive monument is the large equestrian statue of General Greene, sculpted by Francis H. Packer. Unveiled on July 3, 1915, it bears Greene's words: "We fight, get beat, rise, and fight again."

Reenactment: The anniversary of the Battle of Guilford Courthouse is observed every March 15. Demonstrations and reenactments take place and a candlelight tour of the battlefield is offered.

Tannenbaum Park (site)

103 Green Acres Lane, 910-545-5315; Tue–Sat, 10–5, Sun, 2–5. Admission charged.

The Hoskins/Wyrick House served as headquarters for the British Command during the Battle of Guilford Courthouse as well as an interim field hospital for both sides. Today it is a featured exhibit within Tannenbaum Park, site of the North Carolina Colonial Heritage Center.

Halifax

Historic Halifax State Historic Site (site)

St. David and Dobbs streets, 919-583-7191; Apr–Oct: Mon–Sat, 9–5, Sun, 1–5; Nov–Mar: Mon–Sat, 9–4, Sun, 1–4. Free.

Halifax, on the Roanoke River, developed from its founding in the 1720s into a commercial and political center. On April 12, 1776, the 4th Provincial Congress adopted the Halifax Resolves, which directed the North Carolina delegates in the Continental Congress to declare independence in concurrence with any subsequent action to be taken by the other colonies. North Carolina thus became the first colony to come out officially for independence from England.

In November the 5th Provincial Congress wrote the state's first Constitution and bill of rights. They passed into law the next month. A guided walking tour includes four authentically restored buildings, including the 1760 home of a merchant.

Hillsborough

The Alliance of Historic Hillsborough (site)
Orange County Visitors' Center, 150 East King Street, 919-732-7741; Mon–Fri, 9–5. Admission charged for tour.

Hillsborough, site of the 1775 Provincial Congress, was the dominant town of the eighteenth century North Carolina interior. Both armies stayed here during the Revolution. On September 11, 1781, the notorious Tory raider David Fanning single-handedly brought down the North Carolina government in an attack on Hillsborough. Fanning captured Governor Thomas Burke and more than 200 others, including his council and many Continental officers.

Patriots under General John Butler trapped the raiding party at Lindley's Mill, south of Burlington, but Fanning fought through the ambush. The prisoners were delivered to the British base at Wilmington and Burke was paroled to James Island. The events helped weld Patriot support throughout the North Carolina backcountry.

Huntersville

Alexandriana (site)
9921 Old Statesville Road, 704-896-9808.

On May 20, 1775, a rebellious committee convened in Charlotte to address grievances with King George III and Royal rule in the Carolinas. The product was 20 resolutions for the state delegation to present to the Continental Congress. The Mecklenburg Resolves, signed here, were never presented to Congress.

Kinston

Richard Caswell Memorial (mem)
Route 70A.

Richard Caswell served in the Colonial assembly for 17 years. During and after the Revolution he continued to exert strong influence on North Carolina as a military leader, its first governor, speaker of the Senate, comptroller, and second-term governor. The memorial is a display center commemorating Caswell's long public service.

Lenoir

Fort Defiance (site)
Route 268, north of town, 704-754-0951; Apr–Oct: Mon–Sat, 9–5, Sun, 1–5; Nov–Mar: Tue–Sat, 9–4, Sun, 1–4. Admission charged.

William Lenoir became a Revolutionary hero at Kings Mountain, where he helped crush the army of Patrick Ferguson. A Virginian by birth, Lenoir built this house — named for a Colonial fort on the location — between 1788 and 1792. It features original clothing and furnishings.

New Bern

Tryon Palace Historic Sites and Gardens (site)
610 Pollock Street, 919-514-4900; Mon–Sat, 9:30–4, Sun, 1–4. Admission charged.

New Bern, a thriving port at the confluence of the Trent and Neuse rivers, played an active part in the Revolution as the Colonial capital from 1766 to 1776 and as the North Carolina capital from 1776 to 1794. William Tryon won his appointment to the Royal governorship in 1765 amidst growing political unrest in North Carolina. He did little to calm the rebellious mood when he announced plans to build an elegant royal palace — using tax money — on the banks of the Trent River.

When English architect John Hawkes finished Tryon Palace in 1770 it was acclaimed as the finest government building in Colonial America. After just 13 months in his spectacular 38-room Georgian mansion, William Tryon was appointed governor of the New York colony. It was left to his successor, Josiah Martin, to flee Tryon Palace in 1775 ahead of militant Patriots.

After the Revolutionary War, the palace continued to be used for meetings of the General Assembly and as a residence for the elected governors of the state. By the time George Washington visited in 1791 the building was falling into disrepair, and in 1798 the main structure burned to the ground.

In the 1950s Tryon Palace was reconstructed from original plans. The site also includes 14 acres of formal period gardens and other historic homes, including the John Wright Stanly House, the townhouse where Washington stayed during his visit to New Bern.

Salisbury

Old English Cemetery (site)
North Church Street.

In 1770 Lord Granville granted Salisbury the burying ground that has come to be known as the "Old English Cemetery." The oldest remaining tombstone is that of Captain Daniel Little, who died in 1775. In 1781 several British soldiers who served in the army of Lord Cornwallis were buried in the cemetery.

Thyatira Presbyterian Church (site)
White Road, off Route 150, west of town.

At different times during the Revolution in 1781, Salisbury was used as headquarters for British general Cornwallis and Patriot general Greene. In the winter of 1781, Nathanael Greene rode into town and stopped at a public house owned by Elizabeth Maxwell Steele. After listening to Greene's tales of his ragged army, Mrs. Steele gave him two bags of money. Accepting the gift, General Greene noticed the pictures of King George and Queen Charlotte on the tavern wall. Turning the picture of the king to the wall, he wrote on the back with a piece of chalk, "O, George! Hide thy face and mourne." Today, those pictures hang at Thyatira Church, where, in the cemetery, a monument marks the grave of Elizabeth Maxwell Steele.

Sanford

House in the Horseshoe (site)
324 Alston House Road, off Route 42, twelve miles west of town, 910-947-2051; Apr–Oct: Mon–Sat, 9–5, Sun 1–5; Nov–Mar: Tue–Sat, 10–4, Sun, 1–4. Free.

When Philip Alston came to the North Carolina frontier, he selected a hilltop inside a horseshoe bend of the Deep River to build his imposing frame manor house. In the Revolution, Alston became a colonel with the Whigs, waging the Civil War in the backcountry.

The Tory scourge of the Deep River region was David Fanning, who apparently deserted the rebel cause after being plundered by some Americans. When the British moved into Wilmington, Fanning was commissioned a colonel, and he ranged across the Carolina Piedmont waging a bitter guerrilla war against his former neighbors.

Fanning found Alston at home with his band of revolutionaries on August 5, 1781. Gunfire was exchanged for two hours before Fanning rolled a heaping cart of burning straw against the house. Alston quickly surrendered. Fanning granted the Whigs their freedom on the provision they not take up arms again.

Although Alston was distinguished as a lieutenant colonel in the state militia, a justice of the peace, and a state senator, his career was marked by corrupt activities. He was twice indicted for murder, removed as justice of the peace, and suspended from the state legislature for a menu of wrongdoings.

In 1790, Philip Alston sold his house and plantation and left the state. In 1798, four-term governor Benjamin Williams, who had served under Washington as a captain, purchased the 2,500-acre cotton plantation. The "House in the Horseshoe," as the Alston House was known, has been restored to its Colonial appearance. Bullet holes still scar the walls.

Wadesboro

Boggan-Hammond House (site)
206 East Wade Street, 704-694-6694; Mon–Fri, 9–11 and 12–2. Admission charged.

Although in his fifties, Patrick Boggan was an officer of the North Carolina militia of the Salisbury District during the Revolution, serving under his brother-in-law, Colonel Thomas Wade. He engaged in several raids against local Loyalists, sometimes in collaboration with Patriots from South Carolina. The house was built by Boggan — who died in 1817 — around 1780 and is the oldest structure in the town of Wadesboro.

Wilmington

Brunswick Town State Historic Site (site)
Route 133 off Route 17, nineteen miles south of town, 910-371-6613; Apr–Oct: Mon–Sat, 9–5, Sun, 1–5; Nov–Mar: Tue–Sat, 10–4, Sun, 1–4. Free.

Established on the west side of the Cape Fear River, Brunswick Town was the busiest port town in North Carolina prior to the Revolution. Between 1755 and 1770 the Royal government resided here, weathering heated Stamp Act disturbances in 1766.

On May 12, 1776, Sir Henry Clinton declared North Carolina in a state of rebellion and the British razed Brunswick Town. After the Revolution only four families returned to the ashes, and by 1830 the area was completely abandoned.

Excavated foundations of Brunswick Town buildings are presently maintained as archeological exhibits. The trails are dotted with explanatory displays of the bustling Colonial period.

St. James Episcopal Church (site)
3rd and Market streets, 910-763-1628, Sept–May: Mon–Fri, 9–4, Apr–Aug: Mon–Fri, 9–3. Free.

After another costly victory at Guilford Courthouse, Lord Cornwallis regrouped in Wilmington, which had been captured by the British in January 1781. Wilmington was the Colonial capital in 1743 and had been the scene of well-organized resistance to the Stamp Act.

St. James was used as a British stronghold during occupation; across the street is the Burgwin-Wright house, believed to be Cornwallis' headquarters. He marched from Wilmington on April 25 to his eventual defeat at Yorktown. Cornwallis left an efficient Major James Craig in charge of Wilmington. He rounded up and imprisoned known rebels before evacuating after Yorktown. The parish dates to 1751 and the churchyard contains the graves of many Patriots.

Winston-Salem

Old Salem (site)
Old Salem Road, 910-721-7300; Mon–Sat, 9–5, Sun, 12:30–5. Admission charged.

Although the Moravians in Salem took no active military role in the Revolution, their neutrality was tested by both sides. Salem was briefly occupied by the British in February of 1781. Old Salem is a living history restoration from 1766, with many of the 90 buildings reconstructed on the original sites.

Ohio

Revolutionary Status: Part of the Virginia colony

Bolivar

Fort Laurens State Memorial (site)
Route 212, south of town, 330-874-2059, Apr–Oct: daily, 9:30–dusk. Free; admission charged for museum.

Fort Laurens was the site of the only U.S. military fort built during the Revolutionary War in what would become the state of Ohio. A substantial force of 1,200 militia under General Lachlan McIntosh was assembled to pester British and Indian troops between Fort Pitt and Detroit. McIntosh started too late in the season in 1778 and decided to build an advance fort on this site.

The troops withstood months of near-starvation and an Indian siege but held on to the position through the summer of 1779. The inept McIntosh was replaced as commander of the Western Department, and the Americans evacuated Fort Laurens. There were hopes of reoccupying the garrison so it was not destroyed. That never happened and the fort was demolished after the Revolutionary War.

The site is preserved in an 81-acre Ohio park. A museum offers an audiovisual presentation and tells the story of the Revolution in Ohio. The tomb of Ohio's Unknown Soldier, a memorial to the fort's defenders, is located here.

Cary

Crawford Monument (site)
County Highway 29, five miles south of town; Open daily, dawn to dusk.

The original Crawford Monument was erected in 1877 in memory of Colonel William B. Crawford, who had led the Sandusky Expedition sent to quiet the Indian skirmishes in the West. In June 1782, Crawford was captured and brought back to the spot near the monument. Here he was burned at the stake. Crawford remains the only American Army officer ever to die in this manner. In 1994 a new monument was erected and dedicated in Ritchey Cemetery.

Gnadenhutten

Gnadenhutten Monument (site)
Route 36, one mile south of town, 614-254-4143; Memorial Day–Labor Day: Mon–Sat, 10–5, Sun, 12–5; Sep–Oct: Sat, 10–5, Sun, 12–5. Free.

The work of the Reverend David Zeisberger established three Moravian missions in eastern Ohio in the early 1770s. By 1777 he had decided the territory was too hostile and moved the white settlers from the missions. Attempting to remain in the area were Christian American Indians, but by 1781 these peaceful settlers had moved on as well.

In the spring of 1782 about 100 Moravian Indians were revisiting the abandoned settlement when they were attacked and slaughtered by American soldiers under Colonel David Williamson. There are nothing but theories why the friendly Indians were massacred. The white settlers could have been frustrated by the continuing Indian raids on the frontier, regardless of tribe. Another explanation is that a Moravian woman was seen wearing a dress from an American settlement recently savaged by an Indian attack.

Regardless of the reason, the atrocities at Gnadenhutten sparked a new ferocity in Tory-Indian raiding along the Kentucky frontier. The nine-acre memorial includes a log church and a cooper's cabin that have been reconstructed on the site of the original village. A museum discusses Indian life on the frontier and the events of March 7–8, 1782.

Martin's Ferry

Betty Zane Memorial (mem)

Walnut Grove Cemetery.

Ebenezer Zane was the first white settler on what would become the town of Wheeling. The 22-year-old Zane stopped here in 1769 before opening the road west to present-day Maysfield, Kentucky. At Wheeling a fort was built by William Crawford in 1774; it was renamed Fort Henry in 1776.

Fort Henry was attacked many times during the Revolution, the last on September 11, 1782, giving it the distinction, claimed by others, of being the final battle of the Revolution. On this occasion nearly 300 Tories and Indians laid siege to the fort and Betty Zane, Ebenezer's sister, volunteered to leave the fort and retrieve a keg of powder at her brother's cabin, some 60 yards away. She strolled out of Fort Henry as if oblivious to the surrounding warfare as stunned Indians watched in bewilderment. Once in the cabin she grabbed the powder and raced back to the fort.

The Betty Zane Memorial is at the entrance to the cemetery, where many Revolutionary War veterans are buried.

New Philadelphia

Schoenbrunn Village State Memorial (site)

Route 259, one mile southeast of town, 330-339-3636; Memorial Day–Labor Day: Mon–Sat, 9:30–5, Sun, 12–5; Labor Day–Oct: Sat, 9:30–5, Sun, 12–5. Admission charged.

This Moravian mission founded by David Zeisberger in 1772 was the first permanent settlement in Ohio. The town grew to more than 60 log buildings and 300 inhabitants. A civil code was enacted and the first Ohio church and schoolhouse constructed. British and American hostilities during the Revolution caused the prosperous town to be abandoned in 1777. Schoenbrunn was eventually destroyed.

The village has been reconstructed and 17 log buildings now stand amid nearly three acres of cultivated fields. The original mission cemetery is at the site.

Springfield

Battle of Piqua (site)
Route 4, one mile west of town.

A stone sculpture of George Rogers Clark, standing with a rifle in front of him, marks the site of the Battle of Piqua. Clark destroyed the Shawnee Indian village in August 1780. The backside of the monument by Charles Keck portrays an Indian warrior instructing a youth in the handling of a bow and arrow.

Wyandot County Historical Society (col)
130 South 7th Street, 419-294-3857; May–Oct: Thurs–Sun, 1–4:30. Admission charged.

The Wyandot Society museum, housed in an 1853 Normandy-style mansion, has displays and artifacts from the Indian and pioneer history of the region, including William Crawford's tragic Sandusky Expedition.

Upper Sandusky

Indian Mill State Memorial (site)
County Highway 50, three miles north of town, 419-294-4022; Memorial Day–Oct: Fri–Sat, 9:30–5, Sun, 1–6. Admission charged.

Colonel William Crawford first befriended surveyor George Washington in the Shenandoah Valley in 1749. When the Revolution started Crawford was long a proponent of invading the Sandusky region to destroy a major base of Tory-Indian raids. Finally, in 1782 such an expedition was authorized. Crawford believed the time for such a mission had long since passed but he grudgingly consented to lead the 500-man force.

Crawford's men assembled at Mingo Bottom on the Ohio River, north of Wheeling, then in Western Virginia. Their 150-mile advance was watched with interest by Captain William Caldwell, who controlled a small army of Mohawk Valley fighters and Indian allies stationed at Detroit. On June 4, 1782, the two opposing forces made contact at Indian Mill. The long-range sniping favored the American militia, but Caldwell was simply fighting a delaying action until reinforcements could reach the area.

Two days later, the fresh British troops arrived, bringing two cannon with them. Threatened with complete destruction, the American force scattered with most eventually reaching a harassed safety. Crawford attempted to make a stand and was captured along with his nephew and son-in-law. The three men were brutally tortured to death in retribution for the Gnadenhutten massacre three months earlier.

The site is preserved in a three-acre park. A museum is maintained in an old gristmill.

Pennsylvania

Revolutionary Status: Original Colony
Estimated Colonial Population: 240,000
Colonial Capital: Philadelphia
Last Colonial Governor: John Penn
Troops Provided: 10 Continental regiments

Revolutionary Timeline:

September 5, 1774: The First Continental Congress convenes in Philadelphia with 56 delegates from every colony but Georgia

May 10, 1775: The Second Continental Congress convenes as John Hancock replaces Peyton Randolph as president

June 15, 1775: Congress offers command of the Continental Army to George Washington, which he accepts the next day

June 22, 1775: Congress prints the first U.S. paper money

January 15, 1776: The first edition of Thomas Paine's *Common Sense* appears; it will sell 100,000 copies in the next 90 days

July 2, 1776: Congress passes Richard Henry Lee's resolution establishing the 13 colonies as an independent nation

July 4, 1776: The Declaration of Independence is approved

September 9, 1776: Congress decrees that the new nation will be referred to as the "United States" and no longer the "United Colonies"

December 25, 1776: Washington crosses the Delaware River with 2,400 troops to surprise Hessian troops in Trenton, New Jersey

June 14, 1776: Congress adopts the design for a new flag: "thirteen stripes alternate red and white, that the Union be thirteen stars white in a blue field"

September 11, 1777: The Americans endure another major defeat at the Battle of the Brandywine, but Washington's army survives

September 16, 1777: British and rain send Washington retreating in Battle of the Clouds

September 19, 1777: Charles Grey ambushes sleeping Americans in Paoli Massacre

September 19, 1777: Continental Congress flees Philadelphia; the British occupy the city a week later

September 30, 1777: Continental Congress takes refuge in York

October 4, 1777: Washington loses the Battle of Germantown but the engagement revives flagging American spirit

November 11, 1777: Americans surrender Fort Mifflin after enduring one of the heaviest bombardments ever to fall on American soil

November 15, 1777: Congress approves John Dickinson's constitution, the Articles of Federation

December 17, 1777: Washington's Army moves to its winter quarters at Valley Forge;

ravaged by disease and malnutrition, one in four Continentals will never march out

February 23, 1778: Prussian drillmaster, Baron von Steuben, arrives at Valley Forge and begins to convert the Continental Army into a professional fighting machine despite not speaking any English

June 18, 1778: British evacuate Philadelphia

July 3, 1778: John Butler slays 166 Americans in Wyoming Massacre

September 17, 1787: Philadelphia Convention approves draft of new Constitution to replace the Articles of Confederation

---

Allentown

Liberty Bell Shrine (site)

622 Hamilton Mall, 610-435-4232; Mon–Sat, 12–4. Free.

The British occupied Philadelphia in 1777 and being short of ammunition the city's bells were prime targets to be melted down into musket and cannonballs. The bell at the Pennsylvania State House — later to be known as the Liberty Bell — and several other important bells were moved 50 miles north to Northampton Town, today Allentown. On September 24, 1777, a train of 700 supply wagons, guarded by 200 cavalryman, arrived at Bethlehem. The Liberty Bell was hidden under the floor of the Zion Reformed Church. The bell stayed in safety until June 1778.

In 1958 an archaeological dig uncovered the exact spot of the Liberty Bell hiding place. The Commonwealth of Pennsylvania presented Allentown with a full-size reproduction of the original, cast in France and weighing more than a ton, for the town's Bicentennial in 1962, and the shrine was born. Today the replica rests where the original was stored, and a 46-foot interactive mural tells about the Liberty Bell's clandestine adventures and other important Pennsylvania events of the Revolution. The "Liberty Bell" is flanked by the flags of the 13 original colonies.

Trout Hall (site)

Fourth and Walnut streets, 610-435-4664; Apr–Nov: Tue–Sat, 12–3, Sunday, 1–4. Free.

Allentown's oldest surviving home was built in 1770 for James Allen, member of an elite British American family and son of the founder of Allentown. He meant for Trout Hall to be a summer residence, an escape from the heat and epidemic illnesses of Philadelphia summers. During the Revolutionary War, James Allen's diminished legal business brought financial problems, while his loyalism brought political woes. The family moved permanently to Allentown, where they entertained British prisoners of war at Trout Hall.

Altoona

Fort Roberdeau (site)

Sinking Valley, northeast of town off I-99, 814-946-0048; May–Oct: Tue–Sat, 11–5, Sun, 1–5. Admission charged.

The "Lead Mine Fort" was established in 1778 to mine lead for the Continental Army. The reconstructed log fort includes enlisted men's barracks, officers' quarters, a lead miner's hut, a blacksmith shop and lead smelters. Nature trails traverse the site.

Bedford

Fort Bedford Museum (site)

Fort Bedford Drive, 814-623-8891; Jun–Aug: daily, 10–5; May, Sept–Oct: Wed–Mon, 10–5. Admission charged.

This outpost along the Forbes Road wilderness trail in the Allegheny Mountains was settled in 1751. The fort was constructed in 1757 during the French and Indian War; Washington used the town as a headquarters when he led Federal troops into Western Pennsylvania in 1794 to end the Whiskey Rebellion.

Bethlehem

Moravian Museum of Bethlehem (site)

66 West Church Street, 610-867-0173; Tue–Sat, 10–4. Admission charged.

The Moravians founded Bethlehem and built the museum building, GermeinHaus, in 1741. It is the oldest of several buildings in the immediate area that served as hospitals during the Revolution. Casualties were brought to Bethlehem from both the New York and Philadelphia areas but few returned — the mortality rate was nearly 50 percent.

Birdsboro

Hopewell Furnace National Historic Site (site)

Route 345, 215-582-8773; Daily, 9–5. Admission charged.

Mark Bird settled along the French Creek in 1771 and built a furnace, adding to his small empire of forges in the area. During the Revolution he turned his production — some 700 tons of pig iron per year at Hopewell alone — to cannons and shot for America. Bird served as colonel in the militia. With the end of hostilities Hopewell once again cast pig iron for stoves and other iron commodities until 1883.

The 848-acre site is one of the finest remaining examples of an early American iron-making community. Many of the restored structures, including the water wheel and charcoal-fueled blast machinery, operate as they did in Colonial times.

Boalsburg

Pennsylvania Military Museum (col)

Route 322, 814-466-6263; Tues–Sat, 9–5. Admission charged.

Benjamin Franklin organized Pennsylvania's first volunteer unit in the Revolutionary War. The tradition of the Pennsylvania citizen-soldier, carried through the Civil War, is preserved in the exhibits at this museum. The 66-acre park around the museum also features monuments and memorials.

Bristol

King George II Inn (site)

102 Radcliffe Street; Open during business hours.

This 1765 structure is the oldest inn in the country in continuous use. It was the headquarters of Patriot general John Cadwalader during the Revolution. Cadwalader crossed the Delaware too late to join the raid at Trenton in December 1776 but joined Washington for the Princeton campaign.

Bryn Mawr

Harriton House (site)

500 Harriton Road, off Old Gulph Road, 610-525-0201; Wed–Sat, 2–4. Admission charged.

Charles Thomson, an Irish orphan, found passage to America at the age of 10. He prospered first as a schoolmaster and then as a merchant before turning to politics. His service as secretary of the Continental Congress spanned the entire pre–Constitutional government, from 1774 until 1789.

The nearby fields were the site of the Battle of Old Gulph Road. In December 1777, a column of 3,000 British soldiers marched out of Philadelphia, engaging Pennsylvania militiamen in gunfire along a 12-mile front from the city to Old Gulph Road. Washington had wanted to camp here for the winter but the action that day convinced him to march on, choosing Valley Forge, 10 miles away.

Harriton was the home of Thomson's second wife, and he lived here until his death in 1824, immersed in Bible translations. The two-story stone house, set on more than 16 acres, dates to 1704.

Carlisle

Carlisle Barracks (site)

Off Claremont Road, east of town, 717-245-3152; Memorial Day–Labor Day: Mon–Fri, 8–4, Sat–Sun, 1–4. Free.

This Colonial ammunition plant was called Washingtonburg when it was constructed in 1776, the first place in America named for George Washington. He would choose the site as the new nation's first arsenal and military school. The Hessian Powder Magazine, a one-story stone structure, was built by German soldiers in 1777 and houses the site's museum.

First Presbyterian Church (site)
Town Square, High and Hanover streets, 717-243-4612.

In this church the citizens of Carlisle selected Scottish-born lawyer James Wilson and Cumberland County prosecutor George Ross as delegates to the Continental Congress in Philadelphia. Both were signers of the Declaration of Independence. Recently expanded, the original structure on Dickinson Alley counted George Washington among its worshippers.

Molly Pitcher Memorial (site)
Old Graveyard; Carlisle Cemetery, East South Street; Open daily, 24 hours.

Mary Ludwig was a sturdy young servant girl in Carlisle who married a local barber, John Caspar Hays. In 1778 when he marched east to join the Revolution, she went along. At the Battle of Monmouth, near Freehold, New Jersey, record-breaking heat seared the battlefield, and Mary Hays carried water to the troops. When her husband was wounded, "Molly Pitcher" seized a ramrod to keep a musket in operation.

Following Hays' death after the Revolution, Mary remarried George McCauley, a wartime comrade who proved to have little to recommend him as a husband. She deserted the marriage and returned to Carlisle, earning her way as a washerwoman and nurse. She lived to be 79, a colorful character around town known to swill whiskey and chew tobacco. Her gravesite is marked by a life-size memorial provided by the Pennsylvania legislature in 1909.

Also interred in the Old Graveyard are two brigadier generals from the Revolution: John Armstrong and William Thompson. Armstrong was a French and Indian War hero who served in the Philadelphia campaign, but the elderly general saw no action. Thompson was a controversial figure who led the 1st Regiment of Pennsylvania Riflemen from central Pennsylvania to join Washington's troops around Boston in July 1775. The undisciplined frontiersmen soon became the scourge of the battlefield — on both sides. Congress promoted Thompson, an Irish surveyor and justice of the peace, to general on March 1, 1776, before Washington could register his dissenting opinion.

Thompson now led reinforcements up the Hudson River into a reckless conflict with the British at Trois-Rivières and was taken prisoner. He was paroled but Congress refused to make a prisoner exchange to allow him to return to the field. He became so mettlesome in his demands for exchange that he was censured by Congress and lost a costly libel suit. Finally, after four years of agitation he was exchanged but died less than a year later.

Catasaqua

George Taylor House (site)
Lehigh & Poplar streets, 610-435-4664; Jun–Oct: Sat–Sun, 1–4. Admission charged.

George Taylor emigrated from Ireland in 1736 at the age of 20 and was an ironworker for most of his life, gaining recognition as a frontier patriot. When several Pennsylvania delegates to the Second Continental Congress did not demonstrate the desired revolutionary fervor by refusing to vote for the Declaration of Independence on July 4, 1777, the elderly Taylor was recruited to sign the document a month later. He left Philadelphia shortly thereafter, his involvement in politics concluded.

His stone house on the Lehigh River, painted white, was built in 1768 as a summer respite from his work in Easton. His principle residence still stands on South 4th Street in that town.

Chadds Ford

Brandywine Battlefield Park (site)

Route 1; one mile east of Route 100, 610-459-3342; Tue–Sat, 9–5, Sun, 12–5. Admission charged for house tours only.

With the British assault on Philadelphia in late summer of 1777, Washington departed Wilmington, Delaware, and prepared his defensive stand along the meandering Brandywine River, backed by strategic hills. On the morning of September 9, the Colonial leader placed his troops in front of the main fords of the river on the road to Philadelphia. But unfortunately his men had not made a complete topographical survey of the area. The British and General Howe had.

On September 11, Howe sent a diversionary force under Lt. Gen. Wilhelm Baron von Knyphausen into the expected attack point across the river in Chadds Ford, while his main force and that of Maj. Gen. Charles Lord Cornwallis forded the river some 12 miles upriver and began to march on the American's right flank. Washington had no knowledge the upstream ford even existed.

British cannons opened fire at 4:00 P.M. Outmaneuvered and confused, the Americans were unable to successfully defend their position. Washington rallied his troops until nightfall, when he was able to retreat with most of his army intact. British captain John André wrote in his journal, "Night and the fatigue the soldiers had undergone prevented any pursuit."

Washington's shattered army lost 11 guns, and 300 men were killed. Twice that number were wounded, including a young 19-year-old Frenchman who had landed in America only three months before the Battle of the Brandywine to volunteer his services. Wealthy nobleman the Marquis de Lafayette was immediately given the rank of major general, despite his complete lack of military experience. He impressed Washington, however, and distinguished himself in his first military action before being struck in the leg. Lafayette would prove instrumental in securing the French-American alliance, which was to sustain the Revolutionaries.

The Battle of the Brandywine was the largest battle of the Revolution. The action spread over ten square miles, although the state park today encompasses but 50 acres. In the park is a small visitor center with artifacts and displays and two stone buildings: Washington's Headquarters (restored) and Lafayette's Quarters (original). The houses are open for guided tours.

A driving tour of the area, described by a British officer as "a hell of a fine country," is available, although there are few interpretive signs and memorials. The scenic drive does, however, wind through much unspoiled countryside, the same terrain that thwarted both armies over 200 years ago.

Reenactment: "Revolutionary Times at Brandywine" has become the major event of the year at the park. There is a day-long battle and demonstrations of life during the Revolution. The date is on the Sunday closest to the September anniversary of the Battle of the Brandywine.

Chester Springs

Historic Yellow Springs (site)
Yellow Springs and Art School roads, off Route 113, 610-827-7414; Mon–Fri, 9–4. Free.

Between 1721 and 1750, patients from Philadelphia began to partake of the mineral springs gurgling up from the grounds west of the city. By 1760 travelers from as far away as the West Indies came to use the bath houses built around the iron and sulfur springs. In 1773, Dr. Benjamin Rush, who would later sign the Declaration of Independence, wrote of the healing water in Yellow Springs, prompting friends — Washington, Monroe, Madison and others — to visit the health spa.

In 1777 a hospital was built at Yellow Springs, and Washington sent his sick soldiers from Valley Forge, five miles away, to the spa. The hospital served the Continental Army until 1781. Yellow Springs is operated today as a 145-acre eighteenth and nineteenth century village. Ruins of the Revolutionary War hospital remain on the grounds.

Cornwall

Cornwall Iron Furnace (site)
Rexmont Road at Boyd Street, 717-272-9711; Tue–Sat, 9–5, Sun, 12–5. Admission charged.

In 1742, a 30-foot sandstone pyramid rose above the Cornwall Ore Banks, then the greatest known deposit of iron yet discovered in Colonial America. The iron furnace built by Peter Grubb was the seventh to be constructed in the province of Pennsylvania, and the first in what is today Lebanon County. At first it produced stoves, kitchenware and tools, but during the Revolution workers learned how to cast cannon, albeit after several initial failures. In 1777, German prisoners helped to cut wood to fuel the great charcoal cold-blast furnaces.

In the 1800s, Cornwall Furnace was the bustling heart of a 10,000-acre "iron plantation," a self-sufficient community that existed solely for the production of cast iron. By 1878, Cornwall was the oldest furnace in America still in operation. But its glory days were running out. In 1883, the now-obsolete charcoal-fired furnace went out of blast forever.

Remarkably, the entire complex has survived. Nowhere else in the United

States, and only a few places in the world, has a colonial furnace been so well-preserved. The charcoal house is now a visitor center with displays demonstrating mining operations, charcoal making and iron making. Particularly striking is a giant 24-foot iron and wood gear, part of the steam-powered mechanism that blasted air into the furnace. One of Cornwall's failed attempts at making a Revolutionary War cannon sits in front of the furnace.

Devon

St. David's Church (site)
Valley Forge Road; Open daily, dusk to dawn.
The churchyard is the final resting place for General Anthony Wayne, in a plot just north of the 1715 stone church. Wayne was originally buried at Fort Presque Isle in Erie upon his death in 1796 but was reinterred here, down the road from his birthplace, in 1809.

Farmington

Fort Necessity National Battlefield (site)
Route 40, 412-329-5512; Daily, 10–5. Admission charged.
In 1753, when the British decided to drive the French from the Ohio Valley, Lt. Gov. Robert Didwiddie of Virginia selected a 21-year-old major, George Washington, to deliver the eviction notice. In the spring of 1754, Washington's vehicles and artillery were the first to cross the Alleghenies. Meanwhile, the French forced a British fort-building detail at the Forks of the Ohio — now Pittsburgh — to desert the area.

Meeting the returning British, Washington learned of the action and interpreted it as an act of war. At Great Meadows on the morning of May 28, Washington and some 60 men surprised a French scouting party and attacked at Jumonville Glen, a wooded area surrounded by 30-foot walls. Ten French, including commander Joseph Coulon de Villiers, Sieur de Jumonville, were killed. Another 21 were taken prisoner, but one man escaped to bring the tale to Fort Duquesne.

Knowing retaliation was certain to come, Washington hastily began to fortify Great Meadows, which he referred to as "Fort Necessity" in a journal entry. The French entered the area on a rainy July 3, buoyed with some 600 troops and 100 Indians. The British trenches filled with water, and after exchanges of small arms fire Washington was induced to surrender and was allowed to withdraw under the honors of war. It was the future Continental Army leader's first command and the start of the French and Indian War.

The reconstructions of the earthworks have risen on their original sites. A visitor center houses exhibits and offers a ten-minute audiovisual presentation. Admission to the park includes access to the fort, Mount Washington Tavern (which served travelers along the National Road), Jumonville Glen and General Edward Braddock's grave.

Fort Washington

Hope Lodge (site)

553 Bethlehem Pike, 215-646-1595; Daily, 9–5. Admission charged.

The eighteenth century Georgian estate was built by Quaker entrepreneur Samuel Morris between 1743 and 1748. During the Revolution, in the fall and winter of 1777-78, Hope Lodge served as Surgeon General John Cochran's headquarters. On the morning of November 2, 1777, Cochran welcomed over 11,000 of George Washington's troops who encamped in the fields surrounding the house.

Sir William Howe left the comfort of Philadelphia to try and lure Washington into battle, but Washington was unwilling to leave his strong position in the hills. Still, the skirmishes convinced the American commander that his position at Whitemarsh was too vulnerable to surprise attack, so on December 11 he began marching his men westward, planning on a winter camp at Gulph Mills. That too would prove untenable and the Continental Army would eventually spend that famous winter at Valley Forge.

Frazer

Battle of the Clouds (site)

Immaculata College; Villa Maria Hall, Route 352 off of Route 30; Open daily, dusk to dawn.

Washington withdrew across the Schuylkill River after retreating from Brandywine but still desired to contest Howe's march on Philadelphia. He recrossed the river and took position on the Swedesford Road, north of the historical marker in front of the Immaculata College administration building. On September 16, as a decisive battle loomed, a torrential rainstorm ruined nearly every musket cartridge recently issued to the Continental Army — 40,000 in all. The British, with properly designed cartridge boxes, forced Washington into retreat again.

The name "Battle of the Clouds" is local, derived from the ridge, the highest ground between Philadelphia and Harrisburg. Otherwise the aborted action is given the name "Admiral Warren" or "White Horse Tavern."

Harrisburg

Paxton Presbyterian Church (site)

Paxtang Boulevard and Sharon Street; Open daily, 24 hours.

The graveyard of the Presbyterian Church, in use since 1740, holds the remains of the Reverend John Elder, the "fighting parson" of the Revolution.

Hartsville

The Moland House (site)

1641 Old York Road, 215-345-6439; Saturday, 9–12. Free.

The historic farmhouse is restored to its appearance in 1777, when General George Washington directed the Continental Army from the farm.

Lancaster

Rock Ford (site)
Lancaster County Park, 881 Rock Ford Road, 717-392-7223. Admission charged.

Irish doctor Edward Hand came to Philadelphia in 1767 with the 18th Royal Irish Regiment. He mustered out in 1774 and set up a medical practice in Lancaster. Taking quickly to the cause of the American rebels, he fought with Washington in 1776 and 1777 and became the Army's adjutant general in 1781. He remained in politics and was appointed inspector of revenue by Washington during his first term as president.

Hand moved into the two-story brick house on the banks of the Conestoga Creek and lived here until his death in 1802 at the age of 58. A museum is also available in the barn.

George Ross (mem)
King and Lime streets.

During the Revolutionary War, Lancaster was the largest inland city in the colonies. As Congress fled from Philadelphia in the fall of 1777 it stopped in Lancaster, making it the U.S. capital for one day. The memorial to George Ross, a Lancaster lawyer and signer of the Declaration of Independence, is at the site of his home.

Ligonier

Forbes Road Gun Museum (col)
Route 711, north of town, 412-238-9544; Daily 9–5. Admission charged.

General John Forbes built a major British stronghold near here in 1758, named for Sir John Ligonier, commander-in-chief of the British Army. The exhibits include the history of the area, war relics and firearms dating to 1450. The fort is reconstructed on Route 30 and contains interpretive exhibits from the site, which was abandoned in 1766.

Malvern

Historic General Warren Inne (site)
West Old Lancaster Highway, 610-296-3637; Open during business hours as a restaurant.

Less than two weeks after the British victory at Brandywine, British soldiers brought a local blacksmith to this public house and tortured him until he revealed the location of General Wayne's nearby secret camp. During the night of September 20-21 the British moved on the camp.

Paoli Massacre Site (site)
Malvern Memorial Park, Monument Road; Open daily, dawn to dusk.
As the American army retreated north from the Brandywine battlefield, Washington ordered a detachment of 1,500 men under General Anthony Wayne to patrol and harass the British. Wayne camped off the main road near Paoli on September 19, but his position was detected by British scouts. The next night British general Howe ordered an attack under Maj. Gen. Charles Grey.

Desiring a surprise bayonet charge, Grey insisted that his men remove the flints from their muskets before the two-hour march so there would be no chance of an accidental shot alerting the Americans. Shortly after midnight, Grey's men burst into the poorly guarded camp and inflicted extreme casualties in a brief flurry. Many Americans were sliced up as they emerged from their shelters and many others died in blazing huts. The British casualties were only four killed and four wounded, while the American toll was over 300.

Grey returned with over 70 prisoners after what had been, to him, standard tactics. The Americans, however, called the slaughter a "massacre" and took to calling Grey "No-Flint Grey" for his barbaric treachery. Wayne was court-martialed for negligence in the affair but acquitted on November 11, and the Americans had still another rallying cry to sustain them in their revolt: "Remember Paoli!"

Much of the events on the night of September 20 took place a half-mile east of the park. Inside a wooden-capped stone wall is a burial mound with the remains of 53 patriots who died in the Paoli Massacre. In the center is a weathered six-foot stone obelisk, now entombed in Plexiglas. Nearby is a 30-foot monument, erected on the centennial in 1877, upon which much of the original's inflammatory rhetoric is carved. Such inscriptions as "cold-blooded cruelty" and "the atrocious massacre which this stone commemorates" were typical descriptions of American defeats during the Revolution.

Nazareth

Jacobsburg Village (site)
435 Belfast Road, 215-759-9029; Apr–Oct: fourth Sunday, 1–5. Free.
William Henry opened a gun factory in 1750. He was armorer for the Braddock Campaign of 1755 and for the Forbes Expedition of 1758. Deeply involved with the political affairs of the American Revolution, Henry became a member of the Continental Congress. His son William II arrived in Northampton County in 1776 and established the long-standing tradition of Henry gunmaking in the Jacobsburg area.

The site of the 1832 Henry House is administered as part of a national historic district by the Jacobsburg Historical Society.

New Milford

Old Mill Village (site)
Route 848, 717-465-3448; Open 12–5 on scheduled event days. Admission charged.

Reenactment: John Sullivan marched through New Milford on his sortie up the Susquehanna River in 1777. An encampment of Selin's Independent Rifle Company, a Revolutionary War unit of riflemen attached to General Sullivan, is presented each year. The village recreates life in eighteenth century northern Pennsylvania.

Newtown

Bird in Hand (site)
111 South State Street, private residence.

George Welch purchased the 1690 home in 1726 to retail "rum and strong liquors by either the gill or small measure." The building contained a public inn for the next 150 years. In February 1778 the British raided the tavern, killing five Continental soldiers and capturing several others. Several Tories lost their lives in the quick skirmish. The current name dates to 1820, when the owner rechristened the tavern with a picture of Franklin's adage, "A bird in the hand is worth two in the bush." William Alexander, Lord Stirling, used the house two doors away as his headquarters while recuperating after the Battle of Trenton.

Old Presbyterian Church (site)
Sycamore Street; Open daily, dawn to dusk.

The church was constructed in 1769, replacing a wooden structure a half-mile to the west, at the instigation of the Reverend James Boyd. Boyd served the community as minister for a half-century. Hessian prisoners were kept in the church following the Battle of Trenton, and 22 Revolutionary War soldiers are buried in the adjoining cemetery.

Site of Washington's Headquarters (site)
2 South Sycamore Street.

The original house, owned by the Widow Hannah Harris and used as General Washington's headquarters, was built in 1757 and torn down in 1863. Washington stayed here before and after the Battle of Trenton in December 1776. In this house he wrote his two famous letters to Congress giving the official report of his victory at Trenton. The rebuilt house was demolished in 1964.

Newville

Colonel Denning State Park (mem)
1599 Doubling Gap Road (Route 233), eight miles north of town, 717-776-5272; Open daily, dawn to dusk. Free.

William Denning, a Revolutionary War veteran for whom the park is named, served as a sergeant in Nathanial Irish's Company of Artillery Artificers. Denning was stationed outside Carlisle at the Washingtonburg Forge, providing armaments for the Continental Army. While at this forge Denning welded strips of wrought iron in successive layers to produce a cannon lighter and less likely to fail during fire than a cast iron cannon.

Unfortunately, none of Denning's cannon have survived, so its appearance can only be imagined from documents. Also left to the imagination is how Sergeant Denning survived into history as "Colonel" Denning. William Denning, regardless of his rank, lived into his 93rd year before passing away in 1830. He is buried in the Big Spring Presbyterian Church in Newville. His monument reads: "Blacksmith and Forger of Wrought Iron Cannon."

Paoli

Waynesborough (site)

2049 Waynesborough Road, off Route 252, 610-647-1779; Mar–Dec: Tue and Thurs, 10–4, Sun, 1–4. Admission charged.

General Anthony Wayne was born in this house on New Year's Day 1745. An adventurous spirit, Wayne was seemingly destined to live out his life as a tanner, as his father had before him, until the Revolution erupted. He gained a commission in the new Continental Army as a colonel on January 3, 1776, and helped lead the American retreat from its spring 1776 Canadian invasion. Placed in charge of Fort Ticonderoga in New York, Wayne weathered impending mutiny and was promoted to brigadier general on February 21, 1777.

Wayne joined Washington and commanded the center of the American line at the Battle of the Brandywine. At Valley Forge, Wayne was so successful in combing the countryside for horses and cattle he became known as "The Drover." Chasing the British across New Jersey, Wayne served with distinction at Monmouth and became a national hero while leading a daring nighttime raid at Stony Point on the Hudson River. Wayne retired to Waynesborough in 1779.

Wayne returned to the field in 1780 at Washington's bequest and eventually took part in the final siege at Yorktown. A decade later, Wayne was fighting on the frontier, most notably in a defeat of Indian forces at Fallen Timbers, Ohio, in 1794. He died in the West in 1796. A century later, Theodore Roosevelt remembered Anthony as one of the greatest fighting generals in American history.

The beautiful brown fieldstone house, the oldest part of which dates to 1724, has been restored to its eighteenth century appearance. In addition to the Wayne family period furnishings, a slide presentation relates the history of the house and the general, nicknamed "Mad Anthony" Wayne.

Philadelphia

Atwater Kent Museum (col)

15 South 7th Street, 215-922-3031; Wed–Sun, 10–4. Admission charged.

The Atwater Kent Museum is the official history museum of Philadelphia, tracing over 300 years of development. With a population of nearly 40,000 at the time of the Revolution, Philadelphia was nearly twice as large as any Colonial city. Many of the museum's 100,000 artifacts relate to Philadelphia's status as the center of the American rebellion.

B. Free Franklin Post Office and Museum (site)
316 Market Street, 215-592-1289; Daily, 9–5. Free.
Still an operational post office, it commemorates Benjamin Franklin's appointment as the first postmaster general in 1775. Although a branch of the U.S. Postal Service, it is the only branch not to fly the American flag. Rather, it carries the name Franklin used, apparently in reference to the struggle for freedom. Thus the hand-canceled letters mailed here carry Franklin's unique signature cancellation. The Postal Museum is on the second floor.

Bell Printing Shop (site)
Thomas Paine Place & South Third Street, historical marker only.
On this site in January 1776, Robert Bell published the first edition of Thomas Paine's revolutionary pamphlet *Common Sense*, arguing for a republican form of government under a constitution.

Benjamin Franklin (mem)
37th Street, east side of Locust Walk.
One of nine memorials to Benjamin Franklin in Philadelphia, this was created by George Loundeen in 1987. Franklin is seated on a bench; the pigeon is part of the statue.

Benjamin Franklin (mem)
Locust Walk, west of 37th Street.
This rendering of Franklin is one of the city's oldest. It was dedicated in 1899, sculpted by John J. Boyle.

Benjamin Franklin and His Kite (mem)
Coxe Park, south side of Cherry Street, east of 22nd Street.
This statue of Franklin celebrates his life as inquisitive scientist. It was created in 1994 by Agnes Yarnell.

Benjamin Franklin, Craftsman (site)
Municipal Services Building, Broad Street and John F. Kennedy Boulevard, north side of City Hall.
Although his contributions as a craftsman of the creation of America are Franklin's lasting legacy, his life as a printer and tinkerer was his soul. This monument by Joseph Brown was erected in 1981.

The Betsy Ross House (site)
239 Arch Street, 215-627-5343; Tue–Sun, 10–5. Free.
In 1870 Elizabeth Griscom became one of the most famous women in America —

34 years after her death. With the American Centennial approaching, a story began circulating about a grandmother who was a seamstress hired to sew the first American flag. The story had been preserved in Betsy Ross's family for generations until her grandson told the tale in public for the first time.

No one had ever been credited with creating the American symbol before, but now historians began collecting information to fuel the myth. Betsy Ross, it seemed, had outlived three husbands. She eloped with John Ross, an upholsterer on Arch Street, in 1773. He died a member of the Pennsylvania militia in early 1776. She took to sewing to support herself and was suggested as a seamstress to the new American Congress by her deceased husband's uncle. Betsy Ross sewed the first Stars and Stripes from a design by Continental Congressman Francis Hopkinson. On June 14, 1777, Congress adopted the new design.

Ross remarried Joseph Ashburn, who died as a prisoner in March of 1782. She took a third husband, John Claypoole, the following year. Still, she continued sewing "naval colors," as flags were called, for nearly 50 years.

A multilevel brick house has been restored in the manner of a Colonial-era working class home in which Betsy Ross might have lived. She is buried in the courtyard beside the house. "American Attic," a play for children, is performed in the courtyard.

Big Ben at Franklin Town (mem)

17th and Vine streets.

This modern homage to Franklin was created by Tom Miles in 1992. It features a giant frame head with four lightning bolts on poles, two gates topped with kites and a series of eight posts which spell out "Franklin."

Carpenters' Hall (site)

320 Chestnut Street, below Fourth Street, 215-925-0167; Mar–Dec: Tue–Sun, 10–4; Jan–Feb: Wed–Sun, 10–4. Free.

The Carpenters' Company, comprised of master builders, banded together in 1724 "for the purpose of obtaining instruction in the science of architecture and assisting such of their members as should by accident be in need of support, or the widows or minor children of members." In 1771 the Carpenters completed an especially attractive guildhall.

In the fall of 1774, delegates from 12 of the original colonies (Georgia declined to attend) arrived in Philadelphia to consider united action to "redress their grievances against the mother country, Great Britain." The Pennsylvania State House was the obvious choice as a meeting place for America's first full Revolutionary body, but Carpenters' Hall, offered by the Company, afforded the deliberations greater secrecy as a privately owned, more neutral building.

For eight weeks the 56 men attempted to find common ground and unity among radicals and conservatives. Before adjourning and returning to their homes and farms, the First Continental Congress pledged support to Boston with a trade embargo against Great Britain and drafted letters to the British people and to King George III. Patrick Henry avowed, "I am not a Virginian, but an

American," as the delegation pledged to reconvene on May 10, 1775, if their grievances were not settled.

Later, in December 1775, Americans John Jay, Benjamin Franklin and Francis Daymon met secretly for three days in the upstairs rooms of Carpenter Hall with French spy Julien Archard De Bonvouloir to negotiate the support of King Louis XVI in their struggle for freedom from the British. It was an especially sensitive situation for the French envoy since his country was at peace with England and he was offering French support to the rebels.

The Carpenters' Company, the nation's oldest trade guild, still maintains the Hall free for the public. In addition to chairs, flags and other artifacts of the Revolution, in the first floor chamber there is a collection of early carpentry tools.

Christ Church (site)

2nd Street between Arch and Market streets, 215-922-1695; Mon–Sat, 9–5, Sun, 1–5. Free.

The Episcopal parish organized in 1695, and in 1727 one of the finest Colonial churches in America was started. When it was completed in 1744, there were few structures as large in the Americas. Benjamin Franklin organized a lottery to outfit the church with bells and a steeple. Its Palladin windows are among the oldest in America.

At the time of the Revolution the 200-foot Christ Church steeple dominated the Philadelphia skyline. While 15 signers of the Declaration of Independence worshiped here the bells were spirited away to Allentown with the Liberty Bell. Their pews are marked with brass plaques.

Seven of those signers are buried at Christ Church. Robert Morris and James Wilson rest in the churchyard, and a few blocks away, at 5th and Arch streets in the Christ Church Burial Ground, are Franklin, Francis Hopkinson, Benjamin Rush, Joseph Hewes and George Ross. Also interred here is Charles Lee, the flamboyant but incompetent (at best) and traitorous (at worst) major general. There are more Colonial and Revolutionary leaders buried at Christ Church than any nonmilitary cemetery in the United States.

City Tavern (site)

2nd and Walnut streets; Open during restaurant hours, daily 11:30 for lunch, 4:00 for dinner.

City Tavern was erected at great expense by voluntary subscription for the "principle gentlemen" of Philadelphia in 1774. It was the informal center for political discussions, business transactions and social events. Many members of the Continental Congress lodged, dined and celebrated here. John Adams called it "the most genteel" tavern in America.

On July 4, 1777 — the first Fourth of July celebration — Congress picked up the tab for both public entertainment and a special dinner for dignitaries at the City Tavern. That day Continental ships and watercraft filled the Delaware River, cheered on by waterfront crowds. A parade and fireworks were presented to the crowd, beginning enduring traditions. At 3 o'clock in the afternoon Congress and other leaders gathered at City Tavern while Hessian prisoners provided the music. Musket volleys mingled with toasts of rum and spirits.

The original tavern building was destroyed in 1874 but was reconstructed for the Bicentennial in 1975. The tavern is again open for dining and features dishes of the Revolution: roast turkey, prime rib, baked ham, meat pies, sausages, salmon, shad, prawns and lobster, as well as tongue, mutton, venison, turtle, woodcock, pigeon and hare.

Cliveden (site)

6401 Germantown Avenue, 215-848-1777; Apr–Dec, Thur–Sun, 12–4. Admission charged.

After embarrassing the Americans at Brandywine in the fall of 1777, General Howe marched on Philadelphia, taking a circuitous westerly route and occupying Germantown, northwest of the central part of the city. He fortified a line of over two miles, stretching across from the Schuylkill River to the west. But when Washington learned that Howe had split his forces, sending some foraging and others south towards Philadelphia, he planned a bold counterattack with the mass of his entire army of 11,000 regulars and militia.

He would attack in four waves. General John Sullivan would march against the British near the river; Nathanael Greene would attack on the opposite flank three miles to the east; and Washington's main force would travel down either side of the Germantown Road in dual thrusts, hoping to shatter the British middle.

The morning of October 4, 1777, broke into dense fog and the attackers could see little more than 75 feet as they advanced on the British. Still, the Americans carried the early battle. Sullivan smashed into an outpost led by Lt. Col. Thomas Musgrave and forced the outnumbered British into a rare retreat. Musgrave and about 120 men holed up in Cliveden, a grey stone building completed about ten years before as a country retreat for Colonial chief justice of Pennsylvania, Benjamin Chew.

Sullivan continued to harass the British line, but his support from Greene never materialized — he had become lost in the fog. Meanwhile, the main force approaching down the Germantown Road encountered the British-fortified Cliveden. General Henry Knox demanded Musgrave's surrender. When he refused, Knox, following traditional military procedures, ordered an assault on the house, although Cliveden was now isolated impotently behind American lines. The Continental six-pound cannon shells had no effect on the thick stone walls. A frontal charge achieved only American dead. They attempted to burn the British out, but there was little that was flammable in the building.

But there were even greater ramifications of the fruitless half-hour assault than loss of time and American lives. Hearing musket fire behind them, Adam Stephen from Greene's flanking assault violated orders and marched toward the sound. Through the still foggy morning air his troops began firing on American General Anthony Wayne's troops. The chaos disintegrated Greene's advance as Sullivan was running out of ammunition. The Americans broke in disorganized retreat.

Still, the Battle of Germantown buoyed the spirits of the Americans. If they had not defeated Howe's army, they had at least been on the verge of winning a great victory. More importantly, Washington's audacious strike convinced European observers of American commitment to freedom. French military assistance would be shortly forthcoming.

The house that withstood American onslaught stands today, having remained in the Chew family for over 200 years. Tours reveal original Chippendale and Federal-style furniture from its days as a pre–Revolution summer home. Benjamin Chew refused to endorse either side in the conflict and was jailed for a time in 1777. He once again became a justice in Pennsylvania after the war, serving until 1808, two years before his death.

A small visitor center displays a map of the Battle of Germantown, most of which is an urban area today. The main house, with its battle-scarred walls, is fronted by garden statuary, including two stone lions on the doorstep, which observed the events of the morning of October 4, 1777.

Reenactment: The Battle of Germantown is reenacted on the first Saturday in October. Continental troops again march down Germantown Avenue and chased the British into the sanctuary of Cliveden.

CoreStates First Pennsylvania Bank (site)
16th and Market streets, 215-786-5980; Mon–Fri, 9–5. Free.

In the Bank of North America Room is a reconstruction of the original office established in 1782 by Robert Morris, financing officer of the Revolutionary government. The room features eighteenth century furnishings and artifacts.

Declaration House (site)
7th and Market streets, 215-597-8974; Daily, 10–3. Free.

While Jacob Graff, a modest stonemason, lived on the ground floor of his townhouse, a studious Virginian boarder upstairs was crafting the most influential document in American history. At 33, Thomas Jefferson was the second youngest delegate to the Second Continental Congress in 1776, but he was one of five selected to work on a resolution of independent government. In the end, John Adams thought Jefferson best suited for the task of authorship. Jefferson, reasoned Adams, was a Virginian and the declaration should come from a Virginia man. Further, Adams considered himself too obnoxious a presence to shepherd the document to approval and, finally, he thought Jefferson to be a far superior writer than himself.

Jefferson worked on his draft from June 11 until June 28, 1776. He wrote completely from memory, borrowing phrases and ideas and adding his own ideals. What emerged was dissected by Congress before being passed by a vote on July 2. The names of the signers were kept secret until January 18, 1777, after the successful battles of Trenton and Princeton.

Declaration House is a reconstruction. The two rooms that Jefferson rented upstairs have been recreated to invoke Jefferson's life. His passion for music, for instance, is represented by a violin. A film on Jefferson's time in Philadelphia is screened.

Deshler-Morris House (site)
5442 Germantown Avenue, 215-596-1748; Apr–Dec: Tue–Sun, 1–4. Admission charged.

The Germantown Road was the main route to Reading, Bethlehem and the northwest in Colonial days and has been declared a national historical landmark. George Washington visited the area often, both on personal affairs and in preparing the defenses of Philadelphia. This was Washington's residence in Germantown in the fall of 1793 and the summer of 1794. Built in 1772, the house has been restored to that era.

Fort Mifflin (site)
Fort Mifflin Road at the foot of Island Avenue, off I-95, 215-685-4192; Apr–Nov: Wed–Sun, 10–4. Admission charged.

British engineer Captain John Montresor applied his genius to the defenses of the Delaware River in 1771. On the western shore south of Philadelphia he laid out stone walls and against his southern exposure. But formidable Fort Mud became an American stronghold in the fall of 1777, when it was occupied by Lt. Col. Samuel Smith and renamed for Maj. Gen. Thomas Mifflin.

But the river assault by the British on Philadelphia never materialized. General William Howe succeeded in taking the leading Colonial city overland on September 26. But the prize would be worthless without the capture of Fort Mifflin, which impeded British supplies from coming up the river. Howe turned to the master builder Montresor to dismantle the fortifications he had once built.

Montresor's first bombardment began on October 15. The guns at Fort Mifflin easily turned the British back. Heavy rains further deterred the attackers as they laid siege to the fort. The doomed fate of the Americans was certain, however, as Montresor prepared batteries against the unprotected land side of Fort Mifflin — an inconceivable threat only six years earlier.

By November 9 the batteries on nearby Providence Island were ready: two 32-pounders, six 24-pounders, one 18-pounder and many lesser guns were leveled at Fort Mifflin. Also in the artillery were two floating batteries. The bombardment began on November 10. American guns were silenced but the defenders fought valiantly. By November 15 seven British ships joined the assault. At its height 1,000 British cannonballs rained on the fort every 20 minutes. Finally the Americans deserted Fort Mifflin after one of the most memorable defensive stands ever made on American soil.

President John Adams ordered Fort Mifflin rebuilt in 1798 and it remained in use as late as 1962. The 13 restored buildings are mostly interpreted from the 1800s, but the tours and demonstrations cover its Revolutionary origins. The riverside is original and much of the 1770s foundation was used in the reconstruction 20 years later.

Franklin Court (site)
Between Market and Chestnut streets and 3rd and 4th streets, 215-597-1785; Daily, 9–5. Free.

For most of his life, Benjamin Franklin — publisher, inventor, scientist, diplomat, writer — was too busy to build a house of his own. Nearing 60, he began to incorporate his many ideas into a brick house, set off the main streets to afford him views of gardens and grassy spaces. Before he could finish his retreat he was sent to England on behalf of the colonies in the 1760s. He would not return for more than a decade and could only follow the progress of the house in letters from his wife Deborah.

By the time he returned to Philadelphia his wife had died and the Revolution afforded him little time to enjoy his new home. Soon he was back in Europe. After the war ended he was finally able to live in his home, now filled with grandchildren from his daughter's family. Franklin died here in 1790.

The property has been imaginatively developed in a manner befitting Franklin's genius. The house was torn down by his descendants in 1812 but a "ghost house" designed by Robert Venturi depicts Franklin's home. Archaeological remnants of the original building can be viewed underground at four observation stations.

Around his house Franklin purchased five tenant homes in 1786, which have been maintained in exterior appearance. The interior of one has been gutted, except for a wall with detailed archaeological explanations that can be viewed in striking contrast from a five-story steel walkway. Another building features the "Aurora," a reproduction of a newspaper office, complete with a 1785 printing press and bindery.

The complex includes an underground theater that contains Franklin possessions, and his varied endeavors are on display in an impressive audiovisual presentation. A short film reviews Franklin's productive life in Philadelphia after he arrived from Boston as a young man in 1722.

Franklin Institute Science Museum (col)
20th Street and Benjamin Franklin Parkway, 215-448-1200; Daily, 9:30–5. Admission charge.

One of America's leading science centers, the museum is home to the Benjamin Franklin National Memorial and presents many of Franklin's personal possessions. The colossal statue of Franklin in the rotunda was executed by James Earle Fraser.

General Anthony Wayne (mem)
Philadelphia Art Museum, 26th Street and Benjamin Franklin Parkway.

John Gregory designed this rendering of General Wayne in Colonial military uniform riding on a prancing horse. The horse's right front leg is raised high in the air. The gilded bronze was dedicated on September 17, 1937.

General Francesco de Miranda (mem)

20th Street, the Benjamin Franklin Parkway and Winter Street.

Miranda was a freedom fighter from Caracas, Venezuela, who served in the American Revolution, the French Revolution and the emancipation of Latin America. Of him, John Adams said, "Miranda knew more of the families, and connections in the United States, than any other man in them ... he knew more of every campaign, siege, battle and skirmish that had ever occurred in the whole war, than any other officer in our army, or any statesman in our councils."

Germantown Historical Society (col)

5501-03 Germantown Avenue, 215-844-0514; Mon–Fri, 1–5, Sun, 10–4. Admission charged.

Germantown was founded in 1683 when William Penn deeded an area six miles northwest of Center City Philadelphia to a group of German settlers. The society maintains a museum featuring Revolutionary war artifacts from the Battle of Germantown, an extensive research library and a cadre of 12 historic homes.

Historical Society of Pennsylvania (col)

1300 Locust Street, 215-732-6200; Tue, Thurs–Sat, 10–5, Wed, 1–9. Admission charged.

The exhibit "Finding Philadelphia's Past" is a multimedia exploration of 500 items documenting the town's history from the 1660s. Among the Revolutionary items on display are George Washington's desk, Charles Wilson Peale's portrait of Benjamin Franklin, and James Wilson's handwritten draft of the Constitution.

Independence Hall (site)

Chestnut Street, between 5th and 6th streets, 215-597-8974; Daily, 9–5. Free.

The most famous building in America had outlived its usefulness in 1816 and was scheduled to be torn down. Some Philadelphia citizens saw historical value in the old Pennsylvania State House, built in 1732, and lobbied for its preservation.

The sometimes nefarious business of Pennsylvania was conducted in this brick building with its spacious hallways and flanking wings, beginning in 1735. In 1775 the Pennsylvania Assembly moved upstairs, relinquishing its assembly room to a new body, the Second Continental Congress, who hammered out a Declaration of Independence here and chose a Virginia farmer named George Washington to head the Continental Army. Washington would return in 1787 and lead another congregation into forming a totally new government in the world under a written constitution. Here he became America's first president.

The Pennsylvania State House was saved, known thereafter as Independence Hall.

Visitation to Independence Hall is by tour only. The assembly room has been restored to look as it did when the Founding Fathers debated here from 1775 through 1787. Some furniture, including Washington's influential "rising sun" chair, are original. Other rooms housing Revolutionary government functions have also been restored. A statue of George Washington faces America from the front of Independence Hall. It was sculpted by Joseph Alexis Bailly in 1869.

Reenactment: The city of Philadelphia sponsors a week-long "Welcome America!" celebration before July 4. The Declaration of Independence is read on the 4th by the mayor at Independence Hall. Descendants of the signers of the Declaration of Independence touch the Liberty Bell to begin a national bell-ringing ceremony.

Independence National Historical Park (col)
3rd and Chestnut streets, 215-597-8974; Daily, 9–5. Free.

The visitor center features exhibits on America's struggle for freedom, including the 28-minute film *Independence*, directed by John Huston. Information on Philadelphia's historical area and tickets to several of the buildings administered by the park in the four-block area can be obtained at the center. The Bicentennial Bell, a gift to America from the British people, hangs in the visitor center's 130-foot bell tower. A variety of walking tours originate from the visitor center.

Independence Square (site)
Walnut Street between 5th and 6th streets; Open daily, 24 hours.

Demonstrations of liberty were commonplace in the square during the mid–1770s. The Declaration of Independence was first read from here to the public by Colonel John Nixon on July 8, 1776. A statue of Commodore John Barry, the "Father of the Navy," graces the center of the grassy park.

Reenactment: A highly entertaining reading of the Declaration of Independence takes place in the square every July 8, complete with hecklers and slaves protesting their lack of representation in the proclamation.

Liberty Bell Pavilion (site)
5th, 6th, Market and Chestnut streets, 215-597-8974; Daily, 9–5. Free.

Colonial leaders ordered a bell from a London foundry in 1751 to honor the 50th anniversary of William Penn's Charter of Privileges. Weighing nearly 2,000 pounds, the bell was delivered the following year. It bore an inscription from Leviticus around its crown: "Proclaim Liberty throughout all the Land unto all the Inhabitants Thereof." In spite of this engraving the bell was not known as the Liberty Bell until 1839, when it was associated with the abolitionist movement.

The bell was tested and cracked. It was recast locally and rung on public occasions from the bell tower in the Pennsylvania State House, including the first reading of the Declaration of Independence on July 8, 1777. It was spirited away and hidden in Allentown during the British occupation of Philadelphia. Upon its return the bell continued to be rung during special events. It cracked again during Chief Justice John Marshall's funeral in 1835 and was silenced forever after a ringing on Washington's birthday in 1846.

Still, no one ever considered this bell a symbol of the American Revolution. In 1847 a Philadelphian penned a fictional account of an ancient Patriot waiting to ring the bell on July 4, 1776. The story popularized the bell, which was moved to the first floor of Independence Hall in 1852. It remained on display there, except for periodic trips around the country, until being moved to its current home in front of Independence Hall during the Bicentennial in 1976.

In 1950, 53 replicas of the Liberty Bell were cast in France and given to the U.S. government by several private corporations. The dimensions and tone are identical to the 1776 original. Many are displayed on state capital grounds around the country.

The Liberty Bell rests in a glass structure and can be viewed when the pavilion is not open. During visiting hours park rangers tell stories about the bell's history.

Market Square (site)

5500 block of Germantown Avenue; Open daily, 24 hours. Free.

A marker denotes the center of the British line during the Battle of Germantown on October 4, 1777. The artillery was parked here. The left wing extended along Schoolhouse Road to Ridge Road. The right wing extended along Church Lane, comprising the command of Brig. Gen. Matthews and the fearsome Grenadier Guards.

Mount Pleasant (site)

Fairmount Park, Fountain Green at 35th Street and Columbia Avenue, 215-684-7922; Tue–Sun, 10–4. Admission charged.

Benedict Arnold rose from humble beginnings to enjoy society life as a successful merchant. His desperation to maintain that garish lifestyle led him to the treasonous plan of selling West Point to the British. His love of the finer things in life led him to Mount Pleasant, which he purchased on March 22, 1779, while serving as commandant of Philadelphia after the British deserted the city in June 1778. John Adams had called the ornate Georgian mansion, first built for a Scottish privateer in 1763–64, "the most elegant seat in Pennsylvania."

Arnold had an eye for more than fine houses; he married 19-year-old Peggy Shippen, reputedly the most beautiful woman in Philadelphia, a month later. But the Arnolds never lived in Mount Pleasant, although other family members resided there. It was at this time he began his notorious negotiations with the British, which would cause the state to confiscate the house in 1780. It passed through several other hands, including Arnold's again through a secret repurchase through his father-in-law, until the city of Philadelphia bought it in 1868.

National Archives — Mid-Atlantic Branch (col)

United States District Courthouse & Post Office, 9th & Chestnut streets, 215-597-3000; Mon–Fri, 8–5, second Saturday of each month, 8–4. Free.

Compiled military service records for the Revolutionary War period are fragmentary because many of the original records were lost in a fire on November 8, 1800, in the offices of the secretary of war. Still more records were lost when the British ransacked Washington in 1814. What remains are available through the National Archives. The Mid-Atlantic Branch houses records and pictures from the states of Delaware, Pennsylvania, Maryland, Virginia and West Virginia.

New Hall Military Museum (col)

Chestnut Street between 3rd and 4th streets, 215-597-8974; Daily, 9–5. Free.

Housed in a restored 1791 building in front of Carpenters' Hall, the two floors of exhibition space trace the origins of the American Marines, Army and Navy. The building was the nation's first War Office, the direct ancestor of the Pentagon, run by just six employees.

A timeline spiced with artifacts traces the history of America's sea force from November 10, 1775, when Congress resolved to raise two battalions of marines and named Philadelphian Samuel Nicholas its captain. The first Continental fleet was ready by 1776 and featured the *Alfred, Columbus, Cabot, Andrew Doria, Providence, Hornet, Fly* and *Wasp*. Ship models include the brig *Raleigh*, the first to carry the Stars and Stripes into action on August 12, 1777. The *Raleigh* was lost in Penobscot Bay in September 1778.

The museum also recognizes the 5,000 black soldiers — both slave and free — who fought in the Revolutionary Army and Navy. Ironically, their new country would exclude blacks from the military until the Civil War.

Old Pine Street Presbyterian Church (site)

412 Pine Street, 215-925-0821; Sunday service, 10:30. Free.

The only Colonial Presbyterian church in Philadelphia was designed by Robert Smith and home to John Adams and Dr. Benjamin Rush. The church sent 75 men to the Revolutionary forces.

Old St. Joseph's Church (site)

321 Willings Alley, off Walnut Street between 3rd and 4th streets, 215-923-1733; Mon–Fri, 9–5, Sat, 10–6, Sun, 9–3:30. Free.

Philadelphia's first Roman Catholic church was organized on this site by the Jesuits in the 1730s, although the original building has been replaced by a church constructed nearly a century later. The Marquis de Lafayette was among the important Revolutionary figures to worship here.

Old St. Mary's Church (site)

252 South 4th Street, 215-923-7930; Mon–Fri, 9–5, Sun, 8–1. Free.

St. Mary's, established in 1763, was the preeminent Catholic church in Philadelphia during the Revolution, hosting Washington, Adams and other members of the First Continental Congress at Sunday Vespers. Among those buried in the cemetery are Commodore John Barry and General Stephen Moylan.

Philadelphia Museum of Art (mem)

Rear walkway above Kelly Drive.

When General William Reilly of the Pennsylvania National Guard died in 1890, his will provided for monuments to honor the leaders of the American Revolution. By 1938 the fund had accumulated enough money to begin work on the project. The first four to be memorialized were volunteers from other lands who "threw themselves into the cause of emancipating the colonies from the yoke of British tyranny": Richard Montgomery (1946) by J. Wallace Kelly; Marquis de Lafayette (1947) by Raoul Josset; Casimir Pulaski (1947) by Sidney Waugh; and Frederick von Steuben (1947) by Warren Wheelock. John Paul Jones, by Walter Hancock, was added in 1957. The final addition to the walkway leading from the Schuylkill River was Nathanael Greene by Lewis Iselin, Jr., in 1960. It bears Greene's words: "We fight, get beat, rise, and fight again." Also along the back steps of the museum is a rendering of Peter Muhlenberg by J. Otto Schweig, erected in 1910.

Polish American Cultural Center Museum (col)

308 Walnut Street, 215-922-1518; Mon–Sat, 10–4. Free.

The focus of the museum is a portrait gallery of "Great Men and Women of Poland." Included are two Polish Revolutionary heroes, Thaddeus Kosciuszko and Casimir Pulaski, "Father of the American Cavalry." Pulaski was a Polish patriot bitter about the inability of his homeland to wrest itself from Russian rule. He came to America with a letter of introduction from Benjamin Franklin and immediately found action at the Battle of Brandywine. After distinguishing himself as a volunteer aide-de-camp to Washington, he was commissioned four days later as a brigadier general with four regiments in his command. Included in the artifacts on display is the Pulaski Banner, sewn by the Moravian Sisters of Bethlehem, which is the earliest documented use of the monogram "U.S."

The Powel House (site)

244 South Third Street, 215-627-0364; Jun–Aug: Thur–Sat, 12–5, Sun, 1–5; Sep–May: Thur–Sat, 12–4, Sun, 1–4. Admission charged.

In 1769 Samuel Powel, working from an inherited fortune, completed one of the most magnificent Colonial dwellings in Philadelphia. Samuel and Elizabeth Willing Powel soon gained a reputation as the preeminent hosts in the second largest city in the British empire. The social whirl of the Continental Congress centered in the Powel home. The Washingtons danced here on their wedding anniversary and John Adams praised the house as "a splendid seat."

Samuel Powel was elected Philadelphia's last Colonial mayor from 1775 to 1776 and its first mayor under the new constitution in 1789. Tours highlight the elegance that could be enjoyed amidst the turmoil of the American Revolution.

Revolutionary Soldier (mem)

East River Drive.

Erwin Frey crafted the standing figure with a three-corner hat and boots. He holds a rifle by his side with the proper hand, his right hand.

Robert Morris (mem)

North side of Walnut Street, between 4th and 5th streets.

The monument honors the contributions to the economic genius behind the Revolution. It reads: "Robert Morris, Patriot, Statesman, Financier."

The Rush House Site (site)

Walnut and Third Streets.

Dr. Benjamin Rush was among the most influential of early Americans in disciplines ranging from medicine to politics. He served as a Continental Congress delegate and signed the Declaration of Independence. Later, Rush published the first treatise on mental illness in America. His three-story townhouse has been destroyed and is memorialized by a small city park.

St. Peter's Church (site)

3rd and Pine streets, 215-925-5968; Sat, 11–3, Sun, 1–3. Free.

This elegant Georgian brick Episcopal church remains virtually unchanged from its construction in 1761, including the original box pews. Washington worshipped in Pew #41, sitting with Colonial mayor Samuel Powel. The churchyard is the final resting place for Lt. Col. John Nixon, a church founder who was chosen to give the first public reading of the Declaration of Independence; Benjamin Chew, owner of Cliveden, where the Battle of Germantown was concentrated; and Gustavus Conyngham, captain of the privateer *Surprise*.

Second Bank of the United States (col)

420 Chestnut Street, 215-597-8974; Daily, 9–5. Admission charged.

On display are nearly 200 eighteenth and early nineteenth century portraits thath comprise the Independence National Park National Portrait Gallery, including many Revolutionary political and military legends. The bank is an impressive Greek Revival edifice completed in 1824.

The Signer (mem)

5th and Chestnut streets.

This 1980 sculpture honors the courage of those who affixed their names to the Declaration of Independence and the U.S. Constitution. Evangelos Frudakis sculpted the bronze figure, which is placed on a granite pedestal.

Stenton Mansion (site)

18th Street and Windrim Avenue, 215-329-7312; Mar–Dec: Tue–Sat, 1–4. Admission charged.

James Logan, a secretary to William Penn and a scientist and Indian nego-
tiator, built this two-and-a-half story brick home, which General Sir William
Howe used as headquarters during the Battle of Germantown prior to the occupation of Philadelphia by the British. The furnishings reflect eighteenth and
nineteenth century Philadelphia.

Thaddeus Kosciuszko (mem)
18th Street and Benjamin Franklin Parkway.
The rendering of the great Polish freedom fighter was presented by Poland
to the American people to commemorate 200 years of independence. Marion
Konieszny envisioned Thaddeus Kosciuszko dressed in Colonial military cos-
tume with hands and arms pulled behind his back.

Thaddeus Kosciuszko National Memorial (site)
Third and Pine streets, 215-597-9618; Jun–Oct: daily, 9–5; Nov–May:
Wed–Sun, 9–5. Free.
Thaddeus Kosciuszko, born of impoverished landed gentry in eastern Poland,
arrived in America shortly after the adoption of the Declaration of Independence
in the summer of 1776. Educated in Warsaw and Paris in military engineering
but lacking in practical military experience, the 30-year-old Kosciuszko offered
his service to the Colonial rebellion. On October 18, 1776, Congress passed a
resolution that "Thaddeus Kosciuszko, Esq., be appointed an engineer in the
service of the United States, with the pay of sixty dollars a month, and the rank
of colonel." For the remainder of the war he would play a part in virtually every
theater of action.

Kosciuszko planned the nearby fortifications along the Delaware River and
so impressed General Horatio Gates that he was entrusted to select and fortify
the Bemis Heights overlooking the Hudson River near the village of Saratoga.
His cunning defenses led directly to the surrender of 6,000 British troops on
October 17, 1777, influencing the French to intervene on the side of the revolutionaries.

He next set about fortifying the bluffs at West Point to protect the Hudson
Highlands against the British Navy. Kosciuszko toiled for 28 months to construct the permanent fortifications, including a 60-ton chain stretched across
the river, that earned West Point the nickname "the Gibraltar of America." The
British never risked an assault.

Hungering for a more active role in the Revolution, Kosciuszko headed south
under General Greene, designing a fleet of flat-bottomed boats to help the American troops maneuver through the Carolina lowlands. Finally, in the final major
conflict of the war, at Yorktown, Kosciuszko commanded a regiment in battle.
His service in the Continental Army ended in 1783, when Congress promoted
him to the rank of brigadier general.

Kosciuszko returned to Poland and led resistance to Czarist Russia's domi-
nation over Poland in the 1790s. The insurrection failed and a badly wounded
Kosciuszko was jailed before being released in 1796 on the condition he never

again return to Poland. Partially paralyzed, he sailed back to Philadelphia and took rented rooms on the second floor of a boarding house at Third and Pine streets. He stayed for nine months, receiving distinguished visitors who came to pay tribute to the "hero of Poland." He returned to Europe on May 5, 1798, settling in Switzerland and working for Polish freedom until his death on October 15, 1817.

The outside of the Colonial townhouse has been restored, and the small museum describes Kosciuszko's achievements through exhibits and audiovisual displays in both English and Polish. Upstairs, the simple bedroom has been restored as a tribute to the man whose fame, William Henry Harrison said, "will last as long as liberty remains upon the earth."

Todd House (site)

4th and Walnut streets, 215-597-8974; Daily, 9–5. Free.

Dolly Payne Todd, who would become First Lady as James Madison's wife, lived here during her first marriage to John Todd, Jr. Todd bought the 1776 house in 1791. Between 1796 and 1807 it was the home of Colonel Stephen Moylan, a close Revolutionary associate of George Washington. Artifacts from his life are on display during free house tours. Tickets are available at the Independence Mall visitor center.

Tomb of the Unknown Soldier (site)

Washington Square, 6th to 7th streets on Walnut Street; Open daily, 24 hours.

The only tomb in the United States erected to the memory of unknown Revolutionary soldiers decorates one of Philadelphia's original five squares. An eternal flame installed during the Bicentennial of 1776 honors the soldiers' remains in Washington Square. The statue of Washington in the square is a copy of the famous execution by Houdoun and bears the inscription: "In unmarked graves within this square lie thousands of unknown soldiers of Washington's army who died of wounds and sickness during the Revolutionary War."

Upper Burial Ground (site)

6300 block of Germantown Avenue; Open by appointment.

Next to the Concord Schoolhouse — a 1775 one-room schoolhouse with its original belfry and bell — is a graveyard of weathered headstones marking the resting place of 57 Revolutionary soldiers who gave their lives in the Battle of Germantown.

Upsala (site)

6430 Germantown Avenue, 215-842-1798; Tue and Thurs, 1–4. Admission charged.

This Federal-style home was the site of an American encampment during the Battle of Germantown. It is part of the annual reenactment that takes place across the street at Cliveden.

Washington Monument (mem)
Eakins Oval, 24th Street and Benjamin Franklin Parkway.

The heroic equestrian statue of Washington was dedicated in 1897, 87 years after the plans were initiated. It is the work of Rudolf Siemering, who created three zones of layers: the hero Washington is at the top, period allegorical figures are below and human representations are at the bottom.

Pittsburgh

Flag Monument (mem)
Schenley Park, Circuit Road and Schenley Drive.

In 1927, to celebrate the 150th anniversary of the American flag, school children in Pittsburgh collected 188,163 pennies in four weeks to create this bronze and granite monument. It was executed by Harvey Schwab.

George Washington (mem)
West Park.

This large equestrian statue of George Washington features fine details carved, despite the hard stone, by Edward Ludwig Albert Pausch. When the statue was dedicated in 1891, the parade to honor the "Father of our Country" was so extensive it required two hours to pass the viewing stand.

George Washington (mem)
Alexander M. Scott High School, Library Road.

A youthful George Washington standing on the site of the Battle of Monongahela was sculpted by Frank Vittor and dedicated on July 9, 1930. Washington served as aide-de-camp to General Edward Braddock in the battle around this site 175 years earlier. A relief attached to the base depicts six revolutionary soldieers pushing a cannon into position.

Jefferson Memorial Park (mem)
Curry Hollow Road.

Frank Vittor created a life-size bronze of Thomas Jefferson inside 30-foot Corinthian columns, once part of a prominent Pittsburgh bank. Also in the park is a copy of Houdon's "George Washington."

Soldiers and Sailors Memorial Hall (col)
Fifth Avenue and Bigelow Boulevard, 412-621-4253; Mon–Fri, 9–4 and Sat–Sun, 1–4. Free.

The 1910 building was modeled after the Mausoleum of Halicarnassus, one of the seven ancient wonders of the world. The massive base — made of Rhode Island granite — covers an entire city block. Inside are historical military exhibits, including the Revolutionary War. Film presentations are also offered.

Reading

Historical Society of Berks County (col)
940 Centre Avenue, 610-375-4375; Tue–Sat, 9–4. Admission charged.
Included in the collection is the county liberty bell that was rung on July 8, 1776.

Schwenksville

Pennypacker Mills (site)
Skippack Pike (Route 73) and Haldeman Road, 610-287-9349; Tue–Sat, 10–4, Sunday, 1–4. Free.
Washington's army encamped on these sprawling farmlands in late September, before the Battle of Germantown, and retreated there following the battle. The property is now operated as a 130-acre gentleman's estate.

Scranton

Soldiers and Sailors Monument (mem)
Court House Square.
The 60-foot shaft of granite was dedicated on November 15, 1900. Atop the center pillar is a female figure representing the Goddess of Victory.

Sunbury

Northumberland County Historical Society (col)
Hunter House, 1150 North Front Street, 717-286-4083; Mon, Wed, Fri, Sat, 1–4. Free.
The Northumberland Society maintains a museum with exhibits pertaining to Fort Augusta, Pennsylvania's largest frontier fort, thought to be named for King George III's mother. Fort Augusta, on the Susquehanna River, was so large it was never attacked; instead, it evolved into an important base for traders and trappers. During the Revolution, General John Sullivan marched against the Iroquois in 1779 from Fort Augusta. The underground powder magazine from the 1756 fort remains.

Towanda

Bradford County Historical Society Museum (col)
21 Main Street, 717-265-2240; Thur–Sat, 10–4. Free.
The Revolutionary War expedition of John Sullivan traversed the wilderness of Bradford County. After the war many of those soldiers returned to the

Endless Mountains as settlers. The museum has a collection of Revolutionary War memorabilia.

Uniontown

General Lafayette (mem)

Fayette County Courthouse.

This memorial to the young French leader of the American Revolution was crafted of painted wood by David Gilmour Blythe. Larger than life, the poplar planks are pinned together and his high hat is fashioned from tin.

Valley Forge

Valley Forge National Historical Park (site)

Route 23, 610-783-1077; Daily: park, 8–10 p.m.; visitor center and museum, 9–5. Admission charged only for General Washington's headquarters.

In the fall of 1777, after failing to hold the Continental capital of Philadelphia, General George Washington began his search for winter quarters. His selection of the tiny village of Valley Forge, named for an ironworks built along the Valley Creek in the 1740s, bore political and military scars.

Washington had been informed that his support from the Pennsylvania militia, upon whom he depended heavily, would evaporate if he retreated more than 25 miles from British-occupied Philadelphia. Valley Forge, 18 miles northwest of the city, was close enough to harass the invaders, yet far enough away to remove the threat of British surprise attacks. In addition, Washington could place his army between the British and the temporary headquarters of the Continental Congress in York, Pennsylvania.

Nearly 12,000 Continentals, weary from marching and battlefield setbacks, struggled into Valley Forge on December 19, 1777, as snow began to fall. Immediately they fortified the defensive position and sheltered the troops. Washington protected himself to the rear with the Schuylkill River and dug miles of trenches along the high ridges facing Philadelphia. Within a month more than 1,000 wooden huts had been built for the men.

Although the winter was comparably mild, more than 2,000 men perished in the primitive conditions. Promised provisions from Congress never arrived, and rations from the individual states were sporadic. The Colonials survived by scavenging the countryside while the British wintered comfortably in Philadelphia. Only the men's fierce loyalty to Washington held the army together.

On February 23, 1778, a former Prussian officer arrived at Valley Forge with a letter of introduction from Benjamin Franklin. Friedrich Wilhelm von Steuben was immediately assigned the duties of acting inspector general with the task of developing and carrying out an effective training program. Although the Continental Army had been in the field over two years, it was still ill-equipped for consistent success in battle.

Von Steuben broke English tradition by working directly with the men, drilling the units from dawn to dusk. He spoke little English and drafted his own training manual in French, which was translated into English late at night. The resulting "Blue Book" took its place alongside the Bible as required reading in camp. Under von Steuben's direction the American Army was born at Valley Forge.

The ordered ranks, martial appearance and revived spirit helped gain French recognition for the Revolutionaries on May 6, 1778. It was a formidable Continental Army that marched from Valley Forge on June 19 to pursue the British across New Jersey and drive them away from the colonies.

In 1777 the largest city in North America was Philadelphia with 40,000 people; New York numbered 19,000. By the spring of 1778, in just a few winter months, Valley Forge became a town of 20,000 people. Today the park preserves that history on 3,600 acres.

The visitor center features the George C. Neumann Collection, an extensive display of period weapons, and an 18-minute film on the encampment. Artifacts are also on view at the Washington Memorial Chapel in the park. A ten-mile self-guided driving tour includes the National Memorial Arch, reconstructed huts and demonstrations, and an overlook of the Grand Parade, where von Steuben drilled the troops. Preserved buildings include the Isaac Potts House, which Washington used as his headquarters.

Washington Crossing

Washington Crossing Historic Park (site)

Route 32, 215-493-4076; Tue–Sat, 9–5, Sun, 12–5. Admission charged to buildings.

Washington's little army had taken one pounding after another as they camped on the western bank of the Delaware in December 1776. Knowing that upcoming enlistments would expire with the new year and probably reduce his 2,400 men by about a thousand, Washington decided to strike the British across the river in Trenton before they swarmed into Philadelphia.

Using specially designed Durham boats — wide and flat and capable of handling heavy loads — the men started ferrying across the 300-yard river late in the afternoon of Christmas Day. It was not until early the next morning that all his men and 18 cannon were on the Jersey side of the river and his successful march to Trenton could begin.

The park is divided into two sections on the Pennsylvania side of the Delaware River. About four miles north of the actual crossing site is Bowman's Hill, where the army camped. A 110-foot observation tower was built in 1930 to commemorate the lookout of the American Revolution. A memorial flagstaff marks the graves of Continental troops who died during the encampment and who were America's first "unknown" soldiers.

Downstream is a visitor center and several eighteenth century village buildings.

Among them, only the brown fieldstone McKonkey Ferry Inn, at the waterline, was on the site in December 1776. Washington is believed to have dined here before the crossing.

Reenactment: Washington's crossing of the Delaware River, one of the Revolution's most dramatic exploits, is theatrically relived each Christmas Day. The Durham boat replicas in the Durham Boat House are used in the crossing. Local dignitaries assume the poses created in Emmanuel Letze's inspiring yet inaccurate painting "Washington Crossing the Delaware." A copy of the famous work is housed in the Memorial Building at the park.

West Chester

Chester County Courthouse Reliefs (mem)
Chester County Courthouse, High and Market streets.

Four panels in vertical sequence on the building facade represent the area's history and include the leading figures of the Battle of the Brandywine: George Washington, Marquis de Lafayette and Anthony Wayne.

Worcester

Peter Wentz Farmstead (site)
Schultz Road, off Route 73, Skippack Pike, 610-584-5104; Tue–Sat, 10–4, Sun, 1–4. Free.

After the British occupied Philadelphia on September 26, 1777, Washington and his army lingered around the perimeter of the city. He settled on Methacton Hill, some 17 miles west, and hatched plans for the Battle of Germantown in this expansive 1758 Georgian-style mansion. The fear of threats against Washington's life were such that his personal cook locked himself in the kitchen day and night, guarding the food supply against the possibility of poisoning. Tours are conducted by costumed guides, and demonstrations of eighteenth century farm life are offered.

Wyoming

Wyoming Valley Massacre Memorial (site)
Wyoming Avenue (Route 11) and Susquehanna Avenue; Open daily, 24 hours.

The Wyoming Valley was the scene of the Yankee-Pennamite Wars, a series of bloody clashes in which Connecticut and Pennsylvania attempted to settle land claims in the area. With the outbreak of the Revolution the opposing sides reorganized, joining either the Tories or the Patriots.

On July 3, 1778, 53-year-old Tory leader John Butler marched 400 troops and 500 Seneca and Cayuga warriors 200 miles from Fort Niagara to strike the Patriots in the Wyoming Valley. A Pennsylvania force of 300 confused militia and 60 regulars was routed and essentially wiped out. Only 60 men were able to escape. The Tories and Indians continued to rampage through the valley, looting and destroying more than 1,000 structures.

That night 14 prisoners were executed by an Indian woman, possibly of French Canadian ancestry, who dispatched the victims at a site now known as "The Bloody Rock." The tale is told by two prisoners who managed to escape the atrocity.

The remains of 166 American victims from the massacre were buried in a mass grave in the fall of 1778. A 63-foot granite monument surmounted the spot in the 1840s, listing the names of 40 some survivors. The Bloody Rock is preserved in a small memorial down the road on Eighth Street.

York

Historical Society of York County (site)

250 East Market Street, 717-848-1587; Mon–Sat, 9–5, Sun, 1–4. Admission charged.

After receiving the surrender of British Lt. Gen. John Burgoyne at Schuylerville, New York, on October 17, 1777, General Horatio Gates was appointed president of the American Board of War in York. Flushed with his success in New York, Gates may or may not have had his sights on Washington's position as commander-in-chief. Local legend has the Marquis de Lafayette spoiling the "Conway Cabel" in an attempt to oust Washington. Regardless, by the spring of 1778 Gates had returned to the field under Washington.

In addition to its collection of Colonial York, the society administers the brick and timber Horatio Gates House, which was built as an addition to the Golden Plough Tavern in 1751. It is the only surviving example of the mid–1700s German influence in the architecture of the region.

York County Colonial Court House (site)

Market Street and Pershing Avenue, 717-846-1977; Mon–Sat, 10–4, Sun, 1–4. Admission charged.

With the British capture of Philadelphia in 1777 the Continental Congress took refuge in York. It served as the nation's capital from September 30, 1777, to June 27, 1778, although never more than half the 64 delegates were in residence at the same time. On November 15, 1777, the Congress adopted the Articles of Confederation in this building, giving York the foundation to claim itself as "the first capital of the United States." It was also in York that Congress learned that France was to throw its support to the colonies, and they also took time to issue the first National Thanksgiving Proclamation. The courthouse has been restored and features authentic documents and a sound-and-light show with a three-screen dramatic narrative. A French-American exhibit traces the evolution of the vital alliance.

Rhode Island

Revolutionary Status: Original Colony
Estimated Colonial Population: 60,000
Colonial Capital: legislature alternated among five towns
Last Colonial Governor: Nicholas Cooke, Jr.
Troops Provided: 2 Continental regiments

Revolutionary Timeline:

June 9, 1772: One of the first overt acts of aggression occurs when Rhode Islanders board and burn the stranded British revenue cutter *Gaspee*

May 4, 1776: Rhode Island declares itself independent from Great Britain

July 9, 1777: William Burton kidnaps British occupation leader Richard Prescott

August 29, 1778: Bungled American and French assault force ends unsuccessfully in the Battle of Rhode Island

---

Coventry

General Nathanael Greene Homestead (site)

50 Taft Street, 401-821-8630; Apr–Oct: Wed and Sat, 10–5, Sun, 1–5. Admission charged.

Nathanael Greene worked in the family iron foundry until being stirred by the cause of liberty. He sat in the Colonial assembly beginning in 1770 and helped organize a local militia in 1774. From that scant military background Greene rose through the Continental Army to become one of the Revolution's great field commanders.

Appointed a brigadier general by Congress in 1775, Greene, a Quaker, joined Washington in the siege of Boston. He greatly impressed Washington, who made him military commander in Boston after the British left the city on March 17, 1776. He continued to distinguish himself on fields throughout the northern theater, and when the British began operations in the South it was Greene, second in command to Washington, who was chosen to retake and hold that region.

The home was built on a bluff looking down on the south branch of the Pawtuxet River in 1770. Greene divided his time between Rhode Island and Georgia until his death in 1786; his family remained in the two-story frame house until 1899. An eight-pound Revolutionary War field artillery cannon in the garden of "the Mount Vernon of the North" is thought to have been fired on the family forge.

Cranston

War Veterans Memorial Flag Pole (mem)

Rolfe Street, Pontiac Avenue and Park Avenue.

The flagpole supports a standing eagle with wings spread in front of the pole base. It was created by F. Ziegler in 1924 in honor of the citizens of Cranston who served their country, first in the Revolutionary War.

East Greenwich

Independent Company of Kentish Guards (col)

Peirce Street, 401-295-5076; Open by appointment.

In 1774, the year it was chartered, the commanders of this militia unit voted to reject an aspiring officer, citing a stiff knee. The young man swallowed his pride and signed on as a private. The next year Rhode Island commissioned him a brigadier general and gave Nathanael Greene the command of its three regiments. Greene became one of the most successful combat leaders of the Revolution, rising to second-in-command to George Washington.

James Mitchell Varnum House (site)

57 Pierce Street, 401-884-1776; Memorial Day–Labor Day: Thur–Sat, 1–4; Sept: Sat, 1–4. Admission charged.

James Varnum was an honor graduate of the first class of Rhode Island College, later Brown University. He rapidly attained fortune as a successful lawyer and, like his friend Nathanael Greene, entered the militia in 1774 with no prior military training. Varnum fought with distinction in the Boston and New York campaigns and was commissioned as a brigadier general on February 21, 1777. He retired in March 1779, eager to return to his lucrative law practice. However, he was back in the war in 1780, now a major general, assisting the French Army. After the war he was elected a U.S. congressman and ventured to Marietta, Ohio, as judge of the Northwest Territory, where he died in 1788 at the age of 42. The Georgian two-story home, which also contained his law office, was built by Varnum in 1773.

Middletown

Green End Fort (site)

Vernon Avenue.

The British occupied Newport for nearly three years during the Revolution, and the Green End Fort served as eastern anchor in their defense lines, protecting against a land invasion. The Americans under General Sullivan directed their siege works against these eastern fortifications from nearby Honyman Hill. A plaque describing the strategic position is all that remains.

Prescott Farm (site)

2009 West Main Road (Route 114), 401-847-6230; Apr–Nov: daily, 10–4. Admission charged.

The summer of 1777 found Americans searching for good news and heroes from the war, which had dragged on longer than many had anticipated. A hero was soon to emerge from an unlikely front — British-occupied Rhode Island.

General Richard Prescott, a longtime professional soldier, commanded the occupying forces. He had already arrived as a hated figure for his harsh treatment of Ethan Allen following his capture in Montreal in 1775 and was soon universally despised for his dictatorial and aristocratic ways. When American General Charles Lee was captured in New Jersey, Major William Barton, commander at Tiverton, began working on a plan to kidnap Prescott to give the Americans a general to exchange for Lee.

Setting off on July 4, Barton rowed slowly through Mount Hope Bay, recruiting raiders for his mission. By the night of July 9 he landed at Prescott's house, five miles north of Newport, with a band of 40 men. Overcoming a sentinel and evading British pickets posted in the area, Barton surprised Prescott in his bedroom. The general was spirited back to Warwick and was eventually exchanged.

Prescott returned to his command and directed the occupation of Newport until the British evacuated the garrison in October 1779. Barton was hailed as a national hero and celebrated for his boldness. The Americans had received the morale boost they were longing for.

In a bizarre postscript, Barton was remanded to debtor's prison for 14 years for refusing to pay a judgment on Vermont land he had purchased. When Lafayette visited the United States in 1824 he discovered Barton in prison and paid the claim.

The building from which Prescott was taken was the country estate of Henry Overing. Overing's name has been obscured in history by the riveting exploits of the night of July 9, 1777. The farm with additional buildings, includes a 1730 guardhouse where Prescott was held.

Newport

Artillery Company of Newport Military Museum (col)
23 Clarke Street, 401-846-8488; Jun–Sept: Wed–Sat, 10–4, Sun, 12–4. Admission charged.

Chartered in 1741, the Artillery Company is considered to be the oldest active military organization in the United States. The collection began only in 1960 but is now one of the most outstanding in the world. Over 100 countries are represented.

Hunter House (site)
54 Washington Street, 401-847-1000; May–Sept: daily, 10–5; Apr and Oct: Sat–Sun, 10–5. Admission charged.

Admiral Chevalier de Ternay sailed his French fleet into Newport in July 1780 and made his headquarters in the elegant mansion built by deputy governor Jonathan Nichols some 30 years earlier. The proud French commodore never had the chance to lead his ships into battle, however. He died of fever before the year was out, his fleet still bottled up in the Newport harbor by the British blockade. The two-and-a-half story home, gracefully capped with a gambrel roof, has been acclaimed as one of the finest Colonial houses extant.

Museum of Newport History (col)
82 Touro Street, 401-841-8770; Mon, Wed–Sat, 10–5, Sun, 1–5. Admission charged.

During the Revolution the British wasted no time securing Newport and its fine natural harbors. When hostilities erupted, Captain James Wallace controlled Narragansett Bay with a small force that remained in place until driven away in April 1776 by fire from shore batteries. General Henry Clinton reestablished British dominance in December, and the British would not leave for three years.

A French army of 4,000 arrived in Newport in 1780 but was frustrated by the British and did not break through their lines until 1781, when the fleet sailed to action at Yorktown. The Newport harbor was essentially closed for the entire Revolution, and the seaport never regained its prominence as a shipping center. The population cascaded from 11,000 in 1775 to barely half that a year later. The population scarcely rose again by 1870.

The museum, contained in the restored 1762 Brick Market, features exhibits on 300 years of Newport history. In the collection is a rifle from the Battle of Lexington.

Old Colony House (site)
Washington Square, 401-846-2980; Open by appointment only.

From this brick assembly house, completed in 1742, came the news of the most important governmental changes of the eighteenth century. The official death of George II and the ascendancy of George III was read here, and so was the Declaration of Independence on July 20, 1776. Rhode Island became the final state to accept the new republic's Constitution in the Old Colony House in 1790.

In March of 1781 General Washington greeted French lieutenant general Count de Rochambeau here in 1781. A portrait of Washington by native son Gilbert Stuart is in the collection of the Old Colony House.

Providence (site)
Fort Adams State Park, Ocean Drive, 401-847-2400; Open daily, dawn to dusk.

Colonial patriots attempted to protect the entrance to Newport harbor with fortifications on this peninsula begun in May 1776. But when the British arrived in December the project was abandoned. In 1793 a complex here was designed to be the most heavily armed fortress in America and was named for President John Adams when dedicated in 1799. A reproduction of the Continental sloop *Providence,* the first authorized ship of the Continental Navy, is on display.

Redwood Library (site)
50 Bellevue Avenue, 401-847-0292; Mon–Sat, 9:30–5:30. Free.

This Georgian structure dates to 1748 and is one of the oldest libraries still in use in the United States. British officers used the building as a clubhouse. A statue of George Washington is out front.

Rochambeau Statue and Monument (mem)

King's Park, 50 Bellevue Avenue.

The statue commemorates the landing of the French allies in America on July 12, 1780. The French troops remained in Newport for 11 months before sailing south to join the southern campaign.

Trinity Church (site)

Queen Anne Square, 401-846-0660; May: daily, 1–4; Jun–Labor Day: daily, 10–4; Sept–Apr: daily, 10–1. Free.

George Washington worshipped here in Pew 81. The original chandeliers, once lowered so candles could be lit, hang from the rafters by ropes, Colonial-style. The Admiral Chevalier de Ternay, who died five months after bringing his allied fleet to Newport, is buried in the adjacent cemetery.

Wanton-Lyman-Hazard House (site)

17 Broadway, 401-846-0813; Open by appointment. Admission charged.

Considered one of the finest examples of Jacobean architecture in New England, Newport's oldest remaining house was built around 1675. In August 1765 Martin Howard, Jr., the local stampmaster, lived here. As such, Howard's house stood at the center of the maelstrom that led to the Stamp Act Riot of 1765. Howard had fled his property, which was ransacked by protesting vandals. Later, Rhode Island's last Royal governor, Joseph Wanton, resided in the house. The state confiscated it upon his death in 1781 but later returned it to his descendants.

Portsmouth

Butts Hill Fort (site)

Off Sprague Street; Open daily, 24 hours.

The failure of the Americans at the Battle of Rhode Island, the only major land battle fought in the state, illuminates most of the difficulties the Continental Army faced throughout the waging of the war. With his success in pushing the British back to New York in the Battle of Monmouth on June 28, 1778, Washington decided to isolate the enemy and retake the city of Newport to their north. The plan called for Newport to be attacked after a coordinated landing effort with a French force, led by Admiral d'Estaing. The French would come ashore from the West and the Americans, under Maj. Gen. John Sullivan, would approach Butts Hill Fort from the East. The combined assault force had sufficient numbers to overwhelm the British in Newport.

On August 5 the fabled French naval commander Pierre Andre de Suffren scattered a small British fleet and opened the passage for d'Estaing to complete his landing according to script. But Sullivan had learned that the British had abandoned Butts Hill Fort and moved ahead of schedule to take the position, fearing an enemy return. Sullivan, always resentful of foreign officers in the war, never bothered to send word to the French about his improvisation.

An outraged d'Estaing had little time to protest as a powerful British fleet was now upon him. For two days the two navies volleyed before a hurricane-force storm dispersed both fleets. As the British withdrew to New York, Sullivan and his army, 10,000 strong, expected the French would now join him as he marched on Newport. But the slighted d'Estaing had no such intentions and sailed to Boston to repair his crippled ships. Even entreaties from Lafayette, who rode to Boston, could not entice the Frenchman and his 4,000 soldiers back into the fray.

With the French withdrawal, Sullivan was no longer able to hold his troops together, and perhaps 5,000 militia, whose discipline was always a concern, deserted the assault. Sullivan's invasion now became a retreat before it had begun. He scrambled back to Butts Hill Fort with the British, coming out of Newport under Maj. Gen. Robert Pigot, in pursuit. Several attacks on the afternoon of August 29 failed to dislodge the Americans. That night Sullivan successfully evacuated his army to Fort Barton on Tiverton, just as 5,000 crushing British reinforcements were on their way.

Some earthworks remain on the site and the area in Portsmouth retains enough of its eighteenth century character to follow the lines of attack and retreat. A marker tells of the battle in which generals Lafayette, Hancock, Greene and Sullivan participated.

Memorial to Black Soldiers (mem)
Routes 114 and 24, northbound.
The flagpole commemorates the site where the first black American army regiment fought in the Battle of Rhode Island on August 29, 1778. When the state could not raise its necessary quota of enlistments, the unit was formed in February 1778 of black volunteers. Colonel Christopher Greene organized and trained the regiment, comprised approximately 95 former slaves and 30 free blacks. The men went to war with the understanding they would receive their freedom and the pay of white soldiers. During the fighting on August 29 the 1st R.I. Regiment earned accolades for bravery for repulsing a Hessian attack three times.

Portsmouth Historical Society (site)
Corner of East Main Road and Union Street, 401-683-9178; Memorial Day–Columbus Day: Sun, 2–4. Free.
The society museum is maintained in the former Portsmouth Christian Union Church. A monument on the grounds marks the site of the initial skirmish of the Battle of Rhode Island on August 9, 1778.

Providence

Admiral Esek Hopkins (mem)
Admiral Esek Hopkins Park, Admiral Street.
A longtime sea captain, 57-year-old Esek Hopkins was lured into the

Revolution by the Rhode Island legislature which gave him command of all its military forces on October 4, 1775. With the help of his older brother Stephen he wrangled an even more prestigious post when he was appointed chief of the new American Navy two months later. Hopkins departed for Philadelphia in early 1776, embarked on an inglorious military career.

Leading a small fleet into the Atlantic, he ignored Congressional orders to engage the British off Virginia and instead sailed to the Bahamas to seize military supplies. He returned to Philadelphia to a censure by Congress and was suspended from command in 1777. A year later, Hopkins was summarily dismissed.

He returned to Providence and served in local politics and as a trustee of Rhode Island College, living in a frame house at 97 Admiral Street, until his death in 1802 at the age of 84.

Brown University (site)

University Hall, College Street, 401-863-2378; Sept–May: Mon–Fri, 8:30–5; Jun–Aug: 8–4. Free.

Begun in 1764 as Rhode Island College, the school, America's seventh oldest, was relocated to Providence in 1770. University Hall was built that year on the main green and served as barracks and a hospital for Colonial troops during the American Revolution.

Governor Stephen Hopkins House (site)

Benefit and Hopkins streets, 401-751-7067; Apr–Dec: Wed and Sat, 1–4. Admission charged.

The oldest part of this pleasant two-and-a-half story house dates to 1707, the year of Stephen Hopkins' birth. A planter, Hopkins became the most powerful man in eighteenth century Rhode Island, leaving his fields to serve ten terms as governor. He purchased this house in 1742 and made several enlargements. Although well into his sixties, Hopkins embraced the Revolution with a spirit lacking in men decades younger. He served in both Continental congresses and signed the Declaration of Independence on August 2, 1776. He did not die until that independence was secured in 1785. Included in the eighteenth century furnishings is a bed used by George Washington when he visited Hopkins in 1776 and again in 1781.

John Brown House (site)

52 Power Street, 401-331-8575; Tue–Sat, 11–4, Sun, 1–4. Admission charged.

Late in the afternoon on June 9, 1772, the hated revenue ship *Gaspee* ran aground in shallow water off Namquit — now Gaspee — Point in the Narragansett Bay. Commander Lieutenant Dudington had in the past permitted his crew to steal local beef cattle and chop down orchard trees for firewood. Men in Providence knew the *Gaspee* would be stranded until high tide at 3:00 A.M. John Brown and Captain Abraham Whipple organized a mob of 64 men who boarded eight longboats and rowed the seven miles from Providence to the crippled ship.

After a brief flurry of hand-to-hand fighting, Dudington and his crew were taken ashore as prisoners. The *Gaspee* was set afire and virtually destroyed when the powder on board ignited. The raiders rowed back to Providence and scattered. Brown was arrested and although there was talk of returning him to England for trial, he was released for lack of evidence. The incident was one of the first overt acts of aggression of the Revolution.

Brown was one of Providence's most aggressive merchants and the first to engage in the China trade. The mid–Georgian style mansion was designed by his brother Joseph and when finished in 1786 was praised by John Quincy Adams as "the most magnificent and elegant private mansion I have ever seen on this continent."

Market House (site)
Market Square, corner of College and South Main streets.
Only two of the three stories on this brick building were constructed during the Revolution, when the Market House was the city's economic heart. It was the site of the "Providence Tea Party" in 1775, when townspeople destroyed bales of herbs in support of Boston's struggle against British law. French soldiers were housed on the second floor.

Old State House (site)
150 Benefit Street, 401-277-2678; Mon–Fri, 8:30–4:30. Free.
Completed in 1762, the General Assembly convened here when in Providence from 1776 until 1900. The Rhode Island Declaration of Independence was signed here on May 4, 1776, as the assemblymen renounced allegiance to King George III two months before the other colonies.

State House (col)
82 Smith Street, 401-277-2357; Mon–Fri, 8:30–4:30. Free.
Modeled after the U.S. Capitol, the Rhode Island State Capitol was completed in 1904 of white Georgia marble and brick. The dome is one of only four self-supporting marble domes in the world. Among the state treasures on display are the only two surviving regimental flags from Rhode Island's Continental Army, a full-length Gilbert Stuart portrait of George Washington, and mementos of native son Nathanael Greene's historic career. A heroic statue of General Greene resides in the State House Plaza.

Saunderstown

Gilbert Stuart Birthplace (site)
Gilbert Stuart Road, east of Route 1, 401-294-3001; Apr–Nov: Thurs–Mon, 11–4. Admission charged.
Stuart, the most famous portrait painter of the late eighteenth and early nineteenth centuries, was born in this two-story frame house in 1755. His father had built the home four years earlier and operated a snuff mill in the basement. He

sailed for England in 1775 to study under Benjamin West, eventually opening his own popular studio. Stuart returned to the United States in 1792, partly to escape creditors and partly to paint the new president, George Washington.

Washington sat for Stuart three times, of which an unfinished head is the most enduring. Stuart became especially adept at churning out replica portraits of this highly desired rendering. Gilbert Stuart lived until 1828, completing portraits of the first six U.S. presidents.

Tiverton

Fort Barton (site)
Highland Road; Open daily, dawn to dusk.

The British occupation of Newport in December 1776 inspired the Tiverton Heights fortifications of July 1777. Its first commander, for whom the fort was subsequently named, was Major William Barton, who left for his heralded kidnapping mission of General Richard Prescott from this point. He had been in command only a week. Fort Barton was the launching point for General John Sullivan's invasion force during the embarrassing Battle of Rhode Island. Three miles of nature trails meander through the stone and dirt ramparts overlooking the Sakonnet River.

Warwick

Pawtuxet Village (site)
Route 1.

On the saltwater beach at Gaspee Point, the ill-fated *Gaspee* ran ashore. Interpretive markers describe the incident, one of the first violent clashes of the American Revolution.

Reenactment: Gaspee Days, the second weekend in June, remembers the capture and burning of the British revenue ship by Rhode Island patriots. Gaspee Days features a parade, Colonial encampment and muster.

South Carolina

Revolutionary Status: Original Colony
Estimated Colonial Population: 145,000
Colonial Capital: Charleston
Last Colonial Governor: John Rutledge
Troops Provided: 6 Continental regiments

Revolutionary Timeline:
June 28, 1776: South Carolina militia in Fort Sullivan turn away British invading force at Charles Town
May 12, 1780: Charles Town falls to the British and Sir Henry Clinton

May 20, 1780: Banastre Tarleton wipes out American detachment in Battle of the Waxhaws to begin a bloody occupation

August 6, 1780: Thomas Sumter defeats British at Hanging Rock

August 16, 1780: Lord Cornwallis deals Horatio Gates one of America's worst defeats in the Revolution at Camden

August 18, 1780: Tories fall into Patriot ambush at Musgrove's Mill

August 18, 1780: "Bloody Tarleton" kills 150 Patriots at Fishing Creek

November 7, 1780: Overmountain Men annihilate Tory army at Kings Mountain

November 9, 1780: Despised Tory raider James Wemyss captured in American victory at Fish Dam Creek

January 17, 1781: Daniel Morgan bests Tarleton at the Battle of the Cowpens in one of the American highlights of the Revolution

April 23, 1781: Americans capture Fort Watson by using a Maham Tower

April 25, 1781: Francis Rawdon overruns American camp in Battle of Hobkirk Hill

May 22, 1781: Nathanael Greene begins the longest Continental siege of the Revolution at Ninety-Six

September 8, 1781: Greene loses a victory at Eutaw Springs when his men break into a looting binge, but he seals the British in Charles Town

---

Beaufort

Beaufort Museum (col)

713 Craven Street, 803-525-7017; Mon, Tue, Thur–Sat, 10–5. Admission charged.

The natural harbor afforded by the islands between Charleston and Savannah long attracted European explorers. The British laid out a town at Beaufort in 1711, the first city established after Charleston. During the final three years of the Revolution the British used Beaufort as a base of operations. The museum is housed in a 1798 arsenal constructed of brick and tabby, a cement first made here by the Spaniards, who burned oyster shells to extract lime, then mixed it with sand and shells to form the durable building material. The collection includes Revolutionary War relics from Beaufort's Colonial period.

St. Helena's Episcopal Church (site)

505 Church Street, 803-522-1712; Mon–Fri, 10–4. Free.

Founded in 1712, St. Helena's congregation is one of America's oldest. Following heavy skirmishing between inexperienced Charleston militia and British regulars at Port Royal south of town, several soldiers from both sides were interred here.

Sheldon Church Ruins (site)

Route 21 off Route 17, fifteen miles northwest of town.

The elegant Sheldon Church was completed in 1753 and proved an attractive target for the British, who burned it to the ground in 1779. The church was not rebuilt until 1826 and was again burned by invading Federal troops during the Civil War. Today, only colonnaded brick walls and columns remain standing. Memorial services are held on the second Sunday after Easter.

Camden

Battle of Camden (site)

Flat Rock Road, Route 58, five miles north of town.

Both the British Army and the Continental Army were marching in mid–August 1780 when they collided in the swampy pinelands north of Camden on August 15. The British, under Lord Charles Cornwallis, were seeking to win the war by conquering the South; the Americans, directed by recent Saratoga hero Horatio Gates, were under orders to liberate the Carolinas.

Almost from the beginning the Americans, despite a large advantage in numbers, were routed. The indecisive Gates, when he did act, could not mount any coordinated attack. He would eventually quit the field and retreat deep into North Carolina. Meanwhile, his dispirited troops were left to deal with one of the most demoralizing defeats of the Revolution.

The terrain of the battlefield is completely undeveloped and unmarked, except for a stone memorial on the spot where Baron DeKalb was mortally wounded.

Camden Archives and Museum (site)

1314 Broad Street, 803-425-6050; Mon–Fri, 8–5, first Sunday in month, 1–5. Free.

In the spring of 1780, after Charleston fell to the British, several military posts were established in the interior of South Carolina, including Camden. At the head of the Wateree River near major Indian trails, Camden was strategically positioned to be the main interior British outpost. General Lord Charles Cornwallis entered Camden on June 1, 1780 and made his headquarters here for nearly a year. Fourteen Revolutionary War battles would be fought in the area before the British evacuated and burned Camden.

In addition to preserving the Revolutionary heritage of the Camden region, the museum is the home of the South Carolina Daughters of the American Revolution library.

DeKalb Monument (mem)

Bethesda Presbyterian Church, 502 DeKalb Street.

Johann Kalb was born on an Austrian peasant farm in 1721 and left home at 16 to find adventure fighting in the French Army as Jean DeKalb. He rose to the rank of major before his marriage to a wealthy woman enabled him to retire in 1765. He returned to the army a decade later as a brigadier general and came to America with Lafayette in 1777 to enhance his military fortunes in the American Revolution.

It took two years for Congress to assign him a rank commensurate with his status in the French Army. He was assigned to command the esteemed Maryland and Delaware Continentals in the South and led these troops onto the field at Camden. While the main of the American Army was routed and Horatio Gates was covering 60 miles in retreat in one day, Baron DeKalb fought heroically, his body riddled with ten bleeding wounds. It was not until felled by an eleventh injury that his men dispersed. He died three days later in Camden.

DeKalb's remains are beneath the granite monument in front of the Bethesda Presbyterian Church. The church was built in 1822 and designed by Robert Mills, a South Carolina native and architect of the Washington Monument. The cornerstone was laid in 1825 by the Marquis de Lafayette, who had sailed with Baron DeKalb to America to fight for freedom nearly a half-century earlier.

Historic Camden Revolutionary War Site (site)

Route 521, south of town, 803-432-9841; Mon–Sat, 10–5, Sun, 1–5. Admission charged for tours; grounds are free.

Less than three weeks after the fall of Charleston, Lord Cornwallis, ignoring orders to passively defend the conquered town, marched 2,500 British troops to the major inland trading center of South Carolina — Camden. The Americans under Horatio Gates moved immediately to destroy Cornwallis' position but suffered the most disastrous American defeat in the southern department in August.

Cornwallis then set about buttressing the town. He surrounded Camden with a stockade wall anchored by a series of six strong redoubts. Cornwallis commandeered the fine house of Camden's founder, Joseph Kershaw, for use by himself and his officers and exiled Kershaw, a staunch patriot, to Bermuda for the duration of the war. Kershaw, who amassed a fortune with diverse business interests before the Revolution, then mortgaged his fortune to outfit several ships with supplies for the war effort. The ships were hijacked and never delivered their vital cargo. After the war the state of South Carolina denied Kershaw's petition for restitution and he spent the waning years of his life trying to satisfy creditors. He died in 1791.

Restorations and reconstructions that recreate life in Colonial Camden on the 90-acre site are reached on walking trails. Included are several of the earthen British redoubts, which George Washington explored during a visit on May 25, 1791, and the 1777 powder magazine with 48-inch walls. The magazine was built for the state of South Carolina under the supervision of Joseph Kershaw. His house, used by the British, has been reconstructed. It was burned during the Civil War.

Reenactment: During Revolutionary War Field Days in early November, British and Continental armies take the field to compete in drill competitions. The battle skirmish and military "court" are highlights of the celebration.

Hobkirk Hill Battle Site (site)

Route 521, north of town.

As the Revolution dragged into 1781, Lord Cornwallis took the major part of his army to Virginia in hopes of winning the war in America's most important state, leaving a force of some 800 under 26-year-old Lord Francis Rawdon.

Nathanael Greene, new southern commander of the American forces, moved on Camden in April, hoping to sweep the British out of the Carolinas.

He approached the fortified town from the north with a force of 1,400 men, camping on Hobkirk Hill, a mile from Camden. Greene realized the futility of attacking the strong British position despite his superior numbers, but while he was awaiting reinforcements Rawdon seized the initiative and attacked the camp on the morning of April 25, 1781.

Caught by surprise, the Continentals were saved only by the staunch resistance offered by the 5th Virginia Regiment. Although Rawdon was able to claim a technical victory on the battlefield at Hobkirk Hill, his heavy losses were enough to force the British to abandon Camden and their isolated position in the Carolina interior. With Rawdon retiring to Charleston, Greene rapidly reassembled his army and marched to Ninety-Six, the last important British outpost remaining on the South Carolina frontier.

The site of the battle at Hobkirk Hill has been covered completely by a residential neighborhood and is not developed historically. All that can be discerned from the area is the ridge above town where Greene and his men camped.

Carlisle

Fish Dam Engagement (site)

Route 121, three miles east of town.

Major James Wemyss and 140 mounted troops from the British 63rd Regiment were assigned to end General Thomas Sumter's rebel activity in South Carolina. On November 9, 1780, Wemyss attacked Sumter's camp before dawn on the east side of the Broad River, near an old Indian fish dam. Surprise was not achieved and the American campfires made the mounted invaders inviting targets. The British were badly defeated and the hated raider Wemyss was captured. He was later paroled and wreaked no further havoc across South Carolina.

The battle site is undeveloped, interpreted only by a sign and stone marker on the east side of the Broad River. The Colonel William Farr Memorial Bridge to the west is named for the veteran of Cowpens, Blackstock and Musgrove Mills. Farr became the first sheriff of Union County and the first representative from the area sent to the South Carolina legislature after the Revolution.

Catawba

Catawba Cultural Center (col)

1536 Tom Stevens Road, 803-328-2427; Mon–Sat, 9–5. Admission charged.

The Catawba Indians fought on the side of the colonists and supported them in the American Revolution. Today their heritage and culture are preserved through exhibits and videos at their cultural center. A nature trail leads to the Catawba River, the focal point of Catawba life.

Cayce

Cayce Historical Museum (site)

1800 12th Street Extension, 803-796-9020; Tue–Fri, 9–4, Sat–Sun, 2–5. Admission charged.

The Cayce Historical Museum is located within the old Saxe Gotha township and represents the earliest settlement in the Midlands of South Carolina. The focal point in the museum is a reconstruction of the trading post established by James Chestnut and Joseph Kershaw at Granby Village in 1765. The British forces seized the trading post in early 1781 and fortified it as Fort Granby.

Emily Geiger, South Carolina's heroine of the Revolution, was held captive by the British here on July 3, 1781. She memorized and swallowed a note from Nathanael Greene to Thomas Sumter and was released for lack of evidence.

Charleston

Miles Brewton House (site)

27 King Street, private residence.

Miles Brewton constructed this outstanding brick Georgian "double house" between 1765 and 1769. It was considered not only one of the finest homes in Charleston but in all of America. Like most Charleston businessmen Brewton was a moderate politically. He disagreed so vehemently with independence from England that he set sail for Europe in 1775 and his family was lost at sea. The home was then inherited by Revolutionary War heroine Rebecca Motte.

When the British gained control of Charleston in 1780 they made their headquarters here. Sir Henry Clinton, Lord Charles Cornwallis and Lord Francis Rawdon stayed in the Brewton House as each commanded the city.

The Charleston Museum (col)

360 Meeting Street, 803-722-2996; Mon–Sat, 9–5, Sun, 1–5. Admission charged.

Although not a chartered city and even lacking a township government, Charleston, with a population of 12,000, was the fourth largest city in America at the time of the Revolution — and by far the most important south of Philadelphia. Unlike its New England cousins, Charleston's founders were not escaping religious persecution and the town grew up with a decidedly more sybaritic bent. Politics and independence were not primary motivators in Charleston, and after William Moultrie repulsed British invaders in 1776 the war did not touch the city for three years. From 1780 until 1782 the town chafed under British occupation.

The Charleston Museum, founded in 1773, is considered the first and oldest museum in America. Exhibits focus on the history of Charleston, including its role in the Revolution.

City Hall Gallery (col)

80 Broad Street, 803-577-6970; Mon–Fri, 9–5. Free.

Originally built as a bank in 1801, the Charleston City Hall features historic relics and a portrait gallery in the council chamber. Among the paintings of important leaders is a 1791 portrait of George Washington by John Trumbull.

Colonial Powder Magazine (site)

79 Cumberland Street, 803-723-1623; Mon–Sat, 10–5, Sun, 2–5. Admission charged.

The Old Powder Magazine, authorized in 1703 and completed about ten years later, is the only public building remaining in the Carolinas from the period of the Lords Proprietors, the group of English noblemen who originally owned and ruled the joint province of Carolina. The original low, stuccoed brick building with 32-inch thick walls stored powder until the siege of Charleston in 1780, when a shell exploded within yards of the magazine. At that point 10,000 pounds of powder were transferred to the Exchange.

Drayton Hall (site)

3380 Ashley River Road, nine miles northwest of town on Route 61, 803-766-0188; Mar–Oct: daily, 10–4; Nov–Feb: daily, 10–3. Admission charged.

William Henry Drayton, born in this Colonial plantation home in 1742, was one of South Carolina's most active Patriots. He published anti–Parliament pamphlets early in his career and was elected president of the South Carolina Provincial Congress in 1775. On November 11, 1775, Drayton took command of the *Defence* in the Charleston harbor and fired upon British ships. No damage was done in the opening volleys of the Revolutionary War in South Carolina.

A member of the Second Continental Congress, Drayton contracted typhus in Philadelphia and died in the Colonial capital. He is buried in Christ Church.

Heyward-Washington House (site)

87 Church Street, 803-722-2996; Mon–Sat, 10–5, Sun, 1–5. Admission charged.

Daniel Heyward, a prominent rice planter, built the three-story brick house in 1772. His son Thomas, Jr., was elected to the Second Continental Congress in 1776 and, despite reservations, affixed his name to the bottom of the Declaration of Independence. Thomas Heyward continued to serve in Congress until 1778, when he returned to Charleston to live in this house. He stayed until 1794, when he relocated to his plantation Whitehall.

When President George Washington was the guest of Charleston in 1791, this house was rented from Mr. Heyward for the president's use. Today, it is the only eighteenth century house open in the city with original kitchen buildings, carriage house and necessary in the courtyard.

Middleton Place (site)

Ashley River Road, 803-566-6020; Daily, 9–5. Admission charged.

Henry Middleton served in both the First Continental Congress, which he presided over for many months, and the Second Continental Congress. Disturbed by the growing agitation for independence, Henry resigned to return to his expansive plantation. His more radical son, Arthur, replaced him in Congress and signed the Declaration of Independence.

Arthur Middleton was active in the defense of Charleston in 1780, and when captured was exiled to St. Augustine, Florida, like many of his fellow rebel South Carolinians. He was not freed until exchanged in July 1781.

Despite the Middletons' Revolutionary activities, more acclaim today is given the landscaped gardens at Middleton Place, reputedly America's first. Laid out by Henry Middleton in 1741, eventually 100 men would work ten years to complete the gardens.

Monument to the Defenders of Fort Moultrie (mem)

White Point Gardens, Murray Boulevard and East Battery Street.

The monument honors the men of the 2nd S.C. Regiment who repulsed the British attack on Charleston on June 28, 1776. Included on the memorial is an inscription bearing the words of Sergeant William Jasper: "Don't let us fight without a flag!" At the height of the bombardment, British fire severed the Patriot flagstaff. Jasper scrambled from his protected parapet to retrieve the flag, attached it to a new mast and reinserted it before returning to his gun.

Old Exchange and Provost Dungeon (site)

122 East Bay Street at Broad Street, 803-727-2165; Daily, 9–5. Admission charged.

The Exchange & Customs House was completed in 1771 after four years of construction on the site where Stede Bonnet, "The Gentleman Pirate," and his crew were imprisoned half a century earlier before their hanging. On December 2, 1773, in protest of British tea sales, 257 tea chests were seized and stored in the copious storage cellars of the house.

South Carolina Patriots met here in the Great Hall to select delegates to the First Continental Congress. Two years later, independence was declared here, and in 1788 politicians from South Carolina once again assembled in the Great Hall to ratify the U.S. Constitution.

The British also used the customs house during the Revolution. The spacious cellars were converted to dank, comfortless cells for their provost prison. The most famous of the captives held here was Colonel Isaac Hayne, a South Carolina planter and horse breeder who served in the local militia. Captured in May 1780, he was paroled back to his plantation but when the British ordered him to take up arms against the rebels he considered his parole invalidated and returned to the militia. Hayne was captured again in July 1781 and charged with espionage. He was executed on August 4, 1781, in part as an example to rebel officers who might be considering breaking their paroles. Quickly made a martyr by the Revolutionaries, the "Hayne Affair" was used to promote recruiting in the militia.

John Rutledge House (site)

116 Broad Street, 803-723-7999; Daily, 10–4. Free.

John Rutledge almost single-handedly was South Carolina's political authority during the Revolution. The 35-year-old was elected to both the First Continental Congress in 1774 and the Second Continental Congress in 1775 and
became president of South Carolina in 1776. He refused to turn the city over
to the British in 1776 — which led to the British defeat at Fort Moultrie — and
for the next two years directed the political activities of the state.

Rutledge spearheaded resistance to the British occupation in the early 1780s
and was the main player in reestablishing the South Carolina government in 1782
after the British departed. After the war John Rutledge was a delegate to the
Constitutional Convention and signed the U.S. Constitution in 1787.

His three-story 1763 house is now operated as an inn offering guided tours.

Cheraw

Old St. David's Episcopal Church (site)

Route 9, east of town.

Founded in 1750 at the navigational head of Pee Dee River, Cheraw was of
considerable strategic importance during the Revolution. Nathanael Greene,
after taking control of the southern department, seasoned 1,000 troops in camp
here from December 20, 1780, until January 28, 1781.

Old St. David's was completed in 1773 and was the last South Carolina church
built under the monarchy of George III. During the Revolution it was used as
a hospital; victims of a smallpox epidemic are buried in the churchyard.

Pegeus Place (site)

Off Route 1, eight miles north of town.

Pegeus Place was the site of the only completed cartel for the exchange of
prisoners during the Revolution. Constructed around 1765, it is private property but visible from the road.

Chesnee

Cowpens National Battlefield (site)

Route 11, three miles east of town, 864-461-2828; Daily, 9–5. Free.

Banastre Tarleton was a British gentryman, schooled at Oxford, and, at the
precocious age of 21, placed in charge of a company of mounted infantry, the
dragoons. He volunteered to combat the rebellion in America and fought well
in the north in the early years of the war. He found his stride, though, when he
followed Cornwallis to South Carolina.

Still only 24, Tarleton commanded the green-uniformed British Legion, a
particularly fierce army of American loyalists. Tarleton was even more aggressive than his mentor Cornwallis and his fast-moving infantry set about successfully clearing the South Carolina countryside of American resistance. In the
process he earned the moniker "Bloody Tarleton."

On January 16, 1781, Daniel Morgan learned that Tarleton was on his trail. Morgan never attended a fancy school; he was a brawling frontiersman, a teamster by trade. He won his experience by fighting Indians and proved himself one of America's best leaders during the Revolution at Quebec and Saratoga. After the American calamity at Camden he came out of retirement to serve under Nathanael Greene. Cowpens was his first independent command.

Morgan's crack troops from Maryland and Delaware harassed the British across the Carolina backwoods as he marched to rejoin Greene in early 1781. Tarleton convinced Cornwallis that he could chase down Morgan's army and, if not destroy it totally, force it into the pincers of the main British force. Cornwallis gave Tarleton a detachment of 1,100 cavalry and infantry, a quarter of his army wintering in Winnsboro.

Morgan was using the network of rivers to protect his march and on January 16 was camped between the Broad and Pacolet rivers. Rather than continuing his flight, Morgan chose to stand and fight between the rivers, in a grassy meadow peppered with trees. The land used to winter cattle was known locally as Hannah's Cowpens.

Although outnumbered almost two-to-one, Morgan knew his opponent. His plan was to use his young pursuer's audaciousness against him. The ground at Cowpens sloped gradually uphill from the point where Tarleton would be approaching; at the far end were two low crests, separated by a wide swell.

Morgan broke his force into three lines. About 120 sharpshooters were deployed on the lower slope; less experienced militia were stationed along the first crest, and Morgan's most seasoned Continentals — about 500 men — manned the line behind the crest. The plan was for the first two lines to fire two well-aimed volleys and fall back, luring Tarleton deeper into the American position.

The British closed so quickly on Morgan on the morning of January 16 that his men left their rations cooking in camp. Tarleton paused long enough only to enjoy the American breakfast and was ready to strike in the darkness before dawn the next day. Tarleton sent an exploratory force of 50 cavalry to feel out Morgan's position, and 15 were blasted from their mounts. Undaunted, and true to form, the impetuous Tarleton charged on, attacking without reconnaissance just after dawn.

The British surged through the first two lines, weathering the American volleys as the defenders fell back in concert, as planned. But as the fighting intensified at the third line, American communication broke down. John Edgar Howard, called by Nathanael Greene "as good an officer as the world affords," ordered his right to fall back and reform, but the order was mistaken as a general retreat and the entire line broke.

Seeing this maneuver, Morgan quickly improvised on his main plan. He rode up, chose new ground for the Continentals to rally on and stopped the retreat. The British, having seen the Americans turn and leave the field, joyfully broke ranks to chase the defeated foe. The redcoats were still cheering when the first return fire struck. The reorganized militia under Andrew Pickens and the cavalry under William Augustine Washington led a withering charge back down the slope.

The British were completely routed as they dashed off the field. Washington raced ahead of his troops and caught Tarleton, briefly engaging him in a sword fight, but the British commander was able to shoot Washington's horse and flee.

The fighting at Cowpens lasted barely one hour, but British losses were staggering: 110 dead and over 700 captured and wounded. Morgan lost only 12 killed and 60 wounded in a victory as complete as any in the Revolution. The performance of the American army at Cowpens demonstrated to Congress that Greene's army was deserving of their full support.

The Continental Congress awarded only 14 medals during the Revolution, and three — for Morgan, Washington and Howard — were given for heroism at Cowpens.

Little of the terrain has changed since 1781. A walking tour through the open forest, well-suited for cavalry action, includes the American lines across the Green River Road. The visitor center features a lighted map tracing troop movements and an audiovisual presentation on the importance of Cowpens.

Clemson

Andrew Pickens Grave (site)
Old Stone Church, 101 Stone Circle.

Andrew Pickens led the partisan fighting in the resistance to British occupation of South Carolina, raiding in the state's interior as Francis Marion did on the coast and Sumter did in the Piedmont. A native of Pennsylvania, Pickens lived and prospered on the Virginia and South Carolina frontiers. In 1780 Pickens surrendered and was paroled to his farm. But after Loyalists plundered his home he declared the parole invalidated and returned to play crucial roles at Cowpens and Eutaw Springs.

Like Marion and Sumter, Pickens served in state politics after the Revolution. The Presbyterian Old Stone Church was built by Pickens and others in 1797. He died in 1817 at the age of 78. Andrew Pickens is buried alongside several of the men who followed him into battle.

Clinton

Duncan Creek Cemetery (site)
Route 56.

Many Revolutionary War soldiers are buried in this old country churchyard from the days before this town of Scotch-Irish emigrants from Virginia was founded.

Cross Anchor

Musgrove's Mill Skirmish (site)
Route 56, three miles south of town.

With the return of the British to South Carolina and the occupation of

Charleston in May 1780, a groundswell of Tory support was feared throughout the region. Major Patrick Ferguson's burgeoning Tory army numbered around 500 when 200 American militia under Colonel Isaac Shelby came upon them at Musgrove's Mill on the Enoree River.

The Americans hastily assembled a defensive fortification of fallen trees and brush two miles up river from the British camp. Captain Shadrack Inman and 25 volunteers advanced on the Tory position and fired into the camp. The Tories eagerly took after the small raiding party and chased Inman's men directly into the ambush. The Tories lost 63 killed, 90 wounded and 70 captured — half of Ferguson's force. Only four Patriots were killed, although Inman was one, mortally wounded near the end of the fray.

The battlesite from August 18, 1780, is undeveloped and only a marker for Captain Inman's grave identifies the ambush, which is significant as one of the few times in the Revolution when untrained militia bested British regulars.

Eadytown

Francis Marion Tomb (site)
Route 45 off Route 6, south of town.

General Francis "Swamp Fox" Marion harassed the British along the South Carolina coast throughout their occupation. Born in St. John's Parish in 1732, Marion gained military experience fighting the Cherokees in 1761, garnering praise for bravery in dispersing an enemy ambush despite having lost two-thirds of his men.

He commanded a militia regiment in the American Revolution until Charles Town capitulated in 1780. Marion then organized a small band of guerrillas, using the marshy Snow's Island as the base for his operations. On August 20, 1780, he routed 250 Tories with just 52 Patriots at Blue Savannah, South Carolina. More than a dozen ambushes followed over the next year, with the loss of only three men.

Marion lost all his personal property when his plantation was ransacked. He lived in various areas around what is now Lake Marion and held occasional political office in the years after the Revolution before his death on February 27, 1795. His grave is marked with a simple monument.

Eutawville

Eutaw Springs Battlefield (site)
Route 6, three miles east of town.

The final major battle in the South took place on September 8, 1781, when Nathanael Greene moved against the last substantial British force in South Carolina at Eutaw Springs. Greene's army was composed of a line of local militia under Francis Marion and Andrew Pickens and two lines of Continental Army regulars. His total force numbered 2,400 men.

The British under Lt. Col. Alexander Stewart still hoped to win the war in the South. The two armies clashed around 9 o'clock in the morning with the Americans crumbling most of the British line. Only Major John Marjoribanks kept the redcoats on the field. When Greene's men broke ranks to loot the British camp, Stewart reorganized his troops and drove the Americans from the field.

The fighting lasted four hours and was among the fiercest of the war. The Americans suffered 139 killed and 375 wounded; the British had 85 men killed and 351 wounded. Although Greene retreated, he forced Stewart back to Charleston, where the British remained trapped until evacuating the city.

The site of the battlefield is now under Lake Morgan. The small park with interpretive signs is actually the site of the British camp.

Georgetown

Hopsewee Plantation (site)

Route 17, twelve miles south of town, 803-546-7891; Mar–Oct: Tue–Fri, 10–4. Admission charged.

Thomas Lynch built this clapboard home of black cypress in 1740. While serving in the Second Continental Congress, Lynch suffered a stroke and became incapacitated in Philadelphia. His son, Thomas Jr., was sent north as an extra delegate and, despite not being adamantly behind separation from England, signed the Declaration of Independence.

The Lynches headed home that fall but the father died in Annapolis. Seriously ill with fever himself, Thomas Lynch, Jr., would set sail for medical assistance in France in 1779 and be lost at sea.

Lafayette-DeKalb Landing Site (site)

Route 17, south of town.

In 1777 the Marquis de Lafayette, a 19-year-old French nobleman, and his shipmate, Baron Johann DeKalb, a Bavarian professional soldier with 35 years of experience, sailed into the Winyah Bay and landed near this site, accessible only by boat, on North Island. They selected this remote spot to evade a British blockade. The event is remembered by a stone monument along the road.

Prince George Winyah Episcopal Church (site)

300 Broad Street at Highmarket Street, 803-546-4358; Mar–Oct: Mon–Thur, 11:30–4:30. Free.

By 1735, "George Town," where four rivers pour into the Winyah Bay, had become a port of entry where the area's rice and indigo planters and merchants thrived. When the British occupied South Carolina in 1780, a small garrison was placed in Georgetown. On November 15, 1780, Francis Marion raided the town and returned in January supported by Light Horse Harry Lee. After the Americans attacked again in July 1781, the exasperated British burned the town on August 2 and departed.

While in Georgetown, the British used the little brick church as a stable. Soldiers from the Revolution are buried in the cemetery.

Great Falls

Fishing Creek Engagement (site)

Route 21, two miles north of town.

Banastre Tarleton rose to national prominence in England with his success in the South Carolina wilderness here on August 18, 1780. Chasing Thomas Sumter with lightning speed, the British rode into an unprepared American camp and cut the Patriots to shreds. While losing only 16 men, Tarleton killed 150, captured 300 and liberated 100 prisoners. Sumter narrowly escaped by leaping onto an unsaddled horse.

The site of one of America's most galling defeats of the Revolution rests at the bottom of Fishing Creek Reservoir. A roadside marker tells the story.

Heath Springs

Hanging Rock Skirmish (site)

Off Route 467, two miles south of town.

The British established an outpost at Hanging Rock, a natural rock formation, from its main interior headquarters at Camden. Thomas Sumter overwhelmed the garrison in August 1780 but failed to destroy the British post when his militia broke ranks to loot the enemy tents. A stone monument has been erected on the site.

Lancaster

Battle of the Waxhaws (site)

Route 522, south of Route 9, nine miles east of town.

After the surrender of Charleston on May 12, 1780, the only remnants of the regular American army in South Carolina were the 3rd Virginia Continental Regiment commanded by Colonel Abraham Buford. Abandoning his quest to render aid to Charleston, Buford turned and headed for North Carolina.

Buford's retreat was not enough for British commander Cornwallis, who wanted rebel South Carolina governor John Rutledge, who was being escorted by Buford. He dispatched a trusted subordinate, Colonel Banastre Tarleton, and a force of 130 cavalry, 100 infantry and 40 seasoned dragoons to take up the chase. Tarleton was spotting his quarry a 100-mile head start.

Covering more than 100 miles in less than three days, Tarleton reached the rear guard of Buford's column just south of the South Carolina–North Carolina state line on May 20. The British horsemen slashed through the Continentals and, despite being outnumbered, Tarleton demanded that Buford surrender the main body of his force. Buford refused.

Tarleton sent his mounted troops against Buford's line, which waited until the cavalry was a mere 30 feet away before firing. The Americans were routed and Buford's company completely destroyed. Of 350 Continentals, 113 were killed and more than 200 wounded and captured. Many were to die later of their wounds. Rutledge, however, had left the procession days earlier.

The cause of the high casualty rate remains a matter of speculation. Buford's men may have continued firing after seeking quarter, or the British may have been excessively zealous in their submission of the rebels. To Americans the affair quickly became known as Buford's Massacre, and the cry "Tarleton's Quarter!" soon echoed around the South. For his part, "Bloody Tarleton" reported in a letter to Cornwallis, "I have cut 170 officers and men to pieces."

The battlefield is undeveloped and unmarked. A stone obelisk was erected at the site where 84 Americans were buried in a mass grave. The common grave is encircled by a pile of white rocks.

McClellanville

Hampton Plantation (site)
1950 Rutledge Road, 803-546-9361; Thurs–Sun, 1–4. Admission charged.

Noe Serre, a French Huguenot immigrant, built a small six-room farmhouse on this site in the 1730s. By the time George Washington arrived for an official visit on May 5, 1790, the small, functional home had evolved into one of the grandest of the Lowcountry's manor houses. Fearing the president would not be suitably impressed, a massive columned, Adamesque portico was installed to the mansion's facade just prior to his arrival.

The mansion was passed from Serre to his son-in-law Daniel Horry in 1757. Horry was a commander in the defense of Charleston in 1776, but when the British returned in 1780 he took an oath of allegiance to the crown. Due to Horry's facile political allegiances, Hampton Plantation — if not his reputation — emerged from the Revolution unscathed.

McConnells

Historic Brattonsville (site)
Route 322 and Brattonsville Road, four miles east of town, 803-684-2327; Mar–Nov: Tue–Sat, 10–4, Sun, 2–5. Admission charged.

On July 12, 1780, British forces under Captain Christian Huck were surrounded and defeated by combined rebel forces, boosting morale in the Carolina backcountry. The battlefield is preserved within Historic Brattonsville, a living history museum interpreting life in the Carolina backcountry from 1780 to 1860.

Mt. Pleasant

Snee Farm (site)
1254 Long Point Road, off Route 17, 803-881-5516; Memorial Day–Labor Day: daily, 9–6; the rest of the year: daily, 9–5. Free.

Snee Farm was part of a 500-acre Royal grant to Richard Butler in 1698. By 1754, when it came under control of the Pinckney family, the plantation comprised over 700 acres. Charles Pinckney was born three years later. One of four

South Carolina delegates to the Constitutional Convention, Pinckney later served four terms as governor of South Carolina. Financial reversals forced him to sell Snee Farm in 1817. Today, 28 acres remain to interpret the emerging United States in the South Carolina lowcountry.

Ninety-Six

Ninety-Six National Historic Site (site)

Route 248, two miles south of town, 864-543-4068; park open daily, dawn to dusk; visitor center, daily, 8–5. Free.

Ninety-Six was supposedly named because the trading post was 96 miles from the Cherokee town of Keowee in the Blue Ridge foothills. On the eve of the Revolution, Ninety-Six sported a dozen houses, a sturdy jail and a sizable courthouse. Political allegiances ran high and on November 18, 1775, a force of 1,890 Loyalists attacked 532 Patriots who had built a crude fort of fence rails, cowhides and straw bales on John Savage's plantation. After three days the Loyalists under Colonel Joseph Robinson could not capture the fort and its swivel cannon.

With the defenders running low on powder and the aggressors fearing impending reinforcements, a treaty was signed. Both sides agreed to withdraw and the Patriots demolished the fort. It was the first major land battle of the Revolution in the South.

When the British assumed control of the South, Augusta, Georgia, and Ninety-Six were made the dominant strongholds in the wilderness. The town was stockaded and flanked by two forts; a stockade to the west and a strong, star-shaped redoubt to the east. All were connected by a covered way.

When Nathanael Greene arrived at Ninety-Six he examined the British position and concluded that, "the fortifications are so strong and the garrison so large and so well furnished that our success is very doubtful." On May 22, 1781, Greene and his army of 1,000 regulars, without heavy artillery, laid siege to the garrison of 550 battle-toughened Tories led by Colonel John Cruger.

Engineer Thaddeus Kosciuszko, in his first siege operation, began digging a system of parallel trenches, protected by a zigzag pattern of approach, up to the star redoubt. With the third trench line only 40 yards from the fort a 30-foot rifle tower was built. It was now mid–June and the longest Continental siege of the Revolution was heading into its 28th day.

When Greene learned a powerful relief column of 2,000 men was marching to Cruger's aid, he had to attack. On June 18 "Light Horse" Harry Lee successfully fought through the defenses at the western redoubt, but Greene's initial assessment of the British position made a month earlier proved correct. The Continentals were not able to break into the star redoubt. After 40 Patriots were killed in the 45-minute assault, Greene ordered a retreat to Charlotte.

Although a tactical loser, Greene's siege once again weakened the enemy resources. A few weeks later the British abandoned the ruined village, now isolated on the frontier, and pulled back to Charleston.

A new town of Cambridge rose near the fortifications in 1783, but an epidemic decimated it in 1815, and in 1855 the railroad passed by two miles to the north. No one then lived near the old frontier post for more than 100 years. The Colonial earthworks were remarkably intact when purchased by the National Park Service in the 1970s.

An interpretive trail traverses the entire village. An observation tower provides an excellent view of the star redoubt and the zigzag trenches used to attack it. Inside the earthworks are the remains of a 25-foot well, dug through hard-packed clay in a futile effort to obtain water for the besieged fort. The Tories were forced to rely on slaves slipping past Greene's pickets at night to bring water into the redoubt.

A memorial along the trail marks the grave of James Birmingham, the first South Carolina man to die in the fight for freedom. A volunteer with the Long Cane militia, Birmingham was killed at Ninety-Six in 1775.

Rock Hill

Landsford Canal State Park (site)
Route 21, twelve miles south of town, 803-789-5800; Thurs–Mon, 9–6. Free.

Lord Cornwallis crossed Lands Ford in his march from Charlotte to Winnsboro after the Battle of Kings Mountain. General Thomas Sumter used the area as a meeting place and campsite. General William Richardson Davie, who fought with Sumter, served as governor of North Carolina and later retired to a home overlooking the ford. The site features the remains of an early American canal system and an eighteenth century log cabin.

Roebuck

Walnut Grove (site)
Off Route 221, south of town, 864-576-6546; Apr–Oct: Tue–Sat, 11–5, Sun, 2–5; Nov–Mar: Sun, 2–5. Admission charged.

Kate Moore Barry's 1765 plantation house had been lived in only a few years when the Revolution erupted on the South Carolina frontier. She served as a scout for General Daniel Morgan at the Battle of Cowpens. Walnut Grove was a community in itself, with a school, doctor's office and various outbuildings. It is fully restored today.

Salley

Battle of John's Town Memorial (mem)
Route 394, two miles west of town.

The memorial commemorates the Battle of John's Town, fought May 4, 1782, by Patriots to defend the two bull pens where British and Tories were imprisoned during the Revolutionary War.

Santee

Fort Watson (site)
Routes 301 and 15; Open daily, dawn to dusk. Free.

To facilitate their occupation of South Carolina, the British established a series of outposts to support the line of communications between Charleston and Camden. When Nathanael Greene assumed command he initiated a campaign to bring down these interior posts. Fort Watson, constructed atop an ancient 30-foot Indian mound overlooking the Santee River, was his first objective.

Lt. Col. "Light Horse" Harry Lee and Brig. Gen. Francis Marion converged at Fort Watson on April 16. They immediately took control of the post's water supply, which lay outside the Indian mound, and demanded the British surrender. British lieutenant James McKay politely declined the offer and instead began digging a well which struck water on April 18.

The Americans had no cannon and they were not about to storm Fort Watson. Lt. Col. Hezekian Maham broke the stalemate. He proposed the building of a tower — which would come to take his name — from which riflemen could snipe into the fort during an attack. The Patriots toiled over the next five days constructing their tower of notched logs, and at dawn on April 23, while two units assaulted the stockade, the riflemen poured shot into the defenders. McKay soon surrendered.

Over the next month the Americans would capture several more outposts, and on May 10 the British withdrew from Camden. No trace of the British fortifications remain but steps lead up the Indian mound, affording the same view McKay and his defenders saw in 1781.

Spartanburg

General Daniel Morgan (mem)
Morgan Square.

Spartanburg was named for the Spartan Regiment, which represented the town during the Revolutionary War. The statue honors Daniel Morgan, the hero of the Battle of Cowpens.

Stateburg

General Thomas Sumter Family Park and Cemetery (site)
Off Route 261, north of town.

Thomas Sumter was born in rural Virginia on August 14, 1734. As a young man he worked as a surveyor, in his father's mill and as a sheep farmer. A sergeant in the Virginia militia, Sumter fought in the Cherokee wars and eventually became an emissary between the British and the Cherokees, even traveling to London as an interpreter.

After the French and Indian War, he fled Virginia to escape an old debt and relocated in South Carolina. He invested well, operated a crossroads store and was elected justice of the peace in 1766 in his new community. When the Revolution started, Sumter was a colonel on the Continental line from 1776 until 1778.

When Charleston fell, Thomas Sumter formed the first militia to renew the struggle. Over the next 18 months he so impressed the British with his daring "hit-and-run" warfare that they nicknamed him the "Gamecock of the Revolution." After the war the people of South Carolina sent Sumter to Congress and in 1801 he was elected a U.S. senator. He died on June 1, 1832, in the 98th year of his life, being the last surviving officer of the Revolution.

Thomas Sumter is buried in the town of Stateburg, which he founded and promoted for state capital. Having failed in that pursuit, the small village never grew beyond a handful of buildings. Sumter is buried behind a small brick chapel that covers the grave of his glamorous daughter-in-law, the Countess Natalie De Lage De Volude Sumter.

Sullivan's Island

Fort Moultrie (site)

1213 West Middle Street, 803-883-3123; Daily, 9–5. Free.

In January 1776 Charlestonians began to defend their town by starting construction of a fort across the Cooper River on Sullivan's Island. Six months later the palmetto log-and-sand fortification showed only two walls facing the harbor and two incomplete walls exposed to Long Island to the rear. Meanwhile, British amphibious forces were massing offshore.

Rather than sail by the American defenses into Charleston itself, the British chose to destroy Fort Sullivan. With nine powerful warships it certainly possessed the firepower, but bungled British movements sabotaged the operation from the outset. Sir Henry Clinton landed with 2,500 troops on Long Island but was unable to ford his troops across the narrow channel to reach the breach in Fort Moultrie. After delaying nearly two weeks attempting to coordinate a planned attack, Admiral Sir Peter Parker decided to launch the assault without Clinton's support.

The British opened fire on the morning of June 28. The crude fort proved to be an ideal bastion, as the spongy palmetto wood received the cannon balls without splintering. The sand mortar absorbed what the palmetto couldn't. Out on the water the British were unfamiliar with the tricky navigation required to maneuver through Charleston harbor, and three ships ran aground.

Inside Fort Sullivan the inexperienced militia under the command of William Moultrie performed brilliantly in returning fire with 30 smoothbore cannon. After nine hours the British fleet and its more than 200 guns was forced to retire in one of the first decisive Patriot victories of the Revolution. Charleston would remain unmolested for three more years.

After the Revolution Fort Moultrie was neglected, and by 1791 little of it remained. Under a nationwide system of seacoast fortifications, Fort Moultrie was rebuilt in 1798 and remained active until World War II. The fort standing today reveals nothing of the original Fort Sullivan. A short film and exhibits reveal the Revolutionary history of the fort.

Winnsboro

Cornwallis House (site)
8 Zion Road, private home.

Although named for prominent Patriot leader Richard Winn, the picturesque town founded in 1775 is better remembered as the winter headquarters of Lord Cornwallis after the disaster at Kings Mountain aborted his first invasion of North Carolina. The British remained in Winnsboro for four months beginning in October 1780, building the army's strength to more than 4,000 troops. This private home is presumed to be the headquarters of the British general; the army camped at the nearby Mt. Zion Institute.

York

Kings Mountain National Military Park (site)
Route 161, twelve miles northwest of town, 864-936-7921; Daily, 9–5. Free.

When the British decided to stop the Revolution by conquering the South they quickly overran South Carolina and Georgia, and the bloody Civil War between Whigs and Loyalist Tories escalated out of control. With the war now at their doorstep, hundreds of Southerners renewed their allegiance to the Crown. Those who didn't suffered retribution, often at the hands of their neighbors.

Lord Cornwallis ordered Major Patrick Ferguson to range the backcountry to recruit Loyalists for the growing redcoat militia. Ferguson, the son of an Aberdeenshire, Scotland, judge, entered the Royal service at the age of 15 and was a rising star during the Revolution. Celebrated as a marksman, he invented an improved breech-loading rifle, but his efforts to integrate the rifle into the British Army were unsuccessful.

Ferguson won no favor from the locals he failed to recruit. He openly referred to the Carolina woodsmen as "mongrels" and "backwater men" as he hunted down and punished rebels who resisted Royal authority. In September 1780 he dispatched a paroled Whig prisoner to Colonel Isaac Shelby with a message threatening the Westerners that "if they did not desist from their opposition to the British arms, he would march his army over the mountains, hang their leaders, and lay their country waste with fire and sword."

Within weeks the opposition to meet this threat mounted. From deep in the mountains, men from 16 to 60 assembled. They were fiercely independent and carried little interest in politics; they didn't want anyone — American or British — dictating how they lived their lives. They disdained uniforms and came to battle in buckskins. Some 600 "Over-Mountain" men covered more than 200 miles to protect their homesteads.

The frontiersmen joined 400 South Carolina militia at Cowpens on October 6, 1780, to begin a march on Ferguson's position at Kings Mountain, 30 miles to the east. Ferguson had chosen to stand at Kings Mountain, a rocky outcropping that rose some 60 feet to a treeless plateau at the summit. The plateau was 600 yards long and 70 feet wide at one end and 120 at the other. Surrounded by a hardwood forest, Ferguson had seemingly found an ideal location to protect his 1,100 men. He bothered to build no defensive fortifications.

After a night march in the pouring rain, the mountain men wasted no time before attacking in the afternoon of October 7. They surrounded the Tory position and worked their way up the slopes, fighting from tree to tree on their way to the summit. The high ground in this case worked against the defenders as they were unable to get clear shots at their attackers.

Ferguson rode frenetically among his men, imploring them and directing maneuvers with a great silver whistle. His fatal mistake of confronting his pursuers on a timberless hilltop came to an end when a barrage of bullets tore through his body and left him dangling from his horse with one foot still hanging in a stirrup. With the death of Patrick Ferguson, the only British soldier in this civil war among Americans, the Tories surrendered.

Or at least attempted to surrender. Many of the frontiersmen did not know the meaning of a white flag and continued to shoot down the terrified, disorganized enemy. Some of those who knew a white flag had no interest in displaying mercy to despised Loyalists who had burned property and killed settlers. When the carnage ended, 225 Loyalists lay dead or dying, another 163 were wounded and 716 were taken prisoner. The "backwater men" suffered 90 casualties, among them 28 killed.

The prisoners were marched northward to the Continental Army jurisdiction at Hillsborough, North Carolina. Many were beaten and hacked with swords before being turned over to a worse fate. In an all-day, outdoor trial, three dozen Loyalists were tried by a panel of Whig colonels and found guilty of "breaking open houses, killing the men, turning the men and women out of doors, and burning the houses." Nine of the convicted were "swung off."

Once the surviving prisoners were delivered, the army from beyond the mountains faded away as quickly and as quietly as it had arrived. Sir Henry Clinton called the defeat at Kings Mountain "the first link in a chain of evils that at last ended in the total loss of America." Ironically, it was men beholden to no government who had set the country free.

An interpretive walking tour around Battlefield Ridge winds around the American lines and up to the Tory position at the crest. The spot where Patrick Ferguson was wounded is marked by a monument, and his grave is covered with a traditional Scottish stone cairn. The visitor center features a film and exhibits on the mountain men who fought at Kings Mountain.

Tennessee

Revolutionary Status: claimed by the North Carolina colony

Charlotte

Revolutionary Monument (mem)

Charlotte Courthouse, Routes 48 and 49.

A monument honoring the 36 Revolutionary War soldiers buried in Dickson County stands on the front lawn of the Charlotte Courthouse. The monument, which lists the names of Carolina and Virginia men mostly, was dedicated on July 4, 1976.

Elizabethton

Sycamore Shoals State Historical Area (site)

Off Route 321, west of town, 423-543-5808; Mon–Sat, 8–4:30, Sun, 1–4:30. Free.

In 1772, three years after the settling of the area, 113 displaced Virginians established the Watauga Association, the first independent government in America. Sycamore Shoals was the capital of the chain of river settlements. It was a violation of colonial laws established for the frontier, but it didn't stop the settlers from buying 20 million acres of land from the Cherokee. The Watauga Association only paid 10,000 pounds for the "Transylvania Purchase," but it wasn't the Cherokee's land to sell anyway.

The settlement survived Indian raids during the early years of the Revolution and was the departure point for the Overmountain Men, frontiersmen who crossed the Blue Ridge Mountains into North Carolina to reinforce American militia. In September 1780 the Overmountain Men reinforced Francis Marion during a smashing victory at Kings Mountain, which caused the British retreat to the Virginia coast at Yorktown.

A museum houses relics from the first permanent American settlement outside the original American Colonies. A 30-minute film relates the history of the Revolutionary Overmountain Men.

Reenactment: Each September, in one of the Revolution's most ambitious reenactments, recreators march the 220 miles to King's Mountain, South Carolina, along the Over Mountain Victory Trail.

Nashville

Fort Nashborough (site)

170 1st Avenue North between Broadway and Church streets, 615-862-8424; Apr–Nov: Tue–Sat, 9–4. Free.

Fort Nashborough was built in 1780, just in time to meet the coldest winter recorded thusfar in American history. Some 60 men were also killed by Indian raids during the first year. After the Battle of the Bluffs on April 2, 1781, founder James Robertson consolidated all his area settlers in Fort Nashborough. With the help of war dogs the Indians were finally driven off, but raids continued until 1794. The restored log fort is near the site of the original and considerably smaller fort; the blockhouse and stockade appear much as they did in the founding days of Nashville.

Piney Flats

Rocky Mount (site)

Off Route 11E, 423-538-7396; Mar–Dec: Mon–Sat, 10–5, Sun, 2–6; Jan–Feb: Mon–Fri, 10–5. Admission charged.

William Cobb built this two-story log house for his family between 1770 and 1772. The home was used as a rendezvous point for the Overmountain Men and in 1790 became the capital of the U.S. territory of the south of the Ohio River. Costumed guides and a museum interpret the history of eastern Tennessee during the period 1763 to 1792.

Texas

Revolutionary Status: Spanish Territory

Austin

George Washington (mem)

University of Texas, South Mall.

Washington is portrayed by Pompeo Coppini standing as commander-in-chief. This is the third and final rendering of Washington by Coppini, completed when the sculptor was 85 years old. The others are installed in Portland, Oregon and Mexico City.

Laredo

George Washington (mem)

1110 Houston Street.

The Society of Martha Washington commissioned this larger-than life portraiture of Washington which was dedicated in 1992. The work was executed by Roberto Garcia, Jr., a native Texan.

Jefferson

Thomas Jefferson (mem)

Thomas Jefferson Memorial Park, 112 Austin Street.

The bust of Thomas Jefferson by Tommie Wurtsbaugh Glick is the center-piece of a riverfront park. Inscribed on the six-foot pedestal of Dakota granite are the three accomplishments by which he wished to be remembered: author-ing the Declaration of Independence and the Statute of Virginia for Religious Freedom, and founding the University of Virginia. The quote from Jefferson on the back reads: "Still one thing more, fellow citizens — a wise and frugal gov-ernment, which shall restrain men from injuring one another, which shall leave them otherwise free to regulate their own pursuits of industry and improvement, and shall not take from the mouth of labor the bread it has earned — this is the sum of good government."

Vermont

Revolutionary Status: Claimed by the New York colony
and the New Hampshire colony

Basin Harbor

Lake Champlain Maritime Museum (col)

Off Basin Harbor Road, 802-475-2022; May–Oct: daily, 10–5. Admis-sion charged.

Local residents have built boats along the lakeshore for over 150 years, and many are displayed at the museum's boathouse. But the most important vessel on display is the *Philadelphia II*, a replica of a Revolutionary War gunboat sunk in Lake Champlain in October 1776. The *Philadelphia II* was part of the com-mand of Benedict Arnold, whose heroics in the Battle of Valcour Bay may well have saved the Revolution.

After the American invasion of Canada failed in 1775–1776, Arnold stayed in Lake Champlain, harassing the British and commencing work on more ships to augment his tiny fleet of three captured vessels. To subdue Arnold, General Sir Guy Carleton was forced to assemble a flotilla of his own before moving on Albany.

On August 24, having incredibly built 10 new craft in two months, the dynamic Arnold, an experienced seaman, was now ready to commence his own naval war with Carleton. By late September Arnold's fleet numbered 15 as he pushed north to engage the greatly superior British numbers. South of a high bluff off Valcour Island, offshore from present-day Plattsburgh, the navies met on October 11. Arnold skillfully forced the invaders to sail into the wind to reach his woefully ill-equipped ships, some with only two guns, with their cannon. By nightfall both sides had lost ships, but the British, knowing they had Arnold trapped against the island, withdrew some 600 yards south to prevent the American escape.

Arnold knew his brave crew could not carry the battle another day, and that night, aided by a shrouding fog, he executed a daring escape, slipping single file through the British armada. In the morning Carleton discovered Arnold's astonishing disappearing act and gave chase down the lake. Arnold ran his flagship *Congress* and four smaller vessels aground at Basin Harbor on October 13 and burned them with their colors still flying. Arnold and 200 men then made good their escape.

Their daring exploits convinced the British to return to Canada before the winter, ending what would almost certainly have been a successful invasion of Albany. A year later, a reinforced and reinvigorated American force repulsed a second British thrust. The Hudson River was never controlled, the Colonies were never divided and the North would never be conquered.

The sunken *Philadelphia* was recovered from the lake bottom in 1935 and is on display at the Smithsonian Institution. A cannonball remained lodged in her hull and human bones were strewn along with eating utensils inside. The *Philadelphia II* is a working replica of that ship. As Arnold knew his troops were inexperienced seamen, he built gundalows like the *Philadelphia* with as little sail as possible, making it essentially a rowboat. It could be outfitted with two 9-pound cannon and a single 12-pounder.

In 1997 researchers from the museum discovered the last of Arnold's 11 missing ships from the Battle of Valcour Bay, an almost exact copy of *Philadelphia*, but unnamed. The 54-foot vessel, its mast still standing over 50 feet high and its large bow cannon still intact, was in excellent condition in Lake Champlain's icy preserving water. It has been left on the lake bottom, in keeping with museum policy towards preserving wrecks.

Bennington

Bennington Battle Monument (mem)

15 Monument Circle, 802-447-0550; Apr–Oct: 9–5. Admission charged.

Although the Battle of Bennington was fought west of town in New York State, the British objective was a cache of ammunition and guns stored in a small hilltop building in Bennington. Through much of the nineteenth century, Vermonters wanted to commemorate the battle with a monument but lacked the funds. With Vermont's centennial on the horizon in 1891, efforts began anew and $112,000 was raised from private contributions, the U.S. Congress and neighboring states.

A design by Boston architect John Phillipp Rinn was selected and the cornerstone laid in 1887. Slowly the obelisk of blue-grey magnesian limestone rose on the site of the old storehouse. On good weeks laborers were able to add ten feet a week. When the Bennington Battle Monument was completed and dedicated in 1891 it stood 306 feet, 4½ inches tall — the tallest battle monument in the world. Inside, Rinn crafted 417 steps, placed on gentle 4-inch risers to allow even the unathletic to reach its observational level. Today, the Battle Monument remains Vermont's tallest building.

On the grounds are additional monuments, the most striking being a 1910 heroic rendering of Colonel Seth Warner, commander of the Green Mountain Boys in the Battle of Bennington. A large granite boulder honors General John Stark and the 1,400 New Hampshire men instrumental in the American victory. An elevator up the monument affords views of three states from the top; also inside is a detailed diorama of the Battle of Bennington, completed in 1964.

Reenactment: The Battle of Bennington is re-created during Bennington Battle Day Weekend on the weekend nearest August 16. The celebration has taken place since the mid–1960s.

The Bennington Museum (col)

West Main Street (Route 9), 802-447-1571; July–Oct: Tue–Thur, 9–5, Fri–Mon, 9–7; Nov–Jan: daily, 9–5.

The Bennington Museum has an extensive collection of Revolutionary War relics, the most prized being the Bennington Battle Flag, believed to be the oldest surviving Stars and Stripes flag. Made of handspun linen, the flag prominently features a white "76." Also in the military gallery are uniforms, firearms and one of four 3-pound French cannons seized in the Battle of Bennington from the Germans.

Old Burying Ground (site)

Old First Church, Monument Avenue, 802-447-1223; Open daily, dawn to dusk.

The church organization dates to 1762, although the church, famed for its beauty, was not begun until 1805. In the burial yard are the graves of soldiers felled at the Battle of Bennington and five Vermont governors. Also next to the church is the final resting place of poet Robert Frost, who chose for his epitaph, "I had a lover's quarrel with the world."

Burlington

Allen Gravesite (site)

Greenmount Cemetery, Colchester Avenue; Open daily, dawn to dusk.

Ethan Allen and his brother Ira were leaders of the Green Mountain Boys in Vermont's struggle for independence from New York and, at times, against the British as well. Their main objective was the formation of the Republic of Vermont, achieved in 1777. Allen died in 1789, two years before Vermont's entry into the United States as the first state after the framing of the Constitution. His grave is marked by an 1855 granite shaft. The standing figure of Ethan Allen demanding the surrender of Fort Ticonderoga was sculpted by Peter Stephenson.

Ethan Allen Homestead (site)

Off Route 127, north of town, 802-865-4556; May–Oct: Mon–Sat, 10–5, Sun, 1–5. Admission charged.

The warship *Liberty*, which wreaked havoc on Lake Champlain during the Revolutionary War, was built on the Winooski River in 1772, but the area was not settled until 1775. Most of these pioneers joined Ethan Allen's marauding Green Mountain Boys, and the rest deserted the region during British counterattacks. Permanent settlement of Burlington did not begin until 1783. Allen farmed this site from 1787 until his death two years later.

The restored timber farmhouse features objects and a multimedia show relating to Allen and his times. Hiking trails traverse the expansive farmstead.

Claredon

Lt. Colonel Joseph Wait (site)

Pinkowski Farm, Alfrecha Road and Middle Road.

The relief carving is of a Revolutionary soldier standing with his feet together and his proper left hand behind his back. He is dressed in a military uniform and wears a tricornered hat. It was erected in honor of Lt. Col. Joseph Wait, an officer in the American Revolution who died on his return from an expedition into Canada in September of 1776.

East Hubbardton

Hubbardton Battlefield State Historic Site (site)

Unfinished road, seven miles north of Route 4 from Castleton, 802-759-2412; May–Oct: Wed–Sun, 9:30–5:30. Admission for museum only.

After British General "Gentleman Johnny" Burgoyne drove the American rebels from Fort Ticonderoga in his opening thrust to split the colonies along the Hudson River in 1777, he chased them east through hilly terrain. Reaching Hubbardton, American major general Arthur St. Clair ordered a rear guard of some 1,000 men to help cover his weary and tattered main army as they moved southwest.

The American force was comprised of a detachment of Seth Warner's Green Mountain Boys, a detail of Massachusetts militia under Colonel Ebeneezer Francis and the 2nd New Hampshire of the Continental Army under Nathan Hale (not the martyred spy). Warner was under instructions to lead the regiment south to Castleton, but after hard marching, decided to camp on the night of July 6, 1777, in Hubbardton, located along Military Road, which connected the garrisons on Lake Champlain with sites on the Connecticut River.

Indian scouts revealed Warner's camp to Brig. Gen. Simon Fraser, himself camped a few miles west over the next ridge of mountains. Fraser and his German counterpart, the colorful field officer Maj. Gen. Baron von Riedesel, plotted a dawn attack and about 4:40 on the morning of July 7 indeed surprised Hale as his regiment was having breakfast. The entire force, including Hale, was captured with scarcely a shot being fired.

The remaining Americans hurriedly assembled behind a stone wall at the top of Monument Hill. The elite British troops pushed valiantly through bush and fallen trees up the steep slope, suffering heavy losses. Still, the American troops held their ground. Then von Riedesel's grenadiers arrived, heralded by the playing of his band. The Germans broke through the Massachusetts line, killed Francis and then splintered the Vermont troops, who left the field under Warner's decidedly nonmilitary order: "Scatter and meet me in Manchester."

The Americans lost more than 300 men, most of whom were captured. About 35 to 40 men were killed on each side. Although the Americans had been forced from the field, their delaying action was accomplished. Further, they had shown the British they were willing to fight. Burgoyne's 1777 drive to divide the colonies, which would end in defeat at Saratoga, was first resisted in Hubbardton.

A visitors reception center houses a museum with artifacts and a three-dimensional fiber-optic map. On the grounds, a one-mile interpretive trail illuminates the troublesome terrain the British were forced to traverse in the only battle of the Revolution on Vermont soil, including their march through a mountain pass and the deadly climb up Monument Hill.

The 1859 Hubbardton Battle monument stands on the spot where Colonel Ebeneezer Francis was supposedly buried by the British troops. His bravery under fire was greatly admired at Hubbardton, and when his body was found after the battle, Baron von Riedesel personally saw to it that the gallant young colonel received a proper military burial from his Brunswick troops.

Manchester

The Soldier's Monument (mem)

Main Street, in front of the First Congregational Church.

This memorial to all wars, dedicated to the "Men of Manchester," was unveiled on Memorial Day, 1905. The standing figure created by W.H. Fullerton is of a Revolutionary War soldier dressed in uniform, with tricornered hat and tailcoat. He strides forward with a proper left foot. For the Revolutionary War 124 men are listed on a bronze tablet.

Montpelier

State Capitol (mem)

State Street; Jul–Oct: Mon–Fri, 8–4, Sat, 11–2:30; Nov–Jun: Mon–Fri, 8–4. Free.

Built of Vermont's famed Barre granite in the nation's smallest state capital city, the State House displays one of the four brass cannons captured from the Hessians in the Battle of Bennington. Also in the portico is a statue of Ethan Allen, carved from Imperial Danby marble on a granite base. Aristide Piccini was the sculptor.

Orwell

Mount Independence State Historic Site (site)

Unfinished road off Route 73, six miles west of town, 802-759-2412; Jun–Oct: Wed–Sun, 9:30–5:30. Free.

After the Americans overran lightly manned Fort Ticonderoga on May 10, 1775, they quickly moved to defend Ticonderoga's weak northern exposure. Across Lake Champlain — only 1,300 yards at this point — General Philip Schuyler ordered the clearing of timber and the construction of a sister fort. The horseshoe-shaped battery, protected by steep cliffs, was named Mount Independence following the arrival of a copy of the Declaration of Independence on July 18, 1776. A floating bridge connected the fortified complex.

During 1777, Mount Independence was even better fortified than Ticonderoga, but even together the forts were no match for Burgoyne's massive invading force from Canada. On July 5 both posts were evacuated. British and German forces remained at Mount Independence until November, when they burned and destroyed the site after the British surrender at Saratoga.

Mount Independence remains an archaeological site with four interpretive trails winding through 400 acres of foundations and remains. Among the ruins are a general hospital — in constant use from the skeleton force of 2,500 men who held the fort during the winter of 1776 — barracks and a blockhouse.

Rutland

Green Mountain Boy (mem)

Main Street Park, South Main Street and West Street.

The statue commemorates those who defended their land from "Yorkers" claiming rights to them in the conflict between New Hampshire and New York grants, before and during the Revolutionary War, when they also fought the oppressive British. The full-length standing figure of a Revolutionary Green Mountain Boy holding a musket was sculpted by Raymond Porter.

Wallingford

Boy with the Boot (mem)

Route 7 and Route 140.

Often called the "Most Mysterious Statue in the World," the drummer boy is either from the Revolutionary War or the Civil War and honors those who risked their lives to bring water to dying soldiers in the field. The standing boy wears a blue cap, a red shirt and blue pants rolled to his knees. In his right hand he holds a boot from which water leaks from the sole. The figure is at the center of a large basin.

Windsor

Old Constitution House (site)

16 North Main Street, 802-828-3051; Memorial Day–Oct: Wed–Sun, 11–5. Admission charged.

The territory that would evolve into Vermont was long in dispute between New Hampshire and New York. In January 1777, disgruntled residents declared their independence from both states and adopted the name "New Connecticut." On June 4, 1777, representatives convened in Windsor in the tavern operated by Elijah West to create a constitutional government. By July 8 they had hammered out the constitution of the Free and Independent Republic of Vermont. The two-story frame house is now a museum tracing the events that led to the Republic of Vermont, its constitution and eventual statehood.

Virginia

Revolutionary Status: Original Colony
Estimated Colonial Population: 490,000
Colonial Capital: Williamsburg
Last Colonial Governor: Edmund Pendleton (Chairman of Committee of Safety)
Troops Provided: 15 Continental regiments

Revolutionary Timeline:

October 10, 1774: Andrew Lewis defeats 800 Shawnees under Cornstalk to end Lord Dumore's War

March 23, 1775: Patrick Henry avows in a speech at St. John's Church in Richmond to "give me liberty, or give me death"

December 9, 1775: British charge to defeat at Great Bridge, the first battle with regular troops since Bunker Hill

January 1, 1776: Bombardment of Norfolk begins

June 12, 1776: Virginia adopts the first bill of rights, drafted by George Mason

October 19, 1781: After a 19-day siege, Lord Charles Cornwallis surrenders the main of the British Army at Yorktown

January 16, 1786: Virginia adopts Thomas Jefferson's Statute for Religious Freedom, which will become a model for the First Amendment

December 14, 1799: George Washington dies at Mount Vernon

Alexandria

Boyhood Home of Robert E. Lee (site)

607 Oronoco Street, 703-548-8454; Mon–Sat, 10–4, Sun, 1–4. Admission charged.

As a 20-year-old in 1776, Harry Lee abandoned plans for a law career and secured an appointment as a captain in the Virginia cavalry. The greatest success for "Light Horse" Harry Lee came under Nathanael Greene in the Carolinas in 1781, which propelled him into state and national politics after the war. Lee worked in the Second Continental Congress and served Virginia as governor between 1792 and 1795. Later, he was a U.S. congressman.

After his son Robert Edward Lee was born in 1807, economic reversals led to his imprisonment and the authorship of a personal history of the Revolution, *Memoirs of the War in the Southern Department of the United States*. Forced to leave the family estate at Stratford Hall in 1811, Lee moved his wife and five children to Alexandria and this stately brick Federal townhouse, built in 1795. It had been home to William Fitzhugh, a Lee relative who entertained Washington here. "Light Horse" Harry Lee died in 1818.

Carlyle House (site)

121 N. Fairfax Street, 703-549-2997; Tue–Sat, 10–5, Sun, 12–5. Admission charged.

British general Edward Braddock made the 1752 stone mansion built in the Georgian style by Scottish merchant John Carlyle his headquarters in the spring of 1755. In the splendid parlor Braddock summoned five Royal governors to plan the financing for his campaign against the French and Indians in America. The result was the detested Stamp Act, which would help provoke the Revolution. George Washington was commissioned as an aide-de-camp to Braddock in this house.

Christ Church (site)

118 North Washington Street, 703-549-1450; Mon–Fri, 9–4, Sat, 9–1, Sun, 2–4:30. Free.

Completed in 1773, the brick Georgian Episcopal church is Alexandria's oldest. When it opened George Washington purchased Pew 60 for 36 pounds and 10 shillings. It is preserved in the active church today. Christ Church is dedicated to the honorary pallbearers of Washington: Charles Simms, Dennis Ramsay, William Payne, George Gilpin, Philip Marsteller and Charles Little.

Fort Ward Museum and Historic Site (site)

4301 West Braddock Road, 703-838-4848; Tue–Sat, 9–5, Sun, 12–5. Free.

Reenactment: Alexandria hosts the nation's largest parade celebrating the birthday of George Washington on the Monday of Washington's birthday weekend. Camp life is demonstrated and British and Colonial uniformed troops engage in skirmishing at Fort Ward.

Gadsby's Tavern Museum (site)

134 North Royal Street, 703-838-4242; Tue–Sat, 10–5, Sun, 1–5. Admission charged.

In Colonial America, Alexandria was the most developed settlement on the main north-south road between Baltimore and Fredericksburg, and the City Tavern, built in 1770, was the hub for social and political goings-on. John Gadsby became proprietor in 1794.

George Washington was a frequent visitor and participated in the first gala in celebration of his birthday in 1798. In November 1799 he made his final military review from the tavern steps. Washington's Birthnight Ball is reenacted each year and visitors can still enjoy authentic eighteenth century fare in the restaurant.

George Washington Masonic National Memorial (col)

Kin Street at Callahan Drive, 703-683-2007; Daily, 9–5. Free.

George Washington served as the first Worshipful Master of the Alexandria Lodge No. 22, and this 333-foot tall landmark in his honor is crafted after the ancient lighthouse at Alexandria in Egypt. The Replica Lodge Room features a collection of Washington memorabilia, including the family Bible, and a 17-foot bronze statue of the general graces Memorial Hall. Dioramas and murals depict scenes from Washington's career.

George Washington's Grist Mill Historical State Park (site)

5514 Mount Vernon Memorial Highway, 703-550-0960; Memorial Day–Labor Day, Sat–Sun, 10–6. Admission charged.

On the original foundation is a working replica of the mill used by George Washington to process his crops. A video presents the history of the mill.

Lee-Fendall House (site)

614 Oronoco Street, 703-548-1789; Tue–Sat, 10–4, Sun, 12–4. Admission charged.

The white frame house was built in 1785 by Philip Richard Fendall, a Lee family relative. The land was owned by "Light Horse" Harry Lee, and it was here he penned the farewell address from Alexandrians to George Washington when Washington left Mount Vernon to become the nation's first president. The house features many Lee family possessions from the 37 family members who lived in the house from 1785 until 1903.

The Lyceum (col)

201 South Washington Street, 703-838-4994; Mon–Sat, 10–5, Sun, 1–5. Free.

Built in 1839 as a lecture hall and reading room, the city's first cultural center now preserves Alexandria history from its founding in 1749. Included in the 1839 Greek Revival building are prints, documents and artifacts from the Colonial period.

Mount Vernon (site)

George Washington Parkway, nine miles south of town, 703-780-2000; Apr–Aug: daily, 8–5; Sept–Oct, Mar: daily, 9–5; Nov–Feb: daily, 9–4. Admission charged.

George Washington moved to Mount Vernon, a family plantation owned by his older half-brother, Lawrence, as a young man of 16 in 1748. When Lawrence died of consumption in 1752, George was made executor of the estate that he inherited a few years later.

The home to which Washington brought his new wife, the wealthy 26-year-old widow Martha Custis, in 1757 was a one-and-a-half-story building overlooking 2,000 acres. When he was not elsewhere engaged, Washington spent much of the next three decades working on Mount Vernon. He raised the roof to add another story and extended the ends of the house. An innovative colonnaded porch was affixed overlooking the Potomac River.

Washington gradually expanded his land holdings to more than 8,000 acres. Although he considered Mount Vernon to be the most ideally situated estate in the country, Washington was never able to make the plantation profitable. Martha Washington's resources, especially in the times of her husband's extensive absences, kept Mount Vernon extant.

George Washington died at Mount Vernon on December 14, 1799. Early in 1801, Martha Washington, a year older than her husband, died as well. Both are buried on the grounds.

Although Mount Vernon is today one of America's treasures, its value was not immediately recognized after the passing of the childless Washingtons. The estate passed through various family members until it was offered for sale to the state and federal government in the mid–nineteenth century. Neither wanted it. Mount Vernon was saved only by the organization of an early private historical preservation group, the Mount Vernon Ladies' Association, headed by Ann Pamela Cunningham.

In addition to the mansion, restored in appearance to the last year of Washington's life and featuring original paint colors, the 30 acres include Washington's tomb, the gardens and many outbuildings. At the Pioneer Farm daily activities of an eighteenth century farm are demonstrated.

Old Presbyterian Meeting House (site)

321 South Fairfax Street, 703-549-6670; Mon–Fri, 9–3. Free.

Still active as a church, the Old Presbyterian Meeting House was built in 1774 and was a popular gathering place for patriots during the Revolution. Memorial services for George Washington were held on this site in December 1799.

Buried in the churchyard is James Craik, the Revolutionary War surgeon who dressed Lafayette's wounds at Brandywine and attended both George and Martha Washington. His three-story brick home, private today, is standing at 210 Duke Street. Also in the churchyard is the Tomb of the Unknown Soldier of the American Revolution, whose identity "is known only to God."

Stabler-Leadbeater Apothecary Shop (site)

105-107 South Fairfax Street, 703-836-3713; Mon–Sat, 10–4, Sun, 1–5. Admission charged.

Edward Stabler, a Quaker pharmacist, opened one of America's oldest apothecary shops in 1792. The family operated the business for 141 years until the Depression forced the drug shop to close. Included in its prescription files are records for George Mason, George and Martha Washington and other Revolutionary notables.

Woodlawn Plantation (site)

Route 1, seven miles south of town, 703-780-4000; Mar–Dec: daily, 9:30–4:30; Jan–Feb: Sat–Sun, 9:30–4:30. Admission charged.

George Washington gave the land for this estate, originally part of Mt. Vernon, as a wedding present to his adopted daughter, Eleanor Parke Custis, and his nephew, Major Lawrence Lewis. The couple then commissioned Dr. William Thornton, architect of the U.S. Capitol, to design the Georgian mansion.

Ashland

Scotchtown (site)

Scotchtown Road, off Route 54, nine miles northwest of town, 804-227-3500; May–Oct: Tue–Sat, 10–4:30, Sun, 1:30–4:30. Admission charged.

The large frame house built by Charles Chiswell circa 1719 became prominent when Patrick Henry moved his wife Sarah and their six children there in 1771. After failing in the mercantile business as a young man, the 24-year-old Henry began practicing law in 1760. He rose to prominence on May 29, 1765, when he presented seven Stamp Act resolutions to the colonial legislature, asserting that the measures were invalid and Virginia enjoyed the sovereignty of self-rule. Thereafter, Henry reigned as the most powerful opposition voice in the House of Burgesses.

Henry lived at Scotchtown until 1777, having served nationally at the First Continental Congress and having been elected the first governor of the independent Commonwealth of Virginia.

Brookneal

Red Hill (site)

State Road 600, five miles east of town, 804-376-2044; Mar–Oct: daily, 9–5; Nov–Feb: daily, 9–4. Admission charged.

Patrick Henry, "The Trumpet of the Revolution," retired to Red Hill in 1794, resuming his private legal practice. He could look back on his five terms as governor of Virginia (having turned down a sixth), his work on the adoption of the Bill of Rights, and one of the leading roles he played in the fight for independence.

The plantation at Red Hill covered 2,920 acres, although the frame manor house was a modest one. Two of Henry's 17 children were born here and two of his daughters were married here. In 1799 death came to Henry here as well.

The main house was destroyed by fire in 1919 and an authentic reconstruction has risen on the original foundation. Of the buildings on the property,

Henry's law office is original. The museum houses the largest collection of Patrick Henry memorabilia in the world, including the renowned oil painting "Patrick Henry Before the Virginia House of Burgesses" by P.H. Rothermel. Patrick Henry is buried on the estate, beneath the inscription: "His fame is his best epitaph."

Burrowsville

Brandon (site)
Route 611, five miles northeast of town, 757-866-8486; Daily 8–5. Admission charged.

Thomas Jefferson designed this estate for Nathaniel Harrison and it remained in the Harrison family until 1926. During the Revolutionary War the house was fired on by a British frigate from the James River. The front portico still bears reminders of the assault.

Charles City

Berkeley Plantation (site)
Off Route 5, six miles west of town, 804-829-6018; Daily, 8–5. Admission charged.

The first official Thanksgiving is said to have taken place on this site in 1619; a little more than a decade later the first Harrisons arrived. The house on the plantation dates to 1726, about the date that Benjamin Harrison V was born. Benjamin V inherited the plantation in 1745 after his father and two sisters were killed by lightning.

That same year Harrison entered the House of Burgesses and remained until it was disbanded 30 years later. He served in both the first and second continental congresses and signed the Declaration of Independence. Harrison continued to serve in politics until his death in 1791, including a stint as governor of Virginia.

Benedict Arnold, then a British raider, plundered the estate in 1781 but did little damage. George Washington visited the estate as president, as did every one of the first 15 presidents until the Civil War. Two Harrisons — William Henry and Benjamin — became presidents themselves.

Shirley Plantation (site)
501 Shirley Plantation Road, ten miles west of town off Route 5, 804-829-5121; Daily, 9–5. Admission charged.

Since 1660 the plantation has been in the Hill and Carter families and was the birthplace of Anne Hill Carter, who married "Light Horse" Harry Lee in the manor house, which dates to 1723. Shirley Plantation, Virginia's oldest, was a supply center for the Continental Army and a post for both sides during the American Revolution.

Charlottesville

Ash Lawn (site)

Route 795 off Route 53, southeast of town, 804-293-9539; Mar–Oct: daily, 9–6; Nov–Feb: daily 10–5. Admission charged.

By the time he was 20, James Monroe had served over two years in the Continental Army, been wounded at Trenton, and promoted to major. Then, in 1778, he resigned to pursue his legal and political career, which would lead to the White House nearly 40 years later. Monroe moved to this frame house on a tobacco plantation in 1799. The site was personally selected for him by his friend and new neighbor, Thomas Jefferson.

George Rogers Clark (mem)

West Main Street.

Clark, conqueror of the British in the Northwest, was born near Charlottesville, and this memorial, just east of the University of Virginia, honors him.

Monticello (site)

Route 53, 804-984-9800; Mar–Oct: daily, 8–5; Nov–Feb: daily, 9–4:30. Admission charged.

Thomas Jefferson began planning a house on this site as a young boy and started construction on Monticello in 1769. He continued work on his beloved estate for more than a half-century despite ongoing financial difficulties, especially in the years after he left the presidency in 1809. For the final 17 years of his life Jefferson scarcely left the shadow of his mountaintop home.

A British raiding party entered central Virginia in 1781 to capture the author of the Declaration of Independence, but Jefferson had been alerted and escaped by minutes. The invaders did, however, take prisoner several bottles of Monticello's best vintages of wine.

The third president is buried in Monticello's small family burial ground, beneath a simple marker, in accordance with Jefferson's instructions. The epitaph is his own: "Here was buried Thomas Jefferson/Author of the Declaration of American Independence/Of the Statute of Virginia for religious freedom/And father of the University of Virginia."

Chesterfield

Chesterfield County Museum (col)

Route 10 in the Courthouse Complex, 804-748-1026; Mon–Fri, 10–4, Sun, 1–4. Admission charged.

Baron von Steuben used the courthouse in Chesterfield as a headquarters and training facility. This unfortunate connection caused Benedict Arnold to torch the courthouse in 1781. The museum building was constructed as a replica of the 1750 courthouse and chronicles its story inside.

Fairfax

Judicial Center (col)
4010 Chain Bridge Road; Open by appointment. Free.

The wills of George and Martha Washington were probated at the courthouse next door, which has been in continuous use since opening in 1800. The original wills are on display in the Judicial Center.

Falmouth

Ferry Farm (site)
Route 3 at Ferry Road, 540-372-6563; Mon–Sat, 10–4, Sun, 12–4. Free.

Augustine Washington moved his family to the Ferry Farm in 1738 when his son George was six. Five years later Ferry Farm was George Washington's inheritance when his father died. His mother remained here until 1772, after which Washington sold the property.

At Ferry Farm Washington received his formal education and taught himself surveying. It was here that the fanciful legends of chopping down a cherry tree and throwing a Spanish dollar across the Rappahannock River would have occurred in Washington's young life.

Fredericksburg

Fredericksburg Area Museum and Cultural Center (col)
Old Town Hall and Market House, 905 Princess Anne Street, 703-371-3037. Admission charged.

With its location in an accessible valley at the head of the navigable Rappahannock River, Fredericksburg, named for King George III's father, became an important rivertown in Colonial America. The museum maintains six permanent exhibit galleries, one of which tells the story of Fredericksburg in the Revolutionary era. The museum building was once the town hall and market building where political ideas and farm produce were exchanged with equal passion.

George Washington Masonic Museum (site)
803 Princess Anne Street, 540-373-5885; Mon–Sat, 9–4, Sun, 1–4. Admission charged.

A 20-year-old George Washington was raised a Mason in Lodge No. 4 in 1752. The lodge museum collection includes the Masonic Bible, on which Washington took his oath of office as president, and an original Gilbert Stuart portrait of Washington.

Hugh Mercer (mem)
Washington Avenue and Faquier Street.

This bronze tribute to Hugh Mercer was erected in 1906 to honor the Scottish warrior who commanded the 3rd Virginia Regiment and the "Flying Camp." Mercer was one of five Revolutionary generals from the Fredericksburg area.

Hugh Mercer Apothecary Shop (site)

1020 Caroline Street, 703-373-3362; Mar–Nov: daily, 9–5; Dec–Feb: daily, 10–4. Admission charged.

Scottish physician and soldier Hugh Mercer took time between tours of duty on the battlefield to open an apothecary shop in Fredericksburg, believed to have been in this small clapboard building. With the advent of the American Revolution, the 50-year-old Mercer signed on as a colonel and quickly became a brigadier general. He served splendidly in New York and New Jersey until his heroic death in Princeton in January 1777 deprived Washington of one of his ablest lieutenants.

James Monroe Museum (col)

908 Charles Street, 703-373-3362; Mar–Nov: daily, 9–5; Dec–Feb: daily, 10–4. Admission charged.

The fifth president of the United States interrupted his studies at William and Mary College to join Hugh Mercer's regiment as a second lieutenant in 1775. After three years of service, James Monroe returned to Virginia to study law under Thomas Jefferson and begin his career in Fredericksburg. The museum, with the largest collection of memorabilia pertaining to Monroe's life, is at the site of his law office.

Kenmore (site)

1201 Washington Avenue, 703-373-3381; Mar–Dec: Mon–Sat, 10–5, Sun, 12–5. Admission charged.

Colonel Fielding Lewis, sporting a prominent Virginian pedigree, married George Washington's cousin Catherine and, after her death, the American commander's only sister, Betty. These personal — and later — business, ties between Washington and Lewis were only strengthened by the Revolution. Poor health prevented Lewis from serving on the battlefield, but he organized and supervised a small-arms factory in Fredericksburg and kept it running through 1781, using loans secured on personal collateral.

Lewis began work on the manor house, then called Millbank, in 1752 and continued refining the Georgian brick house for the next 25 years. When he died in 1782 the state of Virginia did not authorize repayment of his loans used to keep the munitions works afloat, and the Lewis family lost Millbank.

Mary Washington House (site)

1200 Charles Street, 703-373-1569; Mar–Nov: daily, 9–5; Dec–Feb: daily, 10–4. Admission charged.

George Washington bought this townhouse for his mother in 1772, removing her from the rigors of maintaining the family plantation at Ferry Farm. She lived the last 17 years of her life in this home, just three blocks from her daughter Betty at Millbank. Just before her death in 1789, Washington left for his presidential inauguration from this house, having obtained his mother's blessing.

Mary Washington Monument and Grave (mem)
Washington Avenue, at the end of Pitt Street.
Andrew Jackson laid the cornerstone for a marble monument to George Washington's mother in 1833. It was not completed, however, until 1894, when President Grover Cleveland dedicated the present marker, a 40-foot granite shaft.

Rising Sun Tavern (site)
1304 Caroline Street, 703-371-1494; Mar–Nov: daily, 9–5; Dec–Feb: daily, 10–4. Admission charged.
George Washington's brother Charles built this steep-gabled structure as his home in 1760, but by the Revolution it was being used as the Rising Sun Tavern under the congenial ministrations of its host, George Weedon. Born in Germany, Weedon was a fervent Revolutionary, and the public house was known as a center of political activity.
Weedon, a German veteran of the French and Indian War, took up arms as lieutenant colonel of the 3rd Virginia Regiment, second in command to Hugh Mercer. Known to his men as "Joe Gourd," Weedon fought with distinction and was soon promoted to brigadier general. His actions at Brandywine were credited with enabling the Continental Army to effect a successful retreat. At Yorktown Weedon directed the Virginia militia as he concluded his military career.
After the surrender at Yorktown Washington and Lafayette celebrated at the Rising Sun Tavern. Weedon died 12 years later in 1793.

Great Bridge

Battle of Great Bridge (site)
Intersection of routes 165 and 168; highway markers only.
After the clash at Bunker Hill the British regulars did not meet the American rebels in battle again for nearly six months. The next encounter was in a tidal swamp around the Elizabeth River, 12 miles south of Norfolk.
After fleeing Williamsburg, Lord Dunmore occupied Norfolk, which shortly became the only city in Virginia remaining under British control. When Dunmore learned the revolutionary Virginia government was preparing to move against him, he fortified the city and set about raising an army. Around a core of regular soldiers he recruited some 60 Tories, a band of mariners, and more than 200 black troops referred to as the "Ethiopian Corps." By early December Dunmore had 600 men available to defend a small earthworks he had constructed at the east end of a 120-foot bridge at the Elizabeth River.
The advancing Americans under Colonel William Woodford camped at the west end of the bridge, stymied by the superior British defensive position. But Dunmore had no patience for stalemate and on December 9, 1775, he attacked

the Patriot force. In less than a half-hour of fighting the British were repulsed with the loss of more than 60 men. The Patriots numbered only one casualty. Dunmore soon abandoned Norfolk and British rule was extinguished from Virginia.

Nothing remains of the site of the first battle of the Revolution in Virginia.

Lancaster Village

Mary Ball Washington Museum (col)
Courthouse Green on Route 3, 804-462-7280; Apr–Nov: Tue–Fri, 9–5, Sat, 10–3. Free.

Lancaster House, built about 1798, features a museum with Washington family memorabilia. George Washington's mother Mary Ball was born in Lancaster. The four-building complex includes the eighteenth century clerk's office and jail.

Lexington

Lee Memorial Chapel (site)
Washington and Lee University, 703-463-8768; Apr–Oct: Mon–Sat, 9–5, Sun, 2–5, Nov–Mar: Mon–Sat, 9–4, Sun, 2–5. Free.

The school was founded in 1740 as Liberty Academy and saved from bankruptcy by George Washington, who donated $50,000 worth of James River Canal stock in 1796. The chapel was built in 1867–68 under the close supervision of Robert E. Lee and his son, George Washington Custis Lee, a professor at neighboring Virginia Military Institute. The chapel is the final resting place for Lee and his father, Revolutionary general "Light Horse" Harry Lee.

Lorton

Gunston Hall Plantation (site)
Route 242, off Route 1, east of town, 703-550-9220; Daily, 9:30–5. Admission charged.

While lacking in fiery oration, George Mason nonetheless exerted substantial influence on the Revolutionary movement. Born in 1725, Mason was a lifelong associate of Washington, a mentor to George Rogers Clark, and an instructor to Jefferson. In the years prior to the Revolution he wrote repeatedly and persuasively on the promotion of self-rule in the colonies.

While serving in the Fifth Virginia Convention, Mason became the primary author of the Virginia Declaration of Rights, the first state constitution to be adopted in America when it was approved on June 12, 1776. The ideas proposed by Mason in the document were filtered through the Declaration of Independence, the Bill of Rights, state charters and even in pamphlets disseminated during the French Revolution.

Mason helped shape the U.S. Constitution but refused to sign the final draft, believing too much power resided in the central government. His opposition led to the immediate first ten amendments — the Bill of Rights — although there was still no provision to abolish slavery, which Mason passionately abhorred.

The small Georgian house is a masterpiece of craftsmanship by William Buckland, who worked between 1755 and 1758 under an indentureship to the Mason family.

Pohick Church (site)

Route 1, two miles southwest of town, 703-550-9449; Daily, 9–4:30. Free.

George Washington selected the site and George Mason oversaw the construction, completed in 1774, of this brick Episcopal church. Washington reserved two pews and used this church as his regular place of worship before the Revolution. He was a vestryman for nearly a quarter-century.

Norfolk

St. Paul's Church (site)

St. Paul's Boulevard and City Hall Avenue, 757-627-4353; Tue–Fri, 10–4. Free.

In Colonial Virginia, Norfolk was the largest and most prosperous town in America's dominant colony. As the Revolution brewed elsewhere the ruling merchant class in Norfolk was more concerned with business than politics. After being driven from Williamsburg in 1775, Lord Dunmore relocated his Royal government in Norfolk.

In December 1775, after skirmishing at Great Bridge, it became apparent that Dunmore would not be able to hold Norfolk in the face of growing Patriot pressure. The Loyalists boarded ships from the Royal Navy and anchored offshore. Ongoing negotiations with rebel leaders to allow foraging in Norfolk proved fruitless, and Dunmore announced he was going to shell the city.

Before dawn on January 1, 1776, the bombardment began. As waterfront warehouses burned, the intractable rebel militia set fire to prominent Tory homes in spiteful retribution. The conflagration soon became so widespread that Patriot militia decided to destroy the entire town to prevent its use by the British. When Dunmore moved back to Norfolk he built provisional barracks but soon departed. The city would not revive until after the Revolution.

Built in 1739 on the site of an earlier 1641 church known as the "Chapel of Ease," St. Paul's is Norfolk's oldest building and the only structure to survive the British destruction of the city on New Year's Day, 1776. A cannonball fired by Lord Dunmore of the British fleet remains lodged in the southeastern wall.

War Memorial Museum of Virginia (col)

9285 Warwick Boulevard, 757-247-8523; Mon–Sat, 9–5, Sun, 1–5. Admission charged.

The collection of the War Memorial Museum includes 60,000 artifacts of American and Virginian military history dating to the Revolution in 1775. Also on the premises is a research library and a military film history collection.

Oak Grove

George Washington Birthplace (site)

Route 204, off Route 3, east of town, 804-224-1732; Daily, 9–5. Admission charged.

The Washington family saga in America began in 1657 when seafaring John Washington tarried in the Tidewater region of Virginia, befriended Nathaniel Pope and married Pope's daughter, Anne. The couple was given 700 acres on Mattox Creek as a wedding gift to start a tobacco farm. John eventually acquired more than 10,000 acres.

John Washington's grandson, Augustine, father of George, was born on the Mattox Creek farm in 1694. Although he moved to England, Augustine returned to Virginia as a young man to claim his inheritance along Bridges Creek. He later purchased more than a thousand acres on nearby Pope's Creek as well. Augustine married in 1721 and fathered four children, the eldest of whom died in infancy. In 1729 Jane Butler Washington died at the age of 30.

A year after his first wife died, Augustine married Mary Ball, an orphaned daughter of a prominent planter. Their first child, George, was born in 1732 in the manor house at Pope's Creek. Washington lived at Pope's Creek until the age of four, when Augustine moved to Ferry Farm, across the Rappahannock River from Fredericksburg, to enable him to better manage one of his iron businesses. In his adolescence, after his father's death, George returned to Pope's Creek to help work the family plantation.

On Christmas Day, 1779, while Washington was guiding the Continental Army, the manor house of his birth burned. It was never rebuilt.

George Washington's birthplace was excavated in 1936 and the foundations preserved. Its location and dimensions are indicated by an oyster shell outline. A typical Tidewater house of the upper classes of the 1700s has been constructed on the property as a memorial to Washington. Nearby is the kitchen house and Colonial herb garden.

The Washington family burial ground is near Bridges Creek and contains the graves of 32 family members, including Washington's half-brother, father, grandfather and great-grandfather, John Washington. An obelisk of Vermont marble is a one-tenth replica of the Washington Monument in the nation's capital.

Petersburg

Old Blandford Church (site)

319 South Crater Road, 804-733-2400; Daily, 10–5. Admission charged.

Petersburg was a well-established tobacco port before the Revolution, and as the war moved south General von Steuben and an attachment of 1,000 militia were placed in Petersburg to guard military supplies and tobacco stores. It was this prize that lured Benedict Arnold, now a British raider, and esteemed artillery general William Phillips to Petersburg in 1781.

Outnumbered three-to-one by some of the British elite, the Virginia militia managed to hold out for only a few hours before retreating. During the British occupation, Phillips, a Royal Artillery hero for 20 years, contracted typhoid fever and died. He was buried in Blandford Church Cemetery — known as the Brick Church on Well's Hill in the Revolution — in a secret ceremony to preclude vandalism of the grave. William Phillips, the highest ranking British officer of the Revolution buried in America, remains in an unmarked grave somewhere in the churchyard.

Richmond

The Capitol (site)

Capitol Square, 804-786-4344; Apr–Nov: daily, 9–5; Dec–Mar: Mon–Sat, 9–5, Sun, 1–5. Free.

Thomas Jefferson's neoclassical design was patterned after the Maison-Carrée, a Roman temple in Nimes, France. In the rotunda is the famous statue of George Washington by Jean Antoine Houdon. It was the only statue Washington ever agreed to pose for, and in 1788 the French master sailed across the Atlantic Ocean to study his subject and make a mold of his face. He returned to France to complete his masterpiece.

In the work Houdon incorporated a variety of symbols: a civilian's cane, a sword, a ploughshare and a column of 13 rods — one for each state. The life-size bronze is exactly 6'2" tall, and John Marshall remarked that "nothing in bronze or stone could be a more perfect image than this statue of the living Washington." After seeing the finished work, Lafayette commented, "I can almost realize he is going to move."

The noble visage created by Houdon has been called "one of the finest examples of simplification to be found in modern art." In 1853 six copies of the statue were authorized and displayed in Lexington, Virginia; Raleigh, North Carolina; Columbia, South Carolina; St. Louis; New York; and Washington.

At the bicentennial of Washington's birth in 1932, additional copies were made for the Peruvian Embassy in Washington; the Art Institute of Chicago; the Daughters of the American Revolution in San Francisco; the Henry E. Temple Association in Columbus, Ohio; Memorial Hall in Philadelphia; the Washington Memorial Chapel at Valley Forge; and the city of Pittsburgh.

Later copies were displayed at Versailles in France; the University of Virginia; George Washington University; Trafalgar Square in London; the National Statuary Hall in Washington; the State Capitol at Albany; the State House in Newport, Rhode Island; Kansas City; Uruguay; and the Dominican Republic. The final copy of the classic depiction of George Washington was authorized for the Mount Comfort Cemetery in Alexandria, Virginia.

John Marshall House (site)

818 East Marshall Street, 804-648-7998; Tue–Sat, 10–5. Admission charged.

Future Supreme Court Chief Justice John Marshall contributed to the Revolution as a minuteman in the Culpeper militia and later as a lieutenant in the 3rd Virginia Continentals. After fighting throughout the Northern Department, Marshall saw enough of the world to be drawn from his frontier home to Richmond to practice law after the war ended. He built this home in 1790 and lived here for 45 years.

St. John's Church (site)

2401 East Broad Street, 804-648-5015; Mon–Sat, 10–3:30, Sun, 1–3:30. Admission charged.

When Royal Governor Dunmore dissolved the Virginia Assembly it was no longer possible for the radical body to meet in the capital of Williamsburg. The only building in nearby Richmond large enough to accommodate the 120 members was the St. John's Episcopal Church, built during 1740–41.

On March 23, 1775, some of the greatest figures of the Revolution assembled for the Second Virginia Convention at St. John's. In attendance that day were George Washington, Thomas Jefferson, Peyton Randolph, Richard Henry Lee, George Wythe and Benjamin Harrison. They listened as Patrick Henry, in a speech that would electrify the colonies, urged his colleagues of the Second Virginia Convention, a conservative lot, to prepare for armed conflict: "I know not what course others may take, but as for me, Give me liberty or give me death!" The subsequent vote paved the way for Virginia to raise arms.

St. John's, still active, is one of Richmond's oldest wooden buildings. In the surrounding burial yard is the grave of George Wythe, mentor to Thomas Jefferson and first Virginia signer of the Declaration of Independence.

Reenactment: Reenactments of the Second Virginia Convention are held every Sunday afternoon promptly at 2 o'clock, beginning the last Sunday in May and continuing through the first Sunday in September. A commemorative reenactment is held on the Sunday that falls closest to March 23.

Tuckahoe Plantation (site)

River Road, seven miles west of town, 804-784-5736; Open by appointment.

Thomas Jefferson spent much of the first decade of his life in this home of his Randolph cousins, built between 1712 and 1730. The Randolphs were possibly the most powerful family in colonial Virginia and provided Jefferson's entry into learned society. Tuckahoe stands as one of the most architecturally complete plantations remaining from the early eighteenth century, and among the many dependencies is a tiny brick schoolhouse where Jefferson embarked on a lifelong odyssey of intellectual discovery.

Washington Monument (mem)

Capitol Square.

The equestrian memorial to the commander-in-chief is surrounded by figures of Thomas Jefferson, Patrick Henry, John Marshall, Andrew Lewis and General Thomas Nelson, Jr.

Stratford

Stratford Hall (site)
Route 214, off Route 3, 804-493-8038; Daily, 9–4:30. Admission charged.

Thomas Lee, a prominent Virginia planter, built the Stratford plantation in the 1730s using brick made on the site and timber cut from the virgin forests along the Potomac River. In the H-shaped manor house lived Thomas Lee's eight children, including Richard Henry Lee and Francis Lightfoot Lee, the only brothers to sign the Declaration of Independence. Two other brothers, William and Arthur, were active diplomats during the Revolution.

Their cousin, "Light Horse" Harry Lee, the dashing Revolutionary cavalry leader and close friend of George Washington, made Stratford his home for over 20 years after marrying Matilda Lee, who inherited the estate. Their son, Robert E. Lee, was born in an upstairs bedroom at Stratford Hall.

Williamsburg

Bruton Parish Church (site)
Duke of Gloucester Street and the Palace Green, 757-229-1000; Daily, 9–5. Admission charged.

The church and state were one under the Church of England in the colony of Virginia when the Bruton Parish Church was built in 1712–1715 to replace an earlier church on this spot. Washington and Jefferson attended services here, as did most government officials. After the Revolution, Jefferson wrote the Statute of Religious Liberty, which ended the Anglican Church in Virginia.

The Capitol (site)
East end of Duke of Gloucester Street, 757-229-1000; Daily, 9–5. Admission charged.

The original meeting place for the House of Burgesses, Virginia's Colonial legislature, was built between 1701 and 1705. It burned on January 30, 1747. By 1753 a second building was on the site, which lasted until it burned in 1832. The reconstruction on the original foundations is of the original Capitol Building.

It was here that Patrick Henry introduced the Stamp Act Resolutions of May 29, 1765, declaring that, "if this be treason, make the most of it." The course toward Revolution had been set. Eventually the Virginia Assembly would be disbanded by the Crown. The Capitol features period furnishings and displays rare portraits of Washington, Jefferson and Madison.

Governor's Palace (site)
Palace Green, 757-229-1000; Daily, 9–5. Admission charged.

Lord Dunmore was the last of seven Royal governors to occupy the official executive residence before fleeing in 1775. It served as the executive mansion for the commonwealth's first two governors, Patrick Henry and Thomas Jefferson, until the state capital was moved to Richmond in 1780.

The 1722 building was consumed by fire in 1781 while being used as a military hospital for soldiers wounded at Yorktown. The palace, gardens and dependencies have all been restored to period splendor.

Magazine and Guardhouse (site)

Market Square Green, 757-229-1000; Daily, 9–5. Admission charged.

On the morning of April 21, 1775, the citizens of Williamsburg awoke to discover that during the night Lord Dunmore had secretly removed all the gunpowder from the public magazine. Patrick Henry organized a march by the Hanover County militia to confront Dunmore and have the powder replaced. An outraged Dunmore finally agreed to reimburse the Virginia treasury, but he kept the powder.

The octagonal magazine was constructed in 1715 with brick walls nearly two feet thick. On display in the magazine are Colonial firearms and military artifacts.

President's House (site)

William and Mary College, Richmond Road and Jamestown Road at Boundary Street, 757-221-1540; Mon–Fri, 10–5, Sat, 9–5. Free.

On the north side of the Wren Building, built in 1695 and the oldest academic building in the nation, is the President's House. Built in 1732–33, it was used by every president of the college. Cornwallis occupied it briefly in 1781, and later that year French soldiers camping in the area burned the President's House by accident.

Raleigh Tavern (site)

Duke of Gloucester Street, 757-229-1000; Daily 9–5. Admission charged.

Less than a block from the Capitol the Raleigh Tavern, erected in 1742, became a natural meeting place for burgesses and politically inclined Virginians to debate the merits of independence. George Washington, Thomas Jefferson and Patrick Henry were all known to express opinions in this public house. The building was reconstructed after a fire destroyed it in 1859.

Wetherburn's Tavern (site)

Duke of Gloucester Street, 757-229-1000; Daily, 9–5. Admission charged.

The tavern on this site, still the original building, has been operating since the 1950s. The tavern, a favorite stopping place for George Washington, was run by the Wetherburns and their slaves.

Wythe House (site)

Palace Green, south of Prince George Street, 757-229-1000; Daily, 9–5. Admission charged.

The two-story brick house was built around 1750 and occupied by George Wythe, a former clerk of the House of Burgesses and ardent patriot, from 1779 to 1791. Wythe was a brilliant thinker and signer of the Declaration of

Independence, but his greatest fame came after the Revolution, when he gained acclaim as the first professor of law at an American college. His students — Jefferson, Monroe, John Marshall and Henry Clay among them — rose to national prominence.

Wythe lived into his eightieth year when he was poisoned by a grandnephew in 1806. The murderer escaped conviction, however, when the testimony of the only witness was considered invalid in the courts. The witness was black, to whom the rights fought for in the Revolution did not extend.

Winchester

George Washington's Office Museum (site)

South Braddock Street and West Cork Street, 540-662-4412; Apr–Oct: Mon–Sat, 10–4, Sun, 12–4. Admission charged.

In Winchester, long a crossroads town at the head of the Shenandoah Valley, George Washington began his surveying career in 1748, working under Lord Thomas Fairfax. Washington eventually staked out much of the prime land on the Virginia frontier for himself and family members. Later, as a landlord, he required each tenant to plant at least four acres of apples.

Washington returned to Winchester in September 1755 to supervise the construction of Fort Loudoun; he used this small log building as his office for the next 15 months. He remained in Fort Loudoun as commander and was twice elected to represent Winchester in the Virginia House of Burgesses, in 1758 and 1761.

The museum preserves Washington's frontier office and displays a model of Fort Loudoun which was constructed to protect the frontier from French and Indian incursions. Rare surveying instruments from the Colonial period are also exhibited.

Daniel Morgan Grave (site)

Mount Hebron Cemetery; entrance off Kent Street at the end of Boscawen Street.

Daniel Morgan began his military career alongside Washington in the service of Edward Braddock in the French and Indian War after settling in the Shenandoah Valley. In the American Revolution General Morgan covered himself with glory whenever he took the field — in the assault at Quebec, in the defeat of Burgoyne at Saratoga, in the crushing of Tarleton at Cowpens. He was the most renowned rifleman of the Revolution.

In 1779, in nearby Boyce, he began work on an impressive mansion that he named Saratoga. Much of the work was performed by Hessian prisoners. In the decade after the Revolution Morgan acquired over a quarter-million acres of land through speculation, becoming one of the most powerful men in the Shenandoah. In 1797 he was elected to Congress, but ill health, which hampered him throughout his military career, limited him to a single term.

When he returned to western Virginia, encroaching lameness forced him to abandon Saratoga in 1800 and live on Amherst Street in Winchester. He died in 1802 at the age of 66 and is buried along with five members of his Revolutionary bodyguard near the entrance of the Mount Hebron Cemetery.

Yorktown

Nelson House (site)

Main Street and Nelson Street, 757-898-3400; Spring–Fall: daily, 10–4. Admission charged.

The brick Georgian mansion was the home during the Revolution of Thomas Nelson, Jr. Nelson signed the Declaration of Independence, was wartime governor of Virginia in 1781 and commanded the Virginia militia during the siege of Yorktown. When it was learned that his home was being used to shield British soldiers, he reputedly ordered his troops to fire upon it. The home, which still bears scars from the siege, was built around 1711 by Nelson's grandfather, "Scotch Tom" Nelson.

Yorktown Monument to Alliance and Victory (mem)

Main Street.

Within weeks of the British capitulation at Yorktown, the Continental Congress, on October 29, 1781, authorized a monument to be erected in Yorktown to honor the French Alliance and their integral part in the victory of the American Revolution. In 1880, nearly a century later, funds were appropriated by Congress to fulfill the decree. President Chester A. Arthur laid the cornerstone for the 84-foot shaft of Maine granite, surmounted by the allegorical figure of Liberty. Struck several times by lightning, Liberty was replaced in 1956 and now sports a lightning rod for protection. Tablets at the Victory Monument, on a bluff over the York River, list both American and French dead.

Yorktown Battlefield (site)

East end of Colonial Parkway, 757-898-3400; Daily, 8:30–5. Admission charged.

By 1781, fighting in the Revolutionary War had continued for the better part of six years with no real resolution in sight. The French had joined the fray three years earlier but forces remained bottled up in Newport, Rhode Island, and there was no American financing to deliver a mortal blow to the British. The British, meanwhile, frustrated by Nathanael Greene's continuing efforts to thwart their southern expedition, contented themselves with raiding parties in the Colonies.

In the summer of 1781, Lord Cornwallis and some 8,300 troops set about fortifying Yorktown and Glocester Point, across the York River, as Cornwallis waited for further developments from commander Sir Henry Clinton. The decision proved fatal when, on September 5, French Admiral François de Grasse engaged a British fleet intended to reinforce Cornwallis. In the Battle of Virginia Capes, the French did not score a decisive victory but caused enough damage to send the British back to New York for repairs. The French controlled the harbor.

Having learned of the French expedition when it set out weeks earlier, Washington had mobilized his troops in New York and marched to Virginia. By the end of September, Washington's army of 7,000 French regulars, 5,500 Continental soldiers and 3,500 militia had surrounded Cornwallis and laid siege to Yorktown. On October 6 the Allied troops began digging their first siege line and five days later were working on their second line within point blank artillery range of the British.

Allied access to the river was blocked, however, by two small earthen forts, redoubts 9 and 10, which anchored the east end of the British line. No siege could succeed without destroying these positions. On October 14, Washington ordered his men against both redoubts. The Americans under Alexander Hamilton assaulted Redoubt 10 and the French stormed Redoubt 9. Both assaults were successful after intense hand-to-hand fighting. With no hope of escape and no chance for reinforcement, Cornwallis proposed a cease-fire to begin surrender negotiations.

Pleading illness, Cornwallis did not accompany his men — approximately one-third of British forces in America — to the surrender on October 19, 1781. Accordingly, subordinate General Benjamin Lincoln accepted the sword of surrender for the Americans. With the mass of their remaining forces corralled in New York and Charleston, the defeat at Yorktown induced the British to begin the peace talks that would result in American independence.

The Yorktown Battlefield is part of the Colonial National Historical Park, which includes Jamestown at the western end of the Colonial Parkway. The visitor center features an historical film and relics such as Washington's tent and a reconstructed section of a gun deck from a British frigate.

Two driving tours cover the highlights of the 19-day siege of Yorktown. The Battlefield Tour is a circular seven-mile route that includes the reconstructed siege lines. Washington had ordered all siege lines leveled immediately after the surrender. Important stops include redoubts 9 and 10, which were the keys to the British defense, the Moore House, where official negotiations occurred; and the Surrender Field. The nine-mile Encampment Tour describes behind-the-lines activity that contributed to the Allied victory.

Yorktown Victory Center (col)

Old Route 238, 757-253-4838; Daily, 9–5. Admission charged.

This private museum of the American Revolution features exhibit galleries that chronicle the events of the Revolution and describe the decisive battle at Yorktown. Interpreters detail everyday life for soldiers, farmers and townspeople during the conflict.

West Virginia

Revolutionary Status: Part of the Virginia colony

Kearneysville

Traveller's Rest (site)

Off Route 48; historical marker only.

Horatio Gates, a professional British soldier, purchased the land upon which he built Traveller's Rest in 1773, near land owned by his friend George Washington. The two had struck up an association in 1755 during General Braddock's disastrous march on Fort Duquesne.

Gates distinguished himself early in the Revolution and was rewarded with command of the Northern Department. He organized the final blow against John Burgoyne at Saratoga and Gates was promoted again, to president of the board of war on November 27, 1777. There was even considerable support for Gates to replace Washington as commander-in-chief.

Gates would, however, never see such glory again. His plan to invade Canada was disregarded by General Washington, and by 1780 he found himself home at Traveller's Rest. He accepted command of the Southern Department and against advice of his subordinate officers immediately began preparations for an offensive against the British. On August 16, 1780, Gates led the Continental Army into a staggering defeat at Camden, the likes of which were unparalleled during the Revolution. The disgraced Gates was replaced by Nathanael Greene.

For the next two years, Gates immersed himself in a letter-writing campaign to Washington and Congress, seeking to absolve himself from the disaster at Camden. In August 1782, Congress decided not to pursue a formal inquiry, and Gates was able to return to Washington's command for the last days of the war at Newburgh.

Gates returned to western Virginia, where he lived until 1790. That year he released his slaves and moved to a farm in Manhattan for the final 16 years of his life. The restored Traveller's Rest is a private building.

Leetown

Prato Rio (site)

Leetown Road; historical marker only.

Charles Lee came to America with an exalted military pedigree. The son of a British officer, Lee trained in England and Switzerland and was in uniform by the age of 16. He served with distinction in the French and Indian War in America, and after fighting under Burgoyne in Portugal he was retired with half-pay. The Polish Army hired Lee to fight the Turks, and the soldier of fortune advanced to the rank of major general.

When the adventurer, no admirer of the monarchy, moved to western Virginia in 1773 he quickly supported the Revolution. The Americans welcomed so experienced a fighter and Lee became a Continental Army major general, subordinate in rank only to Washington and Artemas Ward. Ward drifted from favor and Lee stood as a contender to replace Washington as commander-in-chief.

But during the Revolution, Lee's deeds never seemed to live up to his advance billing. He was hailed as a savior by the people of Charleston when assigned to fortify the town. Lee advised William Moultrie to abandon his works, but when the British attacked on June 28, 1776, they were easily repulsed. Later that year Lee bungled a retreat in New Jersey and was captured. Considered a great prize, he was held prisoner for over a year.

Apparently, however, even the British had no use for Lee's military talents. While a prisoner, it was discovered in 1858, Lee submitted a plan for defeating Washington's army to General Sir William Howe. Howe ignored the treasonable outline and Lee was exchanged in spring 1778, rejoining the Continental Army at Valley Forge.

As the Americans chased the British across New Jersey that summer, Lee was presented his first combat command at the Battle of Monmouth Court House—to ruinous effect. He retreated at first contact with the enemy and was personally relieved of command by a furious Washington. Lee demanded a court-martial to restore his reputation but was found guilty of insubordination and disobeying orders. Lee was suspended by Congress for one year. On January 10, 1780, he was formally dismissed from the Continental Army.

Lee lived his remaining years at Prato Rio ("near the river"), consumed with bitterness. Remarkably, three of the most notorious generals of the American Revolution had come from the same lightly populated area of western Virginia. The local story circulated that the three suspended officers toasted each other as "Lee, who was cashiered because when he should have advanced he retreated; Gates, who was cashiered because when he should have retreated he advanced; and Stephen, who was cashiered because when he might have advanced or retreated he did neither."

With no interior walls in the house, Lee was known to mark out room borders with chalk lines. Charles Lee died on October 2, 1782, his reputation still not restored, at the age of 51 during a visit to Philadelphia. Prato Rio still stands as a private residence.

Lewisburg

Lewis Spring-Andrew Lewis Park (site)
Jefferson Street and Randolph Street.

General Andrew Lewis, for whom the town is named, gathered his forces at this site, where a spring supplied water for the settlement, before marching to Point Pleasant, where his troops defeated the Shawnee and other Indians led by Cornstalk. The spring is covered by a small limestone building at what was known as Camp Union. A nearby monument listing the names of Lewis' men sits in front of the Greenbrier County Courthouse on North Court Street.

Martinsburg

General Adam Stephen House (site)

309 East John Street, 304-267-4434; May–Oct: Sat–Sun, 2–5. Admission charged.

Adam Stephen built this two-story house from limestone quarried on his property in western Virginia in 1772. Here he founded the town of Martinsburg. Had he stayed on the frontier rather than seeking appointment in the Continental Army at the age of 58, history might have treated General Stephen a little more benevolently.

Scottish-born Stephen served as a surgeon in the Royal Navy before emigrating to Fredericksburg, Virginia, to practice medicine. He served with distinction alongside Washington in the French and Indian War and rose to the rank of brigadier general. The two were fated to face each other for a seat in the House of Burgesses in 1761, a contest which Washington won, 505 votes to 294. Two years later, during Pontiac's Rebellion, Washington became suspicious of Stephen's battlefield actions and concluded they were "theatrical moves of no military value."

Still, Stephen was much esteemed in western Virginia and given a command by Congress on September 4, 1776. Within four months he had run afoul of Washington again, having sent a scouting patrol into Trenton the day before Washington was planning a surprise attack on the Hessians camped there. Fortunately, Stephen's force did not put the Germans on alert.

He was not so lucky on October 4, 1777, when Stephen's troops blundered into Anthony Wayne's brigade at the Battle of Germantown, causing the Americans to fire upon each other. Stephen was court-martialed for conduct unbecoming an officer — he had been discovered sprawled on the field at Germantown in a drunken stupor — and dismissed from the army. Stephen returned to western Virginia and remained influential in Martinsburg until his death in 1791.

Point Pleasant

Point Pleasant Battle Monument State Park (site)

1 Main Street at the Ohio and Kanawha rivers, 304-675-0869; Mon–Sat, 10–4, Sunday, 1–4. Free.

By 1774, atrocities were becoming more and more common on the Virginia frontier. On April 30 several Indians were murdered by white settlers at the mouth of the Yellow Creek on the Ohio River. The Logan Massacre provoked tribal wars in the region.

Lord Dunmore, governor of Virginia, massed a force of more than 1,000 men under Colonel Andrew Lewis to move down the Ohio to put down Indian war parties in the region. On October 10, 1774, Chief Cornstalk led a similar force of Shawnee, Miami, Hiron and Ottawa against the Virginians at Point Pleasant. A daylong pitched battle left over 50 Colonials dead, but the Virginians took possession of the field. Dunmore's War was said to have been the governor's attempt to prevent the frontiersmen from becoming more deeply involved in the Revolutionary cause. Dunmore's War accelerated the settlement of Kentucky.

Part of the battlefield is preserved in the two acres of parkland by the junction of the Ohio and Kanawha rivers. An 84-foot granite shaft commemorates the battle; at its base is a statue of a typical Virginia woodsman. South of the monument is the grave of "Mad Anne" Bailey, Liverpool born and raised, whose husband was killed at Point Pleasant. Anne assumed a man's appearance and became revered for her feats on the frontier as a woman soldier and border scout.

Reenactment: The two-day Battle Days Celebration, held the weekend closest to October 10, commemorates the clash at Point Pleasant, which the local residents like to consider the opening battle of the American Revolution.

Wheeling

Fort Henry (site)

Main Street, between 11th and Ohio streets; memorial marker only.

George Washington and his friend William Crawford prospected this area for land speculations in 1770. Four years later, Crawford returned to fortify the settlement founded by Ebenezer Zane in 1769. The city's name came from the Indian word *Weeling*, meaning "Place of Skulls." Decapitated heads of white travelers were left here on poles by Indians as a warning for other whites to stay away.

During the Revolution, Fort Henry, named for governor Patrick Henry, was targeted for Tory-Indian raids many times. The first came on August 31, 1777, when 400 Indians surprised the town and killed 23 men before they could reach the safety of the fort. Major Samuel McCulluck escaped an Indian war party by forcing his horse over an almost perpendicular, 150-foot cliff. He and his steed survived unhurt. When Indians finally killed McCulluck on July 30, 1782, they respectfully ate his heart to gain some of his courage.

The last attack came five years later, on September 11, 1782. A band of 250 Indians and two score Tories were frustrated in part by the heroics of Betty Zane, sister of the town founder. She retrieved powder from the Zane cabin at the height of the three-day siege. The attack of Fort Henry can qualify as the last battle of the American Revolution.

The site of the original Fort Fincastle, reborn Fort Henry in 1776, is marked by a memorial stone and interpretive plaque.

Wisconsin

Revolutionary Status: Claimed by the Massachusetts colony
and the Connecticut colony

Cudahy

Casimir Pulaski (mem)

Pulaski Park, 5400 South Swift Avenue.

The bronze portrait sculpture by Joseph Aszklar honors the Polish cavalry leader at a park named for him.

Milwaukee

Thaddeus Kosciuszko (mem)

Kosciuszko Park, Lincoln Street.

General Kosciuszko is portrayed in bronze by Gaetano Trentanove. Inscribed on the base are, "Thaddeus Kosciuszko, hero of both hemispheres." The 29-foot-tall monument was dedicated on June 18, 1905.

INDEX